Sino-India Border Dispute
Unresolved Conflict

Sino-India Border Dispute
Unresolved Conflict

Col. R. Lakhanpal (Retd.)

GAURAV Book Centre Private Limited

Publisher
GAURAV BOOK CENTRE PVT LTD
4832/24,Prahlad Lane,S-207 Ansari
Road, Daryaganj, Delhi-110002
Ph.: 43570976, 23278261
Email: gauravbookcentre@gmail.com

Edition: 2025

ISBN: 978-93-83316-51-9

Laser Typesetting
JEE-VEE Graphics # 09911902109

Price: 1295/-

Printed
Neeta Press, Delhi

Preface

Both sides evoke but also dispute the historical record. "Perceptual" differences, the stamping ground of IR constructivism, remain very different between India and China towards their own and each others' claims on the disputed territories. The role of Tibet presents further related ambiguity in Sino—Indian relations. Indian figures like K. Gopalachari, an advisor to the Indian team in the 1960 discussions with China, emphasised in 1963, in the bitter aftermath of India's 1962 military defeats at the hands of China, that "the India-China boundary is not a complicated question left over from history, but one definitely settled by history".

On assuming power, the People's Republic of China (PRC) renounced all prior foreign agreements as unequal treaties imposed upon it during the "century of humiliation" and demanded renegotiation of all borders. The Sino-India border remains the only major territorial dispute, other than South China Sea disputes, that China has not resolved. China's growing assertiveness in its territorial claims, especially on Arunachal Pradesh, and its relentless development of infrastructure in Tibet will shape the prospects of Sino-India relations. The territory stretching from the jungles of northern

Myanmar, westward to the Karakoram Range, and northward to the edge of the Tibetan plateau can be seen as a single geopolitical system referred to as the Himalayan-Tibetan massif. The ruggedness of this terrain makes movement of men and materiel extremely difficult, thus preventing Indian and Chinese civilizations from intermingling or projecting military power in these remote areas effectively. Not until 1962 did the Chinese and Indian armies fight each other over these desolate heights, thus altering the geopolitics of the region significantly.

This work is essentially useful for scholars researchers social activists academics government functionaries and the general reader alike.

—Author

Contents

1

Sino-Indian Territorial Issues

THE "RAZOR'S EDGE"

In terms of "the rise of China" and its "implications for India", the title of this book, the Sino-Indian territorial dispute represents an immediate arena in which India is having to face the uncomfortable implications from having an increasingly stronger neighbour. For India, the ability of China to deny India's hopes of territorial settlement on India's terms has become ever clearer in the wake of China's rise in military power in and around their disputed territory, which remains the biggest amount of land still in dispute in Asia.

As such, "the 4,056—kilometer (2,520 miles) frontier between India and China, one of the longest inter-state borders in the world, remains ... not defined, let alone demarcated, on maps or delineated on the ground". Here, the judgement over a century ago of Lord Curzon, British Viceroy of India 1898-1905 still seems relevant; the most urgent work of Foreign Ministers and Ambassadors ... is now the conclusion of Frontier Conventions in which sources of discord are removed by the adjustment of rival interests or ambitions at points where the territorial borders adjoin", for "frontiers are indeed the razor's edge on which hang suspended the modern issues of war or peace, of life or death to nations".

Admittedly, the territorial issue has been officially decoupled from the wider Sino-Indian relationship; as with the PRC rhetoric that "China and India have already reached consensus on the border issue. Before it is completely resolved, both countries will endeavor to maintain peace and stability in the border areas and will not let the border issue affect the general picture of China and India's cooperation". However, in reality their territorial issues do affect their wider relationship, in PRC terms "the existence of immense territorial disputes between China and India".

In dispute terms, this chapter argues that, in International Relations (IR) theory terms, the territorial disputes between India and China involve *classical geopolitics* entwined with *critical geopolitics*. Each strand of geopolitics, in their different ways, both involve the respective "position" that India and China hold for themselves and for each other in their immediate and extended neighbourhood. Whilst each side argues from history, the chapter argues that in reality the evidence from history is rather ambiguous and inconclusive for both sides' territorial claims. Indeed, history is a sterile area to argue from, as one Indian commentator put it, "can we go beyond history to look at solutions which do not hark back to the past?" The chapter argues that, from the outside, resolution of the issue seems feasible enough in terms of simple seeming territorial trade offs involving Arunachal Pradesh and Aksai Chin; but is complicated by smaller geographic issues surrounding Tawang, and wider geopolitical issues surrounding Tibet and indeed the balance of power in Asia between India and China.

The two main areas of dispute along this Himalayan frontier are the *Western Sector* (Aksai Chin, around 37,250 square kilometres/ 14,380 square miles); and the *Eastern Sector* (Arunachal Pradesh, around 83,740 square kilometres/ 32,330 square miles). On the one hand, Arunachal Pradesh is inhabited by over a million people, Indian citizens, and includes important Buddhist centres like Tawang. On the other hand, Aksai Chin is a virtually uninhabited bleak barren plateau with no permanent settlements. It is the place "where not a blade of grass grows" as Jawaharlal Nehru once dismissively said; but where China's National Highway 219 runs through Aksai Chin as a key geopolitical infrastructure link for the PRC between its provinces of Tibet and Xinjiang. One further complication is China's occupation of the Shaksgam valley; around 5,180 sq kilometres/1,930 square miles, to which Pakistan relinquished its Baltistan-related claims in 1963, but over which India maintains its own Kashmir-derived claims. Smaller pockets of disputed territory are found, the *Middle Sector* fringes of Himachal Pradesh and Uttar Pradesh. Elsewhere along the Himalayas, lingering uncertainty over China's recognition of Sikkim's incorporation into India in 1975 is entwined with continuing PRC claims to the "Finger Area" in the north of Sikkim, with 71 supposed incidents reported of Chinese troop "incursions" in 2008. Nearby territorial disputes between China and Bhutan around the Chumbi Valley triangulation point with India are of further concern to New Delhi, given the Chumbi Valley's location looking down onto the India's sensitive Siliguri corridor which links India's northeastern states with the rest of India.

Wider nuances arise with India's Foreign Secretary (2004–2006) Shyam Saran, and his comments about *the logic of geography*. In front of one audience, it was a question for Saran of "geopolitical reality" in which "I would like to focus particularly on Asia, where the interests of both India and China intersect. It is said that the logic of geography is unrelenting. Proximity is the most difficult and testing among diplomatic challenges a country faces", where "to those who harbour any skepticism about this fact, it would suffice to remind that we share one of the longest [and disputed] land borders in the world with China. In front of another audience, it was again a question that "it is said that the logic of geography is unrelenting and proximity is the most difficult and testing among diplomatic challenges a country faces"; with the following gloss that "frontiers with neighbours are where domestic concerns intersect with external relationships. This is where domestic and foreign policies become inextricable and demand sensitive handling", and in which "it is important for us to look at the [disputed] boundary question from the long-term and strategic perspective of India-China relations, rather than as a mere territorial issue.

The territorial issues between India and China form one of the biggest land disputes in Asia, and are of significance not only for the size of area under dispute, but also because the two disputants are the big countries most evidently on the rise in Asia. Alongside this *logic of geography*, there is then what Neville Maxwell called "the logic of power"; a *logic of power* whereby powerful states "in their expansive phases push out their frontiers until they meet the resistance of a strong neighbour or reach a physical barrier which makes a natural point of rest".

In geopolitical terms, the current point of rest is along the Himalayas/Karakoram range, but in the long term where exactly is the "natural" point of rest between them? Amidst talk of mutual IR *security dilemma* dynamics, China's strengthening of military forces and related infrastructure in Aksai Chin and Arunachal Pradesh zones is now a spur to India's own more halting augmentation of military forces and related infrastructure. Meanwhile, both countries are seeking to expand their wider strategic space at a time when their immediate mountain borders remain unresolved.

RESPECTIVE CLAIMS

Both sides evoke but also dispute the historical record. "Perceptual" differences, the stamping ground of IR *constructivism*, remain very different between India and China towards their own and each others' claims on the disputed territories. The role of Tibet presents further related ambiguity in Sino—Indian relations. Indian figures like K. Gopalachari, an advisor to the Indian team in the 1960 discussions with China, emphasised in 1963, in the bitter aftermath of India's 1962 military defeats at the hands of China, that "the India-China boundary is not a complicated question left over from history, but one definitely settled by history"; in which "the Indian alignment of the 2,4000 mile boundary, one of the longest in the world, has been determined by geography, confirmed by tradition and custom, sanctified by treaties and reinforced by continuous exercise through the centuries of administrative jurisdiction appropriate to the areas concerned. Ironically, the PRC uses the same criteria and lines of argument, complete with its repeated phrase of the issue as being "a question left over by history".

History does not really settle the issue, as witnessed in the voluminous but inconclusive exchange of maps and documents in the 1960 negotiations. In reality, the picture has been a confused vague picture in the past, in which ethnic-tribal lines and power vacuums have generated blurred and unclear Tibetan borders.

China's territorial claims on Arunachal Pradesh stem from China's wider claims to Tibet, hence the PRC's styling of Arunachal Pradesh as *Zang Nan* "Southern Tibet". In terms of implications for India of China's rise, as Brahma Chellaney trenchantly put it, China "covets Arunachal as a cultural patio to Tibet — a classic attempt at incremental annexation". Despite the worried concerns of Vallabhai Patel over the implications of Chinese move into Tibet in 1950, Nehru moved ahead with the 1954 *Agreement on Trade and Intercourse between the Tibet Region of China and India.* This indicated Indian acceptance of PRC control over Tibet, with repeated use in the 1954 *Agreement,* eight times, of the phrase "Tibet region of China". It also included India's renunciation of forward military and economic rights enjoyed in Tibet by British India. More recently in their 2003 *Joint Declaration,* the formulation was that "the Indian side recognizes that the Tibet Autonomous Region [TAR] is part of the territory of the People's Republic of China". In retrospect, some Indian figures have argued that this showed a recurring tendency for India to hand over "unilateral concessions" to China. However, there was some comment on the implications and sub-text of the 2003 *Joint Declaration* seeming to recognize the claims of the People's Republic of China rather than China *per se*; a qualified recognition whereby if the PRC collapses as a regime, then so could Indian recognition of Chinese claims to Tibet? There was also comment that China's favoured term "inalienable" was not applied to Tibet in the 2003 *Joint Declaration*. Of course, there are ambiguities in China's very claim on Tibet. China claims that political links with Tibet go back centuries. In reality, Chinese control was first seen in the intervention of a Qing army in 1720 and arrival of a Chinese resident commissioner (*amban*). Since then, some degree of Chinese control was able to be enforced in Tibet when China was strong, but effectively lapsed (for most of the period) when China was weak.

As to the periphery around Tibet, it would seem that the *Western Sector,* Aksai Chin, was pretty well ignored by most settled surrounding powers in India and China. Admittedly, in 1865, a

British surveyor W H Johnson employed by the Maharaja of Kashmir, had drawn up the so-called "Johnson Line" which had placed the Aksai Chin plateau in Kashmir, but the Chinese government rejected this demarcation, which remained nominal rather than implemented. A later British proposal was submitted in 1899 by Claude MacDonald the British Minister to China, with Aksai Chin allocated to China, but then was not followed through by either government.

With regard to the *Eastern Sector*, Arunachel Pradesh has varied defensive and offensive strategic importance for India, as it (1) provides strategic depth to India's vulnerable Brahmaputra Valley and India's other North Eastern states; (2) provides security to Bhutan on its entire Eastern flank by geographical contiguity; and (3) in any future conflict with China and if India singly (or in coalition with some other power) develops offensive capabilities against China, it offers the shortest cut for India to China proper and to Tibet. The problem for Indian claims is that some traditional and demographic links were present between Arunachal Pradesh and Tibet, with tax links maintained between Tawang and the Lhasa authorities well into the mid 20th century.

Thus, the Imperial Gazetteer map *Political Divisions of the Indian Empire* (1909) showed the British India frontier as the southern (not northern) borderline of present day Arunachal Pradesh. Admittedly more formal boundary lines between India and Tibet seemed laid down under the Simla Convention of 1914 which established the McMahon Line. The Chinese delegate from the Qing Empire, Chen I-fan, may have initially initialled the Simla Convention; but he then repudiated it, as did the central government in Beijing. The People's Republic of China has maintained a rejection of the Simla Convention as an Unequal Treaty and manifestation of imperialism on the part of British India; "the so-called McMahon Line in the eastern sector is a line which the British imperialists attempted to force upon China by taking advantage of the powerlessness of the Chinese ... It is illegal and has never been recognized by the Chinese Government. British India did gradually move into the Himalayan slopes after 1914, calling it the North East Frontier Agency (NEFA); but this can be accurately enough summed by Mohan Guruswamy that India's claim to the north-eastern frontiers "does not rest on any great historical tradition or cultural affinity. We are there because the British went there".

However, China now faces the problem that there has been continuous occupation of the *Eastern Sector* area by the Republic of India since 1950, albeit interrupted briefly in 1962 before Chinese troops withdrew their forces but not their claim. One of the mysteries remains why China withdrew their forces from the NEFA in 1962, given that it was claiming it as Chinese territory. It would seem that PRC concerns over maintaining their grip over Tibet made the key infrastructure role of the Aksai China the crucial element to retain, which is exactly what they did in 1962, with the NEFA perhaps considered as less important geopolitically for China's position in Tibet. Meanwhile, Indian re-occupation in the wake of the Chinese withdrawal in 1962 has led to the granting of full statehood in 1987 to the NEFA, now termed Arunachal Pradesh, and its subsequent participation in Indian politics. Such integration of Arunachal Pradesh within the Indian polity has not been recognised by the PRC; and it was no coincidence that in 1987 there were serious skirmishes at Sumdorong Chu in Arunachal Pradesh.

Faced with a rising India, whose closer security and defence links with the United States were signalled with their 2005 Defence Agreement, Chinese claims to Arunachal Pradesh have been re-invoked with increased vigour. Hence the widely publicized assertion in November 2006 by China's Ambassador to India, Sun Yuxi, that "in our position, the whole of the state of Arunachal Pradesh is Chinese territory. And Tawang is only one of the places in it. We are claiming all of that. That is our position". The clarification in 2007 by the Dalai Lama, that the 1914 Simla Agreement drawing the MacMahon Line to demarcate the Tibet-India border was signed by an independent government of Tibet, has strengthened PRC re-assertions of its own claims; as the Chinese are acutely concerned that the present Dalai Lama's position not only negates the Chinese claim on Arunachal Pradesh, but also questions the very legality of Chinese sovereignty over Tibet, and with it the PRC's incorporation of Tibet in 1950. Arunachal Pradesh's participation in Indian politics continues to attract Beijing's ire, witnessed in PRC denunciations in 2009 over the visit and campaigning in Arunachal Pradesh by national politicians like Manmohan Singh and Rahul Gandhi. Whilst Beijing expressed how it was "strongly dissatisfied" over what it considered "provocative" action by India; the Indian government merely reiterated how Arunachel Pradesh was an "integral part of India. We rest at that".

India claims, simply enough in its eyes, that the Arunachal Pradesh border has already been agreed via the MacMahon Line drawn up and ratified in 1914 under the Simla Convention; which India sees as a sensible reflection of geography and history.

Chinese administrations may have rejected the Simla Agreement, but Tibetan administrations did not. The Dalai Lama's acceptance of the MacMahon Line and of India's claim within it to Tawang, are a continuing feature of India's case; marshalled again following the Dalai Lama's visit, with Indian government permission (and approval?) to Tawang in November 2009, a visit denounced in the PRC.33 China though argues that neither the Tibetan authorities nor the Dalai Lama have had, be it in 1914 or in 2009, the authority to dispose of territory and conduct foreign policy.

In China's eyes, "there has been no such a thing as 'independent Tibet' since the Yuan Dynasty (1271—1368) established its suzerainty over the region. It was the invasion of Tibet by British forces in the late 19th century that made Tibetan sovereignty an issue. When the British forces withdrew after waging two wars, they tried to create an 'independent Tibet' by convening the Simla Convention".34 As to the Simla Convention, the PRC continues to argue that it was an imperialist facade, "UK representative Henry McMahon secretly signed the so-called 'Simla Accord' with the local Tibetan government manipulated by 'Tibet independence' forces during the 'Simla conference' without the knowledge of Chinese representatives. This accord even incorporated a large area of territory in China's Tibet including the Tawang district to British India".

STATUS OF NEGOTIATIONS

In 1981, following the frozen relations prevalent after the 1962 war, border talks at the vice-ministerial level were initiated. Although Beijing had suggested sectoral swapping in 1960 and 1980, this *overall package* predisposition faced India's push for separate *sector-by-sector* agreements. In 1988 more formal Joint Working Group (JWG) discussions were started; with a twin mandate of ensuring "peace and tranquillity" along the Line of Actual Control (LAC) and working on a "fair, reasonable and mutually acceptable" settlement of the boundary question. In September 1993, China and India signed the *Agreement on the Maintenance of Peace and Tranquillity along the Line of Actual Control in the India-China Border Areas,* with a Sino-Indian Expert Group (EG) set up to assist the work of the JWG on the boundary question. The rhetoric was clear in its Article-1; "the India-China boundary question shall be resolved through peaceful and friendly consultations. Neither side shall use or threaten to use force against the other by any means. Pending an ultimate solution to the boundary question...". In November 1996, China and India agreed in their *Agreement on Confidence Building Measures in the Military Field along the Line of Actual Control in the India-China Border Areas* to delimit their Line of Actual Control (LAC) and institute Confidence Building Measures (CBMs) along the frontier. The agreement included pledges on nonaggression, prior notification of large troop movements, a 10-km no-fly zone for combat aircraft, and exchange of maps to resolve disagreements about the precise location of the LAC.

In June 2003, the India—China *Declaration on Principles for Relations and Comprehensive Cooperation between India and China* had the two countries agreeing "to each appoint a special representative to explore from the political perspective of the overall bilateral relationship the framework of a boundary settlement". Some ground rules for actual territorial negotiations seemed to have been achieved in April 2005 with the signing of the *Political Parameters and Guiding Principles for the Settlement of the India-China Boundary Question*. However, the *Joint Declaration by the Republic of India and the People's Republic of China* (2006) and the *Shared Vision for the 21st Century of the People's Republic of China and the Republic of India* (2008), which both expressed hopes that "such [boundary] differences are not allowed to affect the positive development of bilateral relations" in other fields, have perhaps pushed territorial differences but also territorial resolution to one side?

To conclude, varied frameworks have been seen; some eight rounds of vice-ministerial talks from 1981—1987, fourteen Joint Working Group meetings from 1988—2003, and thirteen rounds of Special Representative talks from 2003—2009. Nevertheless, there seems to have been little substantive progress on territorial issues. Specific discussions on core territorial demands and delineation of forces have given way to broader, but some would say vaguer and less useful, political discussions of bilateral relations as a whole. In terms of general confidence, if anything, the situation has deteriorated between India and China, where the last few years have seen growing numbers of incursions, alongside infrastructure and military forces build up along the Himalayas, both on the Arunachal Pradesh and Aksai Chin borderlines. Despite some of the diplomatic rhetoric of engagement and global cooperation, strategic perceptions of each other have deteriorated, whilst public as well as elite distrust of intentions and military capacity has grown.

Even initial specific steps have been minimal and indeed appear somewhat grudging. In terms of establishing the Lines of Actual Control (LAC), maps have only been established with regard to the relatively minor *Middle Sector* (Himachal Pradesh/Uttar Pradesh fringes) where LAC maps were exchanged in November 2000. China then committed itself to an exchange of LAC maps of the *Western Sector* (Aksai Chin) in 2002 and the *Eastern Sector* (Arunachal Pradesh) in early 2003. However, in 2003 this was effectively overturned when China argued that the two countries should instead focus on achieving an overall final political package settlement. Equally well, the 2006 Joint Declaration pledge that "it was agreed to complete the process of exchanging maps indicating their respective perceptions of the entire alignment of the LAC on the basis of already agreed parameters as soon as possible" also has shown no particular signs of being completed; with no LAC maps having emerged for those two major blocks of disputed territory, Aksai Chin and Arunachal Pradesh. This in turn makes the immediate implementation of the 1996 *Agreement on Confidence Building Measures in the Military Field along the Line of Actual Control in the India-China Border Areas* difficult as the agreement refers to controlling military dispositions and deployments to certain distances from Lines of Actual Control, but yet those LACs have not been established.

The speed, or rather lack of speed, over negotiations is noticeable, a "glacial pace" given that current border discussions were first initiated in 1981. The 2005 *Political Parameters and Guiding Principles for the Settlement of the India-China Boundary Question* talked of "an early settlement of the boundary question" It did have its Article-7 provision that "in reaching a boundary settlement, the two sides shall safeguard due interests of their settled populations in the border areas". However, China's strong reassertion of its claims over Arunachal Pradesh, and especially Tawang, cut across such population principles. This population provision also seems undercut by the comments made to Pranab Mukherjee in June 6, 2007 by Chinese Foreign Minister Yang Jiechi, who stated that "mere presence" of settled populations would not affect China's claims. Meanwhile, the 2006 *Joint Declaration* announced that "the Special Representatives shall complete at an early date the task of finalising an appropriate framework for a final package settlement covering all sectors of the India-China boundary", but as of yet there are no signs of any such "early finalisation" let alone "early settlement". Similarly, the *Working Group* set up at the 2007 Special Representatives meeting to prepare a "framework arrangement" has been equally barren on outcomes, so far.

Indian perceptions of Chinese motives remain highly critical. For Kapila it was the opportunity for China "to keep alive the border dispute as a strategic pressure point against India". For Malik it was a case that "Beijing would not want to give up the 'bargaining chip' that an unsettled boundary vis-à-vis India provides it with. An unsettled border provides China the strategic leverage to keep India uncertain about its intentions, and nervous about its capabilities, while exposing India's vulnerabilities and weaknesses, and ensuring New Delhi's 'good behaviour' on issues of vital concern to China".

Discussions, rather than negotiations have then settled down into a regular, but desultory fashion. The press communiqué from the 2009 Special Representative talks was still noticeably bland; "in a friendly and candid atmosphere, the two Special Representatives had an in-depth exchange of views on resolving the boundary question. Both countries agreed to press ahead with the framework negotiations in accordance with the agreed political parameters and guiding principle", so as "to seek for a fair and reasonable solution acceptable to both. Prior to that, both should work together to maintain peace and tranquillity in the border areas2. Candid is often diplomatic euphemism for blunt differences of opinion, whilst the call for working together to maintain peace and tranquillity is a virtual admission that peace and stability has not yet been established. Equally euphemistic are PRC statements that both countries "should respect history and reality, take into account the feelings of both nations, make the most of their political wisdom and come up with a reasonable and mutually acceptable solution to their border issue". Such sentiments fail to give any tangible specifics on what actual solutions might be forthcoming.

NEGOTIATING STRATEGIES

One repeated emerging criticisms of India's negotiating strategy is that "unilateral concessions" have been made too often by India, without similar concessions being made by China. When PRC military forces started moving into Tibet in 1950, the Republic of India quickly moved to (a) give up the Forward Rights inherited from the days of British India, which stemmed from the Simla Convention and Anglo-Tibetan Agreement of 1904; and (b) instead recognise Chinese control over Tibet in stronger terms than the hitherto used term "suzerainty". In effect, a "Tibet Card" was there to be played at a time of PRC uncertainties. A robust Indian intervention might have maintained Tibet as an effective buffer between India and China, or at least enabled concessions to be won by India on the Himalayan—Karakoram borders. This is the reverse logic behind recent Indian comments that "China has failed to appreciate that if Arunachal is claimed to be the southern part of Tibet Autonomous Region (TAR), India cannot accept Tibet to be within China. India's formal position on Tibet articulated in 1954 and 2003 is therefore a tentative and unilateral diplomatic offer that can only be sustained and the circle completed once China recognizes Arunachal as part of India". Reinvoking such a "Tibet Card" has been floated in some Indian circles in the past few years.

Having lost that opportunity, the next criticism of Indian negotiating strategy is that, faced with an immediate PRC military presence in Tibet and renewed Chinese claims over Aksai China and Arunachal Pradesh, Nehru ignored the chance of a trade-off seemingly offered by China in 1960; whereby Aksai China would have gone to China and Arunachal Pradesh would have gone to India. Instead, India refused to engage in sovereignty negotiations in the 1950s, maintained its claims to the fullest, neglected to build up its own military forces, yet still engaged in adventurist forward probing movements in the late 1950s. At the time, Nehru rejected the idea of territorial trade-off; India "will not concede one piece of territory in return for another in the same manner as a similar dispute between China and Burma was settled this year"; for "there is no question of barter in these matters ... facts are facts". His formal position was, in the formal *Indian Note* of June 16 1962; quite simply that "this boundary is well known and well recognized and has been so for centuries and cannot be the subject of any negotiations". The trouble was the precise boundaries were not well known, were not well recognized, and had not been in shape for centuries. The irony is that the territorial agreement reached between Burma and China in 1960 involved China following the MacMahon Line alongside other mutual concessions and swapping of territory; as did the 1963 Agreement between China and Pakistan with regard to mutual concessions over claims and territory in the Karakoram reaches.

Nehru might have said "facts are facts" but the fact of the matter is that China's military superiority and continuing occupation of Aksai Chin created a very different subsequent set of facts in the wake of India's military defeat at the hands of China in 1962. The problem for consideration of negotiated resolution of the territorial dispute is that demands and offers have shifted. From the outside, an obvious trade off would be between the *Western* Sector and the *Eastern Sector*; which is where Noorani argued that "there is no territorial dispute which has been, and still is, more susceptible to a solution than India's boundary dispute with China. Each side has its non-negotiable vital interest securely under its control. India has the McMahon Line; China has Aksai Chin" In other words, China's *de facto* control of Aksai Chin could be reflected in agreed *de jure* sovereignty for China, and India's *de facto* control of Arunachal Pradesh could in turn be reflected in agreed *de jure* sovereignty for India. This had been Zhou Enlai's seeming suggestion in 1960, and was the "Package Plan" floated by Deng Xiaoping during 1980. The problem is that the Indian government has never taken up such trade-off offers, with Chinese comments made about the weakness of the Indian governments in taking any compromise deal to the Indian public. The separate *sector-by-sector* approach advocated by India when discussions resumed in the 1980s, rather than *overall package* trade-off deals suggested by China, has not worked, it has merely led the PRC to maintain its particular claims in all Sectors.

Another possible example of unilateral concessions was Rajiv Gandhi's visit to Beijing in 1988. Various concessions were made by him. He agreed that the settlement of the border dispute no longer was necessary as a precondition for improvement of bilateral relations, secondly he agreed that some members of the Tibetan community in India were engaged in anti-China activities, and thirdly he agreed that Tibet was an internal affair for China. Ganguly considered the results were "clearly asymmetric" as no support on the Kashmir issue was received from China, which "underscored the stark debility of India's negotiating capabilities vis-à-vis China". On the other hand, the earlier unequivocal support for Pakistan's case in Kashmir was moderated by a more neutral position by the 1990s, the PRC eventually announcing it was "not taking sides on Kashmir".

A final example of "unilateral concessions" came in the 2003 *Declaration on Principles for Relations and Comprehensive Cooperation between India and China*, in which India explicitly recognised the sovereignty of China over Tibet. A careful look at the text shows one-way agreement, one-way obligations, one-way concessions. On the one hand, it stated that "The Indian side recognizes that the Tibet Autonomous Region is part of the territory of the People's Republic of China and reiterates that it does not allow Tibetans to engage in anti-China political activities in India"; before going on to immediately say, on the other hand, "The Chinese side expresses its appreciation for the Indian position and reiterates that it is firmly opposed to any attempt and action aimed at splitting China and bringing about "independence of Tibet". As can be seen, there was no recognition of Indian territory (Arunachal Pradesh?) by China; not even return recognition by China of India's sovereignty claims over Sikkim, the Princely State reincorporated into the Republic of India in 1975, an incorporation which China had refused to recognise. Indian commentators may have read the accompanying *Trade Memorandum* designating Natu La as a border trade post as recognition by China of India's sovereignty over Sikkim, but that was implied rather than explicit, *de facto* rather than *de jure*.

Meanwhile, New Delhi has refused to lay out its formal position, other than the reiteration of its full claims of the Indian Parliament in November 1962, a unanimous vote to get China to vacate all Indian-claimed territories that China occupied. Specific territorial negotiations involving sensitive political climb downs or concessions might well be conducted in private out of the public gaze, yet there seems no indications of this either. India could then indicate some sort of territorial trade-off, short of this maximalist reiteration of its full claims which China is unlikely to accept. Of course, India indicating a territorial trade-off would not necessarily meet with Chinese acceptance, given Indian suspicions that China is happy enough to avoid definitive frontier settlement; but at least it would clarify the issue, and in such an eventuality enable India to more straightforwardly strengthen her own presence and power towards China along the border. In IR terms, if *engagement* proved unsuccessful in leading to territorial settlement, then India could go for a degree of *internal balancing* through building up its military presence and power in Arunachal Pradesh and Ladakh. Some Indian commentators have suggested that "when the Agni-III is finally ready for deployment, it is likely that the Chinese will come down to the table for negotiations and there is likely to be further progress on the border dispute". It could also go for a degree of *external balancing* with others vis-à-vis China but that is a much wider issue. It could try adjusting its bigger policy on Tibet, in effect playing a "Tibet Card" to engineer geopolitical shifts in the future; though would be a much more high risk strategy immediately bringing it up against China's perceived "core interest" of averting internal fragmentation.

If India's strategy over the disputed territories has been hesitant, this has been exacerbated by the very opaqueness, the "Chinese whispers" coming from Beijing. What exactly does China really want, what is its bottom line? For example, are PRC reiterations of claims over the whole of Arunachal Pradesh, re-invoked with greater vigour since the 1990s, just a maximalist initial tactic to end up with the Tawang pocket, thereby strengthening its control over Tibet, a line of argument by Chinese commentators like Ma Jiali and others. Are some suggestions in PRC circles of a different trade-off, Aksai Chin to India and Arunachal Pradesh to China, serious? Did China's acceptance in 2003 of Nathu La as an official border trade post between India and China represent full and definitive acceptance by China of Sikkim's incorporation into India; and what is the significance of rising "incursion" incidents into Sikkim during 2008 by Chinese troops; uncertainties that undermine Wen Jiabao's assertions in 2005 that "Sikkim is no longer the problem between China and India." Is talk in the PRC that "China won't make any compromises in its border disputes with India" a tactical ploy by China to get India to make compromises? If it is, then a trade-off deal is likely at some point. If it is not, then indefinite deadline/stand off is likely, unless one or the other disputant state attempts to decide it on the military battlefield.

One emerging line from the PRC, with implications for India, is PRC emphasis and definition of a "core interests" diplomacy, reflecting the rise of China; "as the country becomes stronger,

China is now on the trajectory to develop its own doctrine of diplomacy". This has been a development in the last couple of years, overlapping with rising friction along the disputed Himalayan reaches; generally what the PRC calls "the recalibration of its strategic focus in diplomacy to 'core interests'", over which it is taking a more obstructive/assertive line. This sense of "core interest" can be primarily seen at stake for the PRC in Taiwan and also Xinjiang. It can also be seen with PRC statements with regard to Tibet, whereby "Tibet related issues remain a core interest of China that refers to state sovereignty and territorial integrity. This is neither a religious issue nor a human right issue". The question is how far China's "core interest" framework may be "expanding". If such a "core interest" linkage is also invoked for Arunachal Pradesh (or in PRC eyes *Zang Nan* "Southern Tibet") as "Tibet-related issues", then one would have less expectations of territorial agreements being reached between India and China, and more likelihood of armed resolution in the future. Such trends were the spur for Barat Verma at the *India Defence Review* to warn that for the PRC "the most attractive option is to attack a soft target like India and forcibly occupy its territory in the Northeast...Beijing's cleverly raising the hackles on its fabricated dispute in Arunachal Pradesh to an alarming level, is the preparatory groundwork for imposing such a conflict on India"; a scenario dismissed in China as a "provocative and inflammatory illusion". Nevertheless, IR security dilemma dynamics may indeed lead to increasing military tension as both sides reinforce their military positions, and "war talk" about the disputed territories increases.

Concerned voices are easy to find as "tensions over a boundary dispute between the two sides are escalating". One reason for Indian concerns is the increasing number of "incursion" incidents along the border, though denied by China. The official India leadership downplays such trends, India's Foreign Secretary Niripuma Rao thus asserting in September 2009 that "there has been no significant increase in intrusions across all Sectors of the Line of Actual Control (LAC)", but that such India-perceived incursions were "because there is no mutually agreed or delineated border". This ignores the earlier increase the previous year, whereby the number of India-perceived "incursions" by the PRC has increased from 140 in 2007 to 280 in 2008, with a similar number in 2009. Such incursion incidents involved not just the *Eastern Sector* around Arunachal Pradesh but now also the *Western Sector* around Aksai Chin/Ladakh; a particular widening development that Indian commentators like Bhaskar Roy have found "sinister" and which Kanwal sees as "aggressive tactical posturing" on the part of China. Admittedly, such border incursions, reflecting different perceptions of where the LAC actually is, have often been trivial in themselves; for example Chinese troops painting rocks in red paint or cross-LAC sheep grazing. Chinese troop movements near and around the narrow Siliguri corridor "chicken's neck" linking north-east India to the rest of India do though cause immediate geopolitical concerns to India.

Certainly, a substantive military build up along the Aksai Chin and Arunachal Pradesh borderlines has also been evident. Partly this has been an infrastructure race, in which India has been belatedly trying to catch up and match China's better established road, and now railway, infrastructure in these disputed borderlands. It has also involved increasing military deployment, again by India to match China's already established forces in places like Linzi airbase. This is reflected in India increasing its ground forces in the border regions facing China. In the *Eastern Sector*, this has also involved the Indian Air Force (IAF) deploying advanced long range Sukhoi Su-30 warplanes to Tezpur for potential cross-LAC operation; complemented by six surface-to-air Akash missile squadrons.77 In the *Western Sector*, this has also involved the Indian Air Force reactivating disused high altitude airstrips like Daulat Beg Oldi and Fukche. Such reinforcements have been picked up in the PRC, and denounced as "unwise military moves".

Meanwhile, Brahma Chellaney asked the question in 2006 "will India—China border talks ever end"? He argued that "after a quarter century of unrewarding negotiations with Beijing, India ought to face up to the reality that it is being taken round and round the mulberry bush by an adversarial state that has little stake in an early border resolution"; in which "the more the talks have dragged on, the less Beijing has appeared interested in resolving the border disputes other than on its terms". His prognosis was simple, "it is time for it to draw the line, at least in the negotiations" and "to re-evaluate the very utility of staying absorbed in a never-ending process". Three years later, in the wake of the 2009 talks, his sense was the same, "the latest round of the unending and fruitless India—China talks on territorial disputes was a fresh reminder of the eroding utility of this process". The PRC may indeed wish to keep the issue open as a way of distracting and threatening India; but other dynamics may be leading the PRC to postpone decisive border negotiations. The PRC may well consider tightening its hold on Tibet itself as a greater priority, shaken during the disturbances that swept across Tibet and Tibetan areas in the spring of 2008? The PRC may also want to delay decisive border territorial resolution with India until it has resolved the Taiwan issue first? Garver also has wondered how far Beijing's apparent slowdown and readiness to avoid territorial resolution with India, is because of "understanding between Pakistan and China that neither will settle their territorial disputes with India independently of the other). Such a consideration point to the wider Pakistan—China—India triangle interplay around the disputed territories that stretch along the Himalayas from Arunachal Pradesh in the east to Aksai Chin and Kashmir in the west, which overlap with basic power balancing by the China—Pakistan "nexus" against India. The overlaps between the varied territorial disputes was shown in 2009 when China gave visas for the entry of Kashmiri separatists to visit China, in the wake of India giving permission to the Dalai Lama to visit Arunachal Pradesh.

What is certain is that any quick decisive territorial resolution between India and China is unlikely. Following rising border frictions, the PRC media reported "China—India border dispute turns sour", with hard hitting nationalist blogs being noticeable in the Chinese official and state controlled media in the autumn of 2009.84 Admittedly, the Indian and Chinese leadership did again reaffirm dialogue in autumn 2009. However, this reaffirmation was in cautious terms "to gradually narrow differences on border issues between the two countries ... to continue talks, with the aim of incrementally removing the barriers to a solution that was fair and acceptable to both sides". Despite the euphemistic headline from the official Chinese media that the two countries had reached "concensus on narrowing border differences"; in reality this merely indicated the existence of a gap without showing how and when it would be resolved. Talk of "gradually" and "incrementally removing" barriers to a solution flags up the slowness of any likely process, whilst offering nothing on what solutions could then emerge once such barriers have been, incrementally, removed.

What of solutions? Could outside arbitration be one way forward? Nehru himself had offered such a route in the immediate aftermath of war in the shape of the International Court of Justice (ICJ) at The Hague. However this was badly received in Parliament and Nehru then backed away immediately from this. In reality the ICJ seems ill equipped to deal with direct large scale territorial disputes between major powers, whilst China's reluctance to have outside bodies disposing of sovereignty issues is higher even than India's.

One bilateral solution which we can return to, involves a *logic of geography,* the "watershed/crestline" line along the Himalayas/ Karakoram. It has a degree of clearness, "the advantage of having a border on such a prominent line as the high watershed of the Himalaya is that it is easily identifiable, historically traditional and politically neutral". It may also be sellable to both parties. Thus, "as far as the Indian public is concerned, they have been brought up to believe that the Himalaya is the traditional boundary and they will be willing to concede any territory that lies beyond it without demur"; whilst "such a boundary should also be acceptable to China as it is based on the same watershed principle which they have accepted in defining their boundaries with Myanmar, Sikkim and Nepal. This watershed principle was an angle suggested by Zhou Enlai in the abortive 1960 discussions. In effect, applying the watershed principle would leave Aksai Chin to China and almost all Arunachal Pradesh with India.

Admittedly, Tawang remains problematic. The Tawang District's 2,085 square kilometres is around 2.5% of Arunachal Pradesh's entire 82,743 area, and its population of 38,924 is around 3.6% of Arunachal Pradesh's 1,091,120 inhabitants (2001 figures), relatively small shares on paper. Neutralization of the entire Tawang subdivision pocket might be an option. Within the Tawang District, given that the Tawang Subdistrict and the District capital Tawang (27°34′47″N) itself lies north of the Se la Pass and the Ka crest line (27°32′26″N), whereas the Lumla and Jang Subdistricts lie on the southerly India-facing slopes of that crest line; could a division of Tawang District be carried out, with the Tawang Subdistrict allocated to China and the Lumla and Jang Subdistricts allocated to India? However, local opinion at the District capital Tawang, population c. 20,000, would probably vote in favour of staying in 'India' rather than going into the 'PRC', though an independent 'Tibet' option would provide an interesting third option. Having Tawang subdivision inhabitants relocate further south if they wished might be another solution, though ugly in political and human terms. Meanwhile, if the Dalai Lama's death was followed by any proclaimed rebirth at Tawang, a not impossible scenario, the situation would be still more complicated with the PRC.

Failing dramatic regime change scenarios of regime collapse/ democratization in the PRC, and re-establishment of a genuinely autonomous or independent Tibet, and Tawang notwithstanding; some sort of trade off involving Aksai Chin and Arunachal Pradesh seems the most likely way forward. In using relatively clear cut neutral geographic principles, the deadlocked politics and unclear history could perhaps be sidelined? Such a trade off would give neither side too much geopolitical advantage, but also ensure a degree of security for each? A *logic of geography* for the future for the national leaderships that would enable these two neighbours to get past the inconclusive divisive *logic of history* between them, and would provide a mutually satisfactory *logic of power* in terms of geopolitical equilibrium outcomes. Failing resolution of their territorial issues, the grinding tectonic plates along the Himalayas will continue to have their geopolitical counterpart as the two Asian giants look at each other across these disputed areas.

RESOLVING THE BOUNDARY DISPUTE: CHINA'S REASONS AND INDIA'S CHOICES

The final settlement of the Sino-Indian territorial and boundary dispute is not a question of 'if' but 'when'. Four pertinent reasons suggest that China can be ultimately trusted to settle the dispute.

On its part, India can take certain steps to ensure that China's reasons do not alter and that 'compromise' is seen as mutually beneficial.

One, China has steadily resolved its territorial disputes with almost all of its 15 land neighbours. Negotiations with the Soviet Union and Vietnam began in 1964 and 1977 respectively. However, it was not until much later that the negotiation processes fructified; it was only in October 2004 that the eastern sector of the Sino-Russian border was finally resolved with the signing of the Supplementary Agreement. With Vietnam, China signed a land boundary agreement in 1999, although they continue to meet regularly at the governmental level to thrash out details pertaining to the Beibu Gulf and the placement of border markers. Therefore, boundary negotiations between China and its other neighbours have been long and arduous affairs. The slowness of the boundary negotiations between India and China needs to be seen in this context.

Two, China has settled 17 of its 23 territorial disputes since 1949, according to M. Taylor Fravel, Assistant Professor of Political Science at MIT. Fravel suggests that regime insecurity and legitimacy crises in peripheral border regions best explain why China not only made concessions but also favoured the peaceful resolution of its territorial disputes. Despite a significant rise in China's economic and military strength vis-a-vis weaker neighbours, China received less than 50 per cent of the contested land. China's 'peaceful development' and 'new security concept' are directly responsible for the gradual stabilization of its borders-both concepts demand peaceful and stable borders for sustained economic growth.

Three, the absence of territorial disputes on China's western flank is a consequence of its 'western development' strategy. Starting with Myanmar and Nepal in the 1960s, a flurry of diplomatic activity saw the resolution of China's borders with Tajikistan and Kazakhstan (in 2002), Kyrgyzstan (in September 2004), Russia (in October 2004), and Mongolia (in November 2005). The pacification of China's western border is driven by the need to build cross-border linkages for economic development as well as the suppression of the three evils-separatism, extremism and terrorism. China's two westernmost provinces that border India, Xinjiang and Tibet, are important to China not least due to the fear that an economic imbalance can potentially fuel secessionist sentiments amongst the Uighurs and Tibetans.

Four, China is likely to reserve the use of force to settle heartland disputes. The hard component of China's comprehensive national strength will continue to dictate an inflexible stance on Taiwan's reunification as well as territorial conflicts of strategic value. Therefore, China is unlikely to make concessions on approximately 30,000 square kilometres of Aksai Chin, not least due to the fact that the Karakoram highway that traverses it provides a strategic link between Pakistan, and China and a shorter route between Tibet and Xinjiang. However, even in the case of disputes over territory of great economic value, such as the South China Sea, China has emphasized the joint development and exploitation of resources, albeit without making any concessions.

As emerging powers, India and China will continue to be pitted against each other. The sheer size and altitude of the disputed area is likely to make demarcation a difficult and lengthy process. However, India can take certain steps to ensure it remains in China's interest to settle the dispute. India must do its utmost to convince China that it is not the target of the newly sealed Indo-US strategic relationship. India must clarify that the support for Tibetans in India is humanitarian and cultural and not a challenge to China's sovereign territoriality. China's friendship with Pakistan cannot be wished away; however, India can make itself important to China by promising trade and joint border development projects that make good business sense. India's inclusion into the Shanghai Cooperation Organisation as an observer in July 2005 was an important recognition of India's commitment to curbing cross-border terrorism.

Even though there are reasons to believe that China is not a revisionist state determined to use force to uphold its territorial claims, proactive steps to create lobbies with vested interests in resolving the dispute must be taken. The seventh round of Sino-Indian border talks in March 2006 helped provide a 'constructive and friendly' atmosphere. It is time for India and China to carry that forward and focus on opening Nathu La for trade, reviving the Stilwell Road for trade across India's northeast, building border free trade zones similar to the Sino-Kazakh one and establishing independent inter-linkages between border regions through transport linkages akin to the Kashgar (Xinjiang, China)-Gilgit (Northern Areas, Pakistan) bus service. Discussion on the Sino-Indian boundary talks must therefore go beyond the rhetoric on China's 'concirclement' of India; it must emphasize the domestic constraints and foreign policy concerns of the Chinese government and the resolution of territorial disputes that such a study reveals.

CHINA'S BORDER SPAT WITH INDIA

The recent meeting between India's National Security Adviser MK Narayanan and China's Vice-Foreign Minister Dai Banggio at Coonoor in Tamil Nadu was the continuation of a series of such meetings in the context of the border dispute between the two countries. While this is a good thing to go by, the main point is: what has been the actual progress in the matter? After every meeting, a standard joint communiqué is issued to the effect that the téte-a-téte was fruitful and the dialogue is being maintained in an atmosphere of friendship and mutual cooperation. Diplomatic jargon cannot be limitless; it must end somewhere.

Again, from time to time one hears of Chinese intrusion into Arunachal Pradesh, especially in the area of Sumdorong Chu Valley and the northern range of the Mishmi Hills. There is also the occasional media report that China claims this Northeastern state of ours on the grounds of a combination of history as well as geography.

India's drawback is that our foreign policy has always been linked to the vote bank. In fact it was a vote bank issue that created the border dispute with China in the first place way back in the late '50s and early '60s. The origin of this problem is worth discussing as this itself suggests the solution. Soon after China secured Tibet, Beijing sent a delegation to New Delhi under then Prime Minister Zhou en Lai with a proposal on Aksai Chin in northern Kashmir, adjacent to the Siachen Glacier. The delegation submitted to us that movement from Tibet to Sinkiang province was a huge problem because one had to traverse the inhospitable Kunlun Mountains en route. Hence it was suggested both countries could arrive at an understanding by which India could lease out Aksai Chin to China, as this would enable the latter to build an all-weather highway across this stretch of territory.

Thus movement from Tibet to Sinkiang would not then involve negotiating the Kunluns at all and India, too, could use this highway as a bonus. In any case, Aksai Chin was just an ice desert with an average height of 18,000-19,000 feet and nothing grew there, let alone having any human habitation. New Delhi reacted with its usual brash arrogance, thundering words to the effect that 'not an inch of our sacred motherland' would be given, et al. Zhou en Lai was shown the door gracelessly.

The Chinese delegation went back and decided to implement a tenet in Hindi conveying the meaning that if ghee cannot be taken out by a straight finger then a crooked finger would be used! China militarily attacked India and physically captured Aksai Chin by force in late 1962 and built the desired highway through it. China is still very much in occupation of this area, cocking a snook at India now and then! On our part we bemoaned our fate, blamed Beijing for gerrymandering into our territory and generally made a political nuisance of ourselves. Nothing helped, of course.

During its attack on India, China had also deeply transgressed into what was earlier known as the North East Frontier Agency that later became Arunachal Pradesh. However, after delivering a crushing military-cum-political defeat on India, China moved back to its own side of the border in this area. This apart, China disputes an area along the Uttarkhand-Tibet border named Barahoti.

China has a strong army garrison in this area at a place called Taklakot that keeps a watching brief over Barahoti. India, therefore, has been well and truly boxed in by China, courtesy New Delhi's folly of riding the high horse with Zhou en Lai's delegation of yore. Diplomacy has never been a strong point with us and the country has suffered badly as a consequence. The science and art of statecraft continue to be subservient to the omnipotent vote bank as far as our leaders are concerned.

New Delhi, for reasons best known to itself, brought out a Lok Sabha resolution in 1994 wherein it was categorically stated that we would retake Aksai Chin by force. Obviously this resolution was nothing but a vote bank gimmick that our näive citizens – including many members of our intelligentsia – swallowed all the way. While firmly occupying Aksai Chin, China periodically needles India over Arunachal Pradesh and Barahoti. Normally, Barahoti remains dormant but Arunachal Pradesh makes news, sometimes with alarm. This has been the state of affairs since 1962. No government at New Delhi since that year has tried to accept the reality and taken any pragmatic steps to reconcile the border situation with China, notwithstanding the fact that currently our relations with China are improving virtually by the day.

The question is, what needs to be done in order to resolve the ongoing impasse? There is only one solution: India must formally accept Zhou en Lai's suggestion of yesteryear but cede Aksai Chin to China. It is doubtful whether China will accept the lease aspect now. The Chinese are a very proud race and will never climb down. In any event, China holds the aces in this matter, never mind the McMahon Line's relevancy to us.

Truth to tell, this solution was hinted by China's previous regime under President Jiang Zemin through his then Foreign Minister Tang Jiaxuan during Prime Minister AB Vajpayee's tenure. While the Sikkim issue got reconciled, Aksai Chin could not be followed through due to the change of government in India in 2004.

China is not really interested in Barahoti and Arunachal Pradesh – Beijing uses these two as pressure points on New Delhi to see reason over the border dispute, a dispute that hinges purely on Aksai Chin. The sooner we come to terms with this, the better.

THE CHINA-INDIA BORDER ISSUE IN 2013: POINT AND COUNTER-POINT

On 15 April around thirty Chinese soldiers crossed an unguarded section of the China-India border – the Line of Actual Control (LAC) – and set up camp, reportedly nineteen kilometres inside territory India claims. In itself this was not an unheard of incident; one Indian newspaper reported that in 2012 there were 'over four hundred incursions', ninety per cent of which occurred in the Ladakh region, where the latest incident took place. This time, though, the Chinese troops set up a camp in the disputed territory, the first time they had done so since 1986.

A flag meeting was held by military representatives of the Indian and Chinese armies but to no avail. At subsequent meetings and through diplomatic channels, and amid much pressure from the mass media and the public, India asked China to withdraw to previously-held positions. China, in turn, asked India to remove the "fortified positions" its troops had constructed along the LAC.

The issue created a good deal of debate in China, India and the rest of the world, where it was reported upon and studied so as to deduce China's motivations for the "transgression" and India's strength and diplomatic maturity in how it dealt with it.

It is in this spirit of debate that Future Directions International presents this Associate Paper. Two noted analysts present the perspectives of China and India respectively. Dr. Liu Zongyi is a visiting fellow at the Centre for Strategic and International Studies (CSIS) and a research fellow at the Shanghai Institutes for International Studies (SIIS). Acknowledging the complexity of the border issue, Dr. Liu emphasises the symbiotic relationship between the two countries and observes India stands to gain more by allying with China rather than with the United States of America, with which country it is developing fast-growing ties.

Dr. Jabin Jacob is the Assistant Director & Fellow, Institute of Chinese Studies, New Delhi. Whilst not denying the complexity of the border issue, Dr. Jacob points out that incursions of this type will become the new norm and confidence-building measures will need to acknowledge this fact. He also notes that China, while acknowledging India's rise, appears to be unable to cast off its misgivings in relation to the growing India-US relationship.

2

Border Dispute Remains Unresolved

THE Venerable Lobsang Norbu, a 77-year-old monk who presides over one of several Tibetan Buddhist hilltop monasteries in Arunachal Pradesh, in north-eastern India, recalls the "very horrible" war that China launched 50 years ago this week. Flares lit up the night, then gunfire erupted. Terrified villagers and monks fled through the pine and rhododendron forests to nearby Bhutan. Many of India's poorly led and outgunned soldiers panicked and ran just as quickly.

Other residents remember the sudden appearance of Chinese soldiers, whom Mao Zedong had earlier deployed to put down a Tibetan uprising north of the border. The attackers swarmed over the disputed Himalayan border. They quickly overran Tawang, a monastery town wedged beside Tibet.

Karma Wangchuk was then working for Indian intelligence. He says he hid in the long grass and counted in the tough young soldiers, "some in white hats". When he got beyond 500 he was spotted and fired at. He fled to safety on the Indian plains far below. Other locals, ethnic Monpa, whose language is close to Tibetan, talk of how the Chinese soldiers behaved decently towards civilians. Yet they have no doubts about wanting to remain as part of India.

Although the Indian press has made much of the anniversary this month, officials in Delhi, the capital, have studiously ignored the memory of the country's swift and humiliating defeat in the war. There is, says Ajai Shukla, author of a forthcoming book on Tawang and the Sino-Indian border, "very little glory from 1962".

Tensions had risen in the late 1950s over the disputed border, 3,380km (2,100 miles) long, when India learnt of a new road the Chinese had built through the Aksai Chin at the border's western end. The empty region was claimed by India as traditionally part of Ladakh, but to the Chinese it was (and still is) a strategic link between Tibet and Xinjiang. So confident were Indian generals that the Chinese had neither the will nor the ability to launch a war across the line of control that they established outposts behind the Chinese troops in Aksai Chin. China's Communist leaders had other ideas. Among other things, they were angry at India for granting refuge to the Dalai Lama and other Tibetans who had fled south. They massed troops in Aksai Chin and north of Arunachal Pradesh.

The invaders raced south, and the war claimed around 4,500 lives before China unilaterally declared it over and pulled out. The Chinese had exposed the weakness of India's army. Relations between the Asian behemoths have been cagey, at best, ever since. No shot has been fired since 1993, yet the border disputes persist.

Ordinary Indians have paid a price for that, a senior politician in Arunachal Pradesh complains. He says anxiety over China is to blame for a shortage of central funds for hydropower stations, roads, bridges and railways. Other opportunities have also been missed. China, including Hong Kong, is now India's largest trading partner, exchanging goods worth $74 billion last year. Yet nearly all of the trade takes place by sea, with only a trickle passing directly by land. As a result, India's north-east lies moribund, forgotten between Bangladesh, Myanmar and a forbidding Chinese border. Street markets in Tawang are packed with Chinese crockery, toys and other small manufactures. Yet none have come through the nearby border post. (There had once been a time, even under the communists, when Lhasa, the Tibetan capital, was provisioned via Calcutta.)

Instead of trade, the region is seeing a steady rise in military spending. Worried by China building a railway and all-weather road network on the Tibetan plateau over the past decade, India's border force is upgrading the treacherous, zigzagging track up to Tawang. For the moment it is a two-day drive from the plain to the treeless border. By 2016 the track is due to become a sleek national highway, able to carry troops quickly up to the border.

Indeed, India is raising four new divisions—70,000 soldiers—for the frontier, and establishing new, better-equipped bases. "Half a million men are eyeball to eyeball," says Mohan Guruswamy, a China expert in Delhi. He sees diminishing prospects for settling the border dispute. Despite well-established routines between the two sides' infantry patrols to avoid clashes, he worries about a persistent risk of accidental conflict.

A deal over the border has for years been self-evident: China gets to keep Aksai Chin in the west and India gets to keep the 80,000 square kilometres of Arunachal Pradesh, which China informally calls "South Tibet". In the past China has signalled a readiness to settle the dispute along just such lines. But Indian leaders and parliament have always balked, saying voters would not tolerate losing an inch of territory, even when no settled populations are involved.

China can be capricious, too. It deliberately provoked tensions over the border when it issued visas to residents of Arunachal Pradesh only on stapled pieces of paper rather than in passports, a signal that the Chinese government does not recognise Indian authority over the state. Such steps look calculated to cause offence.

Broader relations have improved over the past couple of years, though with no progress on the border. Occasional plans for joint military operations are announced and then quickly forgotten. Formal border talks exist—a 16th round is due between special representatives—but no one expects anything to follow from them.

As the years slip by, China may grow less interested in a quiet border. Observers in India worry that if either China's generals or its nationalist social-media activists and editors gained sway over border discussions, Chinese diplomats would struggle to propose compromises.

Back in the Tawang valley, Dorjee Khandu Thongdok, a jovial politician, campaigns to raise awareness over the "agony and sufferings during the Chinese aggression" of 1962. Munching on roasted sweetcorn just harvested from nearby fields, he has no trust in talks with China. A military solution is certainly no answer, he insists. But he would, he says, not be surprised if the Chinese again invade Arunachal, just as they did half a century ago. The task of both Indian and Chinese leaders is to ensure that he is wrong.

INDIA-CHINA BORDER DISPUTE

On assuming power, the People's Republic of China (PRC) renounced all prior foreign agreements as unequal treaties imposed upon it during the "century of humiliation" and demanded renegotiation of all borders. The Sino-India border remains the only major territorial dispute, other than South China Sea disputes, that China has not resolved. China's growing assertiveness in its territorial claims, especially on Arunachal Pradesh, and its relentless development of infrastructure in Tibet will shape the prospects of Sino-India relations.

The territory stretching from the jungles of northern Myanmar, westward to the Karakoram Range, and northward to the edge of the Tibetan plateau can be seen as a single geopolitical system referred to as the Himalayan-Tibetan massif. The ruggedness of this terrain makes movement of men and materiel extremely difficult, thus preventing Indian and Chinese civilizations from intermingling or projecting military power in these remote areas effectively. Not until 1962 did the Chinese and Indian armies fight each other over these desolate heights, thus altering the geopolitics of the region significantly.

Chinese President Hu Jintao met with Indian Prime Minister Manmohan Singh in Sanya City, south China's Hainan Province, April 13, 2011. Hu said China is willing to further push forward negotiations on border issues on the basis of peace and friendliness, equal consultation, mutual respect and understanding. The two sides should consider setting up a consultation and coordination mechanism on border issues so as to achieve consensus as soon as possible and to better maintain peace and stability at the border regions before the issues are solved.

China wants India to put behind the 1962 war as an "unfortunate" thing of the past and that the two countries should strengthen their military ties including formalising a border management pact under which their troops will not fire at each other. The Chinese assessment was conveyed to the Indian defence ministry team which visited Beijing on 14-15 January 2013 for the third round of the annual defense dialogue between the two countries.

Border tensions between China and India flared after New Delhi claimed a contingent of 30 to 50 PLA soldiers crossed about 12 miles beyond the Line of Actual Control between the two countries on 15 April 2012 and stayed there for three weeks. According to New Delhi, PLA soldiers frequently conduct border incursions (more than 600 times over the last three years) but do not usually cross more than a few miles over the Line of Actual Control nor stay there longer than several hours.

Beijing denied Chinese troops had crossed into Indian territory. A Chinese Ministry of Foreign Affairs spokesperson said, "China has always acted in strict compliance with relevant agreements and protocols between the two countries on maintaining peace and tranquility in the Line of Actual Control area along the border... Chinese patrol troops have never crossed the line." Chinese Premier Li Keqiang attempted to downplay the incident and the risk of conflict. During a state visit to India, he insisted that "a few clouds in the sky cannot shut out the brilliant rays of our friendship." Premier Li did not directly address the alleged Chinese incursion, though he said "both sides believe we need to improve various border-related mechanisms that we have put into place and make them more efficient, and we need to appropriately manage and resolve our differences."

President Xi Jinping met Indian Prime Minister Manmohan Singh at the BRICS Summit in Durban, South Africa, 29 March 2013. Xi urged both sides to use special representatives to strive for a fair, rational framework that can lead to a solution to the border issue as soon as possible. India will abide by political guidelines set by both sides and seek a solution to the border issue with a commitment to safeguarding peace, Singh said. Since 2003, more than a dozen rounds of talks had been launched to resolve the border disputes. But ties have still been occasionally strained by the issue and overshadowed by closer India-US relations amid Washington's accelerating Asia "pivot" policy.

Beijing and New Delhi resolved the April border impasse in May after a series of talks and agreed to pursue a formal agreement to build trust and confidence between the border troops. The two sides signed the agreement during the Indian prime minister's trip to China in October 2013. China and India concluded a border defense cooperation pact 24 October 2013, making it a highlight of Indian Prime Minister Manmohan Singh's visit to the Asian neighbor. The Indian Express newspaper said the pact also puts no restrictions on India developing border infrastructure or enhancing military capabilities along the border. It quoted India's Ambassador to China S. Jai Shanker as saying: "This principle allows both countries to take appropriate measures according to their own security needs."

Nevertheless, the potential for periodic low-level confrontations between border patrols to escalate likely will persist. Indian media have reported several additional albeit briefer incursions by Chinese troops since the April standoff. Furthermore, both China and India continue to boost their militaries' capabilities on the border, adding to mutual suspicion. This has left both sides sensitive to each other's border activities and disposed toward worst-case perceptions of the other sides' intentions and activities. Ely Ratner and Alexander Sullivan of the Center for a New American Security, warn: "more intense strategic competition between India and China would reverberate throughout the continent, exacerbating tensions in Central Asia, the Indian Ocean, and Southeast Asia. Disruptions to the Asian engine of economic growth caused by these tensions could debilitate the global economy."

THE CHINA CHALLENGE: A STRATEGIC VISION FOR U.S.-INDIA RELATIONS

India is keeping a wary eye on China's rapid global ascent. Unresolved border issues that resulted in the Sino-Indian War of 1962 have been heating up again in recent years.

Indian policymakers are scrambling to develop effective policies to cope with a rising China by simultaneously pursuing both a robust diplomatic strategy aimed at encouraging peaceful resolution of border disputes and forging strong trade and economic ties and an ambitious military modernisation campaign that will build Indian air, naval, and missile capabilities.

By bolstering its naval assets, India will solidify its position in the Indian Ocean and enhance its ability to project power into the Asia Pacific. New Delhi also will continue to boost its medium-range missile programs to deter Beijing and to strengthen its air capabilities to deal with potential flare-ups along their disputed borders.

Meanwhile, China has also been paying increasing attention to India. China's interests on its southern flank have led the People's Liberation Army (PLA) to strengthen its forces in the Lanzhou and Chengdu Military Regions bordering India.

The U.S. must keep a watchful eye on the trend lines in Sino-Indian relations and factor these into its overall strategies in the broader Asia region. A strong India able to hold its own against China is in America's interest.

China's increased assertiveness in the East and South China Seas over the past year has been accompanied by a hardening position on its border disputes with India. Last summer, India took the unprecedented step of suspending military ties with China in response to Beijing's refusal to grant a visa to an Indian Army general serving in Jammu and Kashmir.

Chinese Premier Wen Jiabao's visit to New Delhi last December helped tamp down the disagreement, and military contacts have since resumed. Still, the incident shows the fragility of the Sino-Indian rapprochement and the potential for deepening tensions over the unresolved border issues to escalate.

U.S. Secretary of State Hillary Clinton's visit to India this week for Strategic Dialogue talks provides an opportunity to take India's pulse on China and to discuss new diplomatic and security initiatives that will contribute to maintaining a stable balance of power in Asia. The U.S. should demonstrate support for Indian military modernisation and enhanced U.S.-Indian defence ties.

Despite U.S. disappointment over India's decision to de-select two American companies from its Medium Multi-Role Combat Aircraft (MMRCA) competition, the U.S. is bound to conclude other major defence deals with India as it pursues an ambitious defence modernisation campaign, which includes spending plans of around $35 billion over the next five years.

Indeed, this year, the two sides finalised a deal worth nearly $4 billion for the U.S. to provide India with enough C-17 aircraft to give India the second-largest C-17 fleet in the world. Enhancing Indo-U.S. cooperation in maritime security in the Indian Ocean region is also an area of mutual interest that is ripe for new initiatives.

India's rejection of the MMRCA has added a dose of realism to Indo-U.S. relations and reminded U.S. officials that the burgeoning partnership will not always reach the full expectations of either side. Still, the growing strategic challenge presented by a rising China will inevitably drive the U.S. and India to increase cooperation in defence and other key sectors, such as space, maritime security, and nuclear non-proliferation.

What Drives Sino-indian Competition?

The drivers of the current Indian-Chinese rivalry are varied and complex. While China's economy is several times larger than India's and its conventional military capabilities today outstrip India's by almost any comparison, Beijing has begun to take notice of India's growing global political and economic clout, as well as the broad-based American support for expanding strategic ties with India.

For its part, India, long suspicious of China's close relations and military support for Pakistan, views an increased Chinese presence in northern Pakistan and expanded civil nuclear cooperation between Beijing and Islamabad as particularly worrisome. Indian military strategists believe they must plan for the possibility of a two-front war with Pakistan and China even as they actively seek dialogues with both to diminish the chances of such a dire scenario.

At the same time, Chinese assessments of Indian military planning suggest a view in Beijing that New Delhi sees China as a major threat. One Chinese assessment concludes that the Indian military sees Pakistan as the main operational opponent and China as a potential operational opponent. It also describes the Indians as seeing China and Pakistan as closely aligned in threatening India.

The rivalry is also driven by the rapidly expanding resource requirements of each country, whose economies continue to grow steadily despite the global economic downturn. Competition over energy and water resources will increasingly shape the contours of their competition, as will each country's efforts to expand trade and economic relations with countries that are in the other's traditional sphere of influence.

SIMMERING BORDER TENSIONS

Long-standing border disputes between China and India continue to cause friction between the two countries despite ongoing border talks that started in the 1980s. India claims that China occupies more than 14,000 square miles of Indian territory in the Aksai Chin along its northern border in Kashmir (commonly referred to as the western sector), while China lays claim to more than 34,000 square miles of India's northeastern state of Arunachal Pradesh (commonly referred to as the eastern sector). The two sides fought a brief border war in 1962 after China invaded the eastern and western sectors of their shared borders and ended up annexing the area of Aksai Chin, a barren plateau that had been part of the pre-partition princely state of Jammu and Kashmir. India also is a long-term host to the Dalai Lama and about 100,000 Tibetan refugees that fled after China annexed Tibet in 1950.

Meanwhile, according to Beijing, India is occupying territory unfairly claimed during the era of "unequal treaties." The Chinese Communist Party (CCP) has never accepted the validity of the McMahon Line as the demarcation of the Sino-Indian border in Tibet, viewing it as forced upon weak imperial and republican governments by the British Raj.

In 2003, each side appointed "special representatives" – national security adviser for India and vice foreign minister for China—to upgrade and regularise their border discussions. Since then, the two sides have clarified the mapping of the middle sector of their disputed frontiers (the border that demarcates the Indian state of Sikkim). However, there has been no exchange of maps of the eastern and western sectors under dispute.

China's interest in consolidating its hold on Tibet and its perceptions of India's expanding global influence and closer ties to the U.S. have led Beijing to harden its position on its border disputes with New Delhi over the past five years. China has increasingly questioned Indian sovereignty over the states of Arunachal Pradesh and Jammu and Kashmir and has stepped up probing operations along different parts of their shared frontier. The Chinese are also building up military infrastructure and expanding a network of road, rail, and air links in the border areas.

The hardening Chinese position can be traced back to comments made by the Chinese ambassador to India, referring to the entire state of Arunachal Pradesh as part of China, in the run-up to President Hu Jintao's November 2006 visit.

Moreover, in recent years, Chinese commentators have begun to refer to Arunachal Pradesh commonly as "Southern Tibet." Prior to 2005, there were no Chinese references to "Southern Tibet" in China's official media. In 2009, China opposed an Asian Development Bank loan, part of which was earmarked for a watershed project in Arunachal Pradesh — another demonstration that China is questioning Indian sovereignty over the state more openly.

These moves have signalled to New Delhi that the Chinese may be backing away from a 2005 border agreement, referred to as the "Agreement on Political Parameters and Guiding Principles for Settlement of the Boundary Question." More specifically, since the 2005 accord stipulated that "settled populations will not be disturbed," India argues that China has violated the 2005 agreement by laying claim to Tawang in Arunachal Pradesh. Chinese interlocutors claim Tawang is part of Tibet because one of the Dalai Lamas was born there. The Chinese have objected to recent visits to Tawang by the Indian Prime Minister and the Dalai Lama.

In addition to raising questions about the status of Arunachal Pradesh, China has called into question Indian sovereignty over the state of Jammu and Kashmir. In 2009, Beijing began stapling visas to Indian passport holders from Jammu and Kashmir. Furthermore, in July of last year, China denied a visa to Indian Lieutenant General B. S. Jaswal, chief of Northern Command, which includes parts of Kashmir. General Jaswal had intended to travel to Beijing to participate in a high-level China-India defence exchange. In response to China's refusal to grant General Jaswal a visa, India suspended further bilateral defence exchanges.

The visa issue appears to have been resolved, as India resumed defence contacts with China last month by sending an eight-member Indian military delegation to China. The visit followed media reports that China had begun issuing regular visas to Indian residents of Jammu and Kashmir.

Since the 1999 Kargil border conflict between India and Pakistan, Beijing's position on Kashmir seemed to be evolving toward a more neutral position. During that conflict, Beijing helped convince Pakistan to withdraw forces from the Indian side of the Line of Control following its incursion into the heights of Kargil in Kashmir. Beijing made clear its position that the two sides should resolve the Kashmir conflict through bilateral negotiations, not military force, but the stapled visas issue and Beijing's refusal to grant a visa to the Indian army official from Kashmir have raised concern in New Delhi that China is reverting to a policy of favouring Pakistan's position on Kashmir.

Indian commentators have noted that China's backtracking from its neutral position on Kashmir would likely be met with subtle moves by India that increasingly question Chinese sovereignty over Tibet.

Increasing Military Activities

Meanwhile, Chinese military activities in the region have expanded. In July 2010, the official newspaper of the PLA, People's Liberation Army Daily, reported that units of the People's Liberation Army Air Force (PLAAF) were engaging in armed combat air patrols. These are believed to have been advanced Su-27 or J-11 (domestically produced versions of the Su-27) fighter aircraft.

The combat air patrols were followed by an August 2010 logistics exercise involving the newly constructed Qinghai-Tibet railway. This exercise marked the first PLAAF use of the railway for military purposes, with the Military Transportation Department of the PLAAF Logistics Department overseeing the movement of "combat readiness materials" to Tibet. This would seem to reflect a growing PLAAF role in maintaining security along the Sino-Indian border in the Tibetan area.

In October 2010, there were reports that the PLA had conducted joint (inter-services) live-fire exercises in Tibet for the first time. These reportedly involved armour, artillery, air, and electronic warfare units and a variety of new equipment. Given the emphasis placed on joint operations in PLA doctrine, such exercises are not surprising, but instead reflect the extent to which they are being applied across the military, not just opposite Taiwan.

Indian expert observers do not interpret China's new-found assertiveness as preparation for imminent conflict, and they continue to calculate that the overall probability of another Sino-Indian war is low. However, they believe China may be trying to enhance its bargaining position in the ongoing border negotiations. The Indian observers note that incursions across the disputed borders are likely aimed at gaining tactical advantage to bolster Chinese territorial claims.

India has somewhat belatedly sought to match the Chinese moves and to reinforce its own claims in the disputed border areas by augmenting forces and constructing roads along the shared frontiers. These measures include the deployment of two squadrons of Su-30 MKI fighter jets in Assam and the raising of two mountain divisions for deployment in Arunachal Pradesh. India also has redeployed elements of its 27th Mountain Division from Jammu and Kashmir to the patch of land that intersects India, Tibet, and Bhutan and links India with the rest of its northeastern states.

India is reviving air fields along the border with China, including one in the Ladakh region.

India must increasingly factor the potential threat of conflict over its disputed borders with China into its security planning and projections. While Indian strategists assess that Pakistan poses the most immediate threat to India, they increasingly view China as the more important long-term strategic threat.

In order to deter Chinese aggression along India's border, Indian strategists believe they must develop the capability to inflict severe damage on Chinese forces in Tibet. China has an edge over India with regard to overall air power. Given infrastructure constraints in Tibet, however, China's ability to deploy significant air power on the border with India remains in question.

CHINA'S EXPANDING INFLUENCE IN SOUTH ASIA

China is consciously strengthening ties to its traditional ally Pakistan and slowly gaining more influence with other South Asian states. In addition to developing a port facility in Sittwe, Burma, China has invested in the development of ports in Hambantota, Sri Lanka, and Gwadar, Pakistan, and has offered assistance to Bangladesh in developing its deep-sea port in Chittagong. Because China imports about 70 percent of its energy requirements, its interest in developing these ports is primarily to help ensure uninterrupted access to crucial energy supplies.

China has already invested about $200 million in the Gwadar Port facility in the southwest part of Baluchistan Province in Pakistan off the coast of the Arabian Sea.

Pakistan's defence minister recently claimed that Pakistan had invited China to start building a naval base at Gwadar; Chinese officials publicly dismissed the notion. It is unclear whether Islamabad made the statement without coordinating with Beijing or whether the episode was carefully choreographed to send a signal (mainly to the U.S. and India) about the potential impact of an even cosier Sino–Pakistani military alliance.

China maintains a robust defence relationship with Pakistan and views a strong partnership with Pakistan as a useful way to contain Indian power in the region and divert Indian military force and strategic attention away from China. The Chinese JF-17 Thunder fighter aircraft is currently under serial production at the Pakistan Aeronautical Complex, and an initial batch of 250 to 300 planes is scheduled. China also plans to provide Pakistan with J-10 medium-role combat aircraft with an initial delivery of 30 to 35 planes. Other recent sales of conventional weapons include F-22P frigates with helicopters, K-8 jet trainers, T-85 tanks, F-7 aircraft, small arms, and ammunition.

The China-Pakistan partnership serves both Chinese and Pakistani interests by presenting India with a potential two-front theatre in the event of war with either country. Toward the end of the Indo-Pakistani war of 1965, China reportedly demanded that India dismantle certain posts on the India-China contested borders, but the war ended with Pakistan's acceptance of a U.N.-brokered ceasefire before China had an opportunity to act on its demands. During the 1971 Indo–Pakistani War, China took a less threatening posture toward India, possibly because of Soviet warnings to the Chinese.

China transferred equipment and technology and provided scientific expertise to Pakistan's nuclear weapons and ballistic missile programs throughout the 1980s and 1990s, enhancing Pakistan's strength in the South Asian strategic balance. The most significant development in China–Pakistan military cooperation occurred in 1992, when China supplied Pakistan with 34 short-range ballistic M-11 missiles. Beijing also built a turnkey ballistic missile manufacturing facility near Rawalpindi and helped Pakistan develop the 750 km–range solid-fuelled Shaheen-1 ballistic missile.

China helped Pakistan build two civilian nuclear reactors at the Chasma site in the Punjab Province under agreements made before it joined the Nuclear Suppliers Group (NSG) in 2004. More recently, China is moving forward with plans for two additional new nuclear reactors for Pakistan (Chasma III and Chasma IV), but the U.S. has indicated that Beijing must first seek an exemption from the NSG for any nuclear technology transfers. The NSG members discussed the proposed Chinese reactor sale to Pakistan at their plenary meeting in late June 2011 in the Netherlands. China argued that the proposed sale should be viewed as part of the earlier agreement struck with Pakistan before Beijing joined the NSG.

An Obama Administration decision to allow the China–Pakistan nuclear deal to advance unhindered would contradict earlier statements by U.S. officials that the construction of the two new nuclear plants would be inconsistent with China's NSG commitments. It could also jeopardise nuclear safety and security on the subcontinent, given that Pakistan's increased access to civilian nuclear technology without sufficient legal context and safeguards poses a potential proliferation threat.

U.S. media reports claiming that 7,000 to 10,000 PLA troops were deployed to Gilgit-Baltistan in Northern Pakistan last summer to help rebuild areas devastated by the massive Pakistani floods raised alarm in New Delhi. Indian analysts also noted the presence of PLA logistics and engineering corps in the region to provide flood relief and to build infrastructure projects such as roads, railways, and dams. The troops are most likely construction battalions helping to build transportation links between Pakistan and China, possibly from Gwadar Port. Nonetheless, New Delhi would view with consternation the possibility of Chinese troops stationed on both the eastern and northwestern borders of Indian Kashmir.

China also uses military and other assistance to court the smaller South Asian nations and to help them enhance their autonomy vis à vis India. Beijing has sold modern missile boats to Bangladesh and provided extensive military aid to Sri Lanka to help it win the war against the Tamil Tigers in 2009.

China's main interest in Nepal stems from its concerns over the large Tibetan refugee population there. Close to 20,000 Tibetans reside in Nepal, making it home to the world's second-largest Tibetan refugee community. Beijing increased its involvement with Nepal after the March 2008 ethnic Tibetan uprising against Chinese rule on the eve of the 2008 summer Olympics in Beijing.

Beijing has been pressing Nepal to tighten its borders with Tibet, which has led to a major decrease in the number of Tibetans able to flee to Nepal in recent years. China is also bolstering trade with Nepal and pursuing road-building and hydropower projects.

India "Glancing" East

For its part, India is slowly building political and economic ties with the Association of Southeast Asian Nations (ASEAN) and the individual states of Southeast Asia, which generally welcome India's involvement as a balance to growing Chinese influence. India became a member of the East Asia Sum-mit in December 2005 and signed a free trade deal with the ASEAN countries in2009. India has also enhanced its naval profile in Southeast Asia, holding periodic joint exercises with Singapore, Thailand, Vietnam, and Indonesia.

Also with an eye on China, India has prioritised strengthening relations with Japan through increasing military contacts, maritime cooperation, and trade and investment ties. Tokyo has pledged $4.5 billion in soft loans for the Delhi-Mumbai railway freight corridor, and the two sides inked a joint security declaration in 2008, calling their partnership "an essential pillar for the future architecture of the region." In 2007 and 2009, Japan participated in the Malabar naval exercises in the Indian Ocean.

In a significant turnaround from its past tough stance toward India's nuclear program, Tokyo is currently negotiating a civil nuclear deal with New Delhi.

Contesting the Seas... Indo–Chinese strategic competition increasingly revolves around naval issues. India views with concern the Chinese military presence in and around the Indian Ocean and is carefully considering what it means for energy and sea-lane security. New Delhi is especially worried about Beijing's potential naval expansion, including the development of its first aircraft carrier.

India is steadily increasing its defence budgets and focusing particular attention on building up its naval capabilities. In February, New Delhi unveiled its 2011 budget with an 11 percent increase for defence. India's rising defence budgets and growing navy have begun to concern Beijing, as China's energy lifeline that passes through the Indian Ocean side of the Malacca Straits will increasingly be vulnerable to India's naval presence.

India has the world's fifth-largest navy. It already has one aircraft carrier and is striving to put into place three carriers by 2020 as part of its naval expansion and desire to project power throughout the Indian Ocean. Difficulties in defence procurement and deficiencies in its own shipbuilding sector, however, could stall India's progress in developing its naval capabilities. India has also carefully cultivated ties with the countries of the Indian Ocean rim, including Mauritius, Maldives, Seychelles, and Madagascar, providing these countries with naval support, such as offshore naval patrol vessels and staff and training. In February 2008, India convened the Indian Ocean Naval Symposium, inviting participants from the littoral states to discuss maritime security. The United Arab Emirates hosted the second conference in May 2010.

India is pursuing better ties with Vietnam to try to check Chinese naval influence and access to the Indian Ocean. New Delhi initiated a new security partnership with Hanoi in 2000 that emphasized defence training, supply of advanced weaponry, and the potential for India to gain access to the South China Sea through the Cam Ranh Bay naval and air base. Indian officials have long understood the importance of Vietnam in the South China Sea and its potential to balance the Chinese naval presence in the Indian Ocean. The Vietnamese have demurred on granting India access to Cam Ranh Bay, and the Vietnamese–Indian security partnership remains limited. Vietnam has supported India in its quest for a permanent seat on the United Nations Security Council and has helped to block Pakistan's bid for membership in the ASEAN Regional Forum.

China, meanwhile, increasingly sees India as a maritime as well as a land threat. An assessment of the Indian military published by the PLA's National Defense University Press observes that, since the 1970s, India has increasingly shifted its strategic attention toward the Indian Ocean. In the Chinese view, this shift began in the wake of the 1971 Indo-Pakistani War, with increased construction of naval bases and forces and a concomitant expansion of Indian strategic guiding thoughts (zhanlue zhidao sixiang) to the Indian Ocean, and accelerated in the 1980s with the dispatch of Indian troops to Sri Lanka and the Maldives. While some of this naval effort is seen as being aimed at other states in the Indian Ocean region, especially Pakistan, the Chinese assessment also sees the Indian naval buildup as aimed at extra-regional military powers.

China's growing dependence on maritime commerce to sustain its economy inevitably heightens its concern over Indian naval capabilities. The Chinese assessment is that the Indian military has expanded its area of operations westward to the Persian Gulf and eastward to the Straits of Malacca, encompassing the key sea lanes of communications (SLOCs) that Chinese oil imports must transit.

As China modernizes its navy, there is some potential for the PLA to establish a greater presence in the Indian Ocean. India fears—a fear associated with China's port construction activities in Burma, Sri Lanka, Pakistan, and potentially Bangladesh—that these commercial ports might become naval ports of call. With China's acquisition of several new nuclear-powered attack submarines and additional diesel-electric submarines, and also the introduction of an aircraft carrier (the Shi Lang), the PLA navy may choose to establish a longer-term, sustained presence in the Indian Ocean, in part to help safeguard its SLOCs.

...and Space. India has given indications that it is developing a military space program to match China's expanding space capabilities. New Delhi has an advanced civilian space program and launches satellites for other countries, including Israel. Officials from the Indian Space Research Organization (ISRO) have announced their aim to use satellite-based communication and navigation systems for "security needs." In 2010, the Indian Ministry of Defence unveiled plans for dedicated military satellites for all three of its defence services. Still, India's space budget is one-third of China's, which is publicly stated as about $2.2 billion.

There are also reports that India has shown growing interest in an anti-satellite (ASAT) capability. Media reports from March 2011 about India's ballistic missile defense (BMD) program provide indications that such a system might also have ASAT missions.

Demographic trends feed strategic rivalry

India's population will surpass China's in about 15 years. While not a decisive factor in determining the overall power balance between the two Asian giants, this demographic trend will play a role in regional security dynamics.

The most striking difference in the Indian and Chinese demographic pictures over the coming decades is the onset of India's youth bulge at the same time that China finds its population graying. U.S. Census Bureau analysts estimate that new entrants into China's labour force may be near its upper limits of 124 million as the population of Chinese aged 20 to 24 peaks this year. India's population of 20- to 24-year-olds, on the other hand, is not expected to peak until 2024 when it hits 116 million. While India's workforce will increase by 110 million over the next decade, China's will increase by less than 20 million, according to a Goldman Sachs study.

This demographic dividend could fuel India's economy in ways that make it a peer competitor to China—in particular, pushing Indian growth rates ahead of China's. At present, the Chinese economy is vastly larger than India's. At more than $4.7 trillion, China's GDP is four times India's; its GDP per capita, at about $3,565, is three times India's; and China produces about 12 percent of the world's GDP while India produces about 5 percent. The Chinese also hold socioeconomic advantages over India that could play in Beijing's favour: Adult literacy in China stands at about 91 percent, compared to roughly 61 percent in India.

Trade could mitigate other competitive interests

Trade and business ties between China and India have increased dramatically in the past decade. Bilateral trade has increased from around $5 billion in 2002 to more than $60 billion in 2010. During Premier Wen Jiabao's visit to India last December, the two sides highlighted their growing economic relationship by pledging to boost trade over the next five years to $100 billion annually.

The rapidly expanding trade relationship between the two countries could help encourage a mutual interest in regional stability. While Beijing will almost certainly maintain close strategic ties to Pakistan, its growing economic stakes in India could motivate China to pay more attention to balancing its ties between India and Pakistan. On the other hand, some Indian analysts believe that China is pursuing a two-pronged strategy of lulling India into complacency with greater economic interaction while taking steps to encircle India and undermine its security.

What the U.S. should do

India must include the potential threat of conflict erupting over its disputed borders with China in its security planning and projections. While Pakistan presents the most immediate threat to India, Indian strategists increasingly view China as the most important long-term security challenge. Long-standing China-

Pakistan security ties are a continuing source of angst in New Delhi and reminder of a potential two-front war. While India seeks to avoid conflict with China, Indian military planners also assess that they need to develop sufficient capabilities to deter an increasingly powerful and assertive China.

The U.S. should pursue robust strategic and military engagement with India in order to encourage a stable balance of power in Asia that prevents China from dominating the region and surrounding seas. New Delhi — not unlike many other capitals in Asia — balks at the idea of being part of an American-led China "containment" strategy. Some Indian strategists even favour a go-slow approach to the U.S.-Indian partnership in order to avoid raising Chinese ire. But China's recent posturing on its border disputes with India leaves New Delhi few options other than to play all the strategic cards at its disposal, including deepening and expanding ties with the U.S.

One must also calculate that Chinese alarms over "containment" may in part be a tactic to prevent closer Indian cooperation with nations in the Pacific, including the U.S.

The partnership between the U.S. and India will almost certainly never develop into an "alliance," given India's core foreign policy goal of maintaining its "strategic autonomy." But an elevated partnership that gives a nod to India's growing political, economic, and military strength would signal a solidarity that could help deter Chinese military aggression and temper China's ambitions to revise borders in its favour.

The U.S. and India share a broad strategic interest in setting limits on China's geopolitical horizons. They can work together to support mutually reinforcing goals without ever becoming "allies" in the traditional sense. To this end, the U.S. should:

– Support India's military modernisation campaign, including its quest for increasingly sophisticated technologies related to its strategic weapons programs. The U.S. advanced this goal earlier this year when it removed export controls on several Indian space and defence-related organizations. In January, the U.S. removed several subsidiaries of India's Defense Research and Development Organization and the Indian Space Research Organization from the Department of Commerce's "Entities List," which bars the export of certain dual-use technologies.

During the 1990s, the U.S. had pressured India to modify its nuclear and missile posture and opposed the deployment of India's short-range Prithvi missile and the development of its medium-range Agni missile. The U.S. must recognise India's need to improve its strategic capabilities in order to address potential challenges from a rising China.

Develop new initiatives for keeping the Indian Ocean safe and secure. India and the U.S. have participated together in informal low-level efforts to address piracy off the coast of Somalia and in the Gulf of Aden. However, India has not joined the U.S.-led Coalition Maritime Force with combined task force (CTF-151), which the U.S. established as a major multilateral counterpiracy effort. India has been more interested in coordinating with other countries on a bilateral basis to address piracy rather than joining multinational anti-piracy organisations. In 2008, India initiated the Indian Ocean Naval Symposium to discuss maritime security with the other littoral states but did not include the U.S. in the discussions.

The U.S. should continue to work with India on maritime security while also seeking to convince New Delhi of the merits of adding the U.S., the United Kingdom, and Australia to a forum like the Indian Ocean Naval Symposium. One of the main goals of the forum should be to agree to a code of conduct for naval vessels operating in the region and to develop an action plan for dealing with violations of the agreed code.

Additionally, the U.S. should consider engaging the Indian navy in such areas as anti-submarine warfare training and ocean surveillance capabilities. Improvements in these areas would help to reassure India, especially in the event of a growing PLA naval presence.

Remain engaged with the smaller South Asian states and fully exercise its observer role in the South Asian Association of Regional Cooperation (SAARC). The U.S. needs to remain focused on its relations with Nepal, Sri Lanka, and Bangladesh so that these nations do not perceive China as the main economic and political game in town. India is clearly the dominant power in South Asia, but China is making new inroads with these countries that could come at the expense of stability and democratic trends in the region. The U.S. should participate fully in SAARC gatherings and ensure that its presence and influence are felt throughout the region.

Increase cooperation with India to address cyber security threats. In December 2009, more than 200 computers belonging to top-ranking Indian government officials, including three service chiefs and former National Security Adviser M.K. Narayanan, were compromised in a hacking operation that originated in China. The U.S. and India have been slow to seize opportunities for cooperating on cyber security issues. The two sides should explore joint efforts to monitor foreign investments in critical Internet technologies and telecommunications in order to establish a means of sharing pertinent cyber threat and vulnerability information to enhance the mutual security of their networks.

Keep strategic messaging in the region consistent. The Administration faltered in 2009 when it promoted U.S.–China "cooperation" in South Asia as part of the U.S.–China Joint Statement. South Asia constitutes India's immediate neighbourhood, and America's interests in the region are far more aligned with India than they are with China. Stabilising Afghanistan and ensuring that it never again becomes a safe haven for international terrorists is one example of the convergence of U.S.-Indian strategic interests in the region. If the U.S. is to forge a lasting partnership with India, it must start by recognising India's predominant interests in South Asia, even as it promotes peace, stability, and economic progress throughout the Subcontinent.

Conclusion

Sino-Indian tension, particularly over unresolved border issues and naval competition in the Indian Ocean, will persist in the years ahead and could even precipitate armed conflict, although this remains a relatively remote possibility. The U.S. must seek to build closer strategic and defence ties with India, both to help maintain a peaceful equilibrium in the region and to help deter any potential aggressive action by China.

India's decision to forego American planes to fulfil its fighter aircraft needs has added a dose of realism to Indo–U.S. relations. Nevertheless, the complex challenge presented by a rising China will inevitably drive the U.S. and India to elevate ties and increase cooperation across a broad range of sectors in years to come. There is a great deal the U.S. can do, carefully and deliberately, to facilitate this natural confluence of strategic interests.

SINO-INDIAN BORDER DISPUTE AND THEIR COMPETITIVE SYMBIOTIC RELATIONSHIP

Analysis

Recently, the Sino-Indian border dispute once again became a focus of for the world's mass media. A "tent confrontation" between the Chinese and Indian armies took place and continued near the Line of Actual Control (LAC) for several days. From the Indian point of view, the Chinese army invaded Indian territory, and this incident was "the most serious one in the past 25 years". Level-headed analysis will indicate, however, that China would not wish to provoke simultaneous conflicts with Japan and India, two major Asian powers. In fact, the Indian mass media's reports about Chinese incursions have been heard continually in recent years. Some reports that the Chinese have invaded India for more than 600 times in the past three years are ridiculous.

The Sino-Indian border issue is very complicated. It was left over from the time of British rule in India and has never been resolved. In the 1960s, a military conflict broke out between China and India over territorial boundaries. That conflict became the excuse for India to develop its armed forces vigorously, to get ready for battle, and to make nuclear weapons. The root reason cause of many of the "incursion" incidents reported by India is that the two sides have never reached a consensus on the position of the LAC since the boundary conflict in 1962. They have never delimited the LAC, let alone a formal border. It is therefore debatable to say the Chinese army invaded Indian territory.

Since 1993, however, China and India have signed two agreements and one protocol on the maintenance of peace and tranquillity and the establishment of confidence-building measures in the border areas. They have set up a working mechanism for consultation and coordination on border affairs. These efforts have helped ensure a durable peace and stability in the border areas. The possibility that China and India will come to serious conflict is very small.

Bilateral relations between China and India are very subtle; apart from the boundary problem, the issues of China-Pakistan relations, the Dalai Lama and water resources also hinder the promotion of China-India relations. These problems have given India a deep-seated distrust of China. Some Indians are gradually losing self-confidence as they observe the growing economic gap between China and India. The Indian mass media and some Indian strategic scholars frequently refer to a "Chinese incursion" and the "China threat" and propagate an attitude of no confidence in China's intentions. This situation provides opportunities for some Western countries to undermine Sino-India relations. With the US "rebalancing" toward the Asia-Pacific, the Sino-Indian relationship is undergoing subtle changes these days. Some Indian scholars promote an alliance under the US leadership to counterbalance China. For example, Harsh V. Pant, a professor of defence studies at King's College London, argues that India's strategic interests can only be realised by an Asia-Pacific arrangement in which the US retains its predominant status. The Indian Express columnist C. Raja Mohan similarly urges India to shift its policy of strategic autonomy and strategically cooperate with the US.

So far, India has concentrated on strengthening its "Look East" Policy to enhance strategic and security cooperation with countries such as Japan, South Korea, Malaysia and Vietnam. It has also taken a high profile in the South China Sea disputes. In December 2011, the first trilateral dialogue between the US, Japan and India was presided over by the US. One of the discussion topics was China's growing military and political global position. It is no wonder that many think that India may abandon strategic autonomy to ally itself with the US and contain China.

Currently, Indian policymakers have a relatively clear view of Sino-Indian and India-US relations. India doesn't yet have the ability to directly confront China, and, as a country prioritising economic development, it is in need of a peaceful neighbouring environment. History shows that the US is not a reliable ally for India. Because of the effect of the economic crisis, the US is heavily burdened by its domestic economic problems, and there are doubts about how much money can be invested in counterbalancing China. The US anchors its hope on the strategy of "offshore balancing" to achieve balance with, or even contain, China by stirring up tensions between it and its Asian strategic partners. It is just taking advantage of India's strength to balance China, which, in effect, should kill two birds with one stone.

So, at present, we have the ironic spectacle of articles in both the US and Indian media trying to provoke each other into tensions with China. The Indian media highlights the idea that Uncle Sam is well-prepared to battle China, while the US media points out that India is engaging in military expansion in preparation for possible Sino-Indian boundary conflicts. India still maintains its status as a "swing state" in the international system. Although it has recently become more pro-US, since the US recognised India as a nuclear power despite it not being a signatory to the Nuclear Non-Proliferation Treaty (NPT), India will not abandon its strategic autonomy to ally with the US.

I have published articles that arguing that the Sino-Indian relationship is, in essence, a competitive symbiotic relationship. I say that for the following reasons: First of all, there really are some areas of competitions between China and India, mainly in geopolitics, trade and energy, etc. But that competition is not necessarily cutthroat and zero sum. China and India can cooperate if they have mutual trust. In fact, they do cooperate in fields such as energy and anti-terrorism.

In addition to the aspect of competition, the Sino-Indian symbiotic relationship can be divided into four areas: First, as two big powers that are rising simultaneously, China and India are in similar positions in the current international system. They are beneficiaries of that system, but at the same time, they are constrained by it and also suppressed by the dominant power in the system. They want to gradually advance the reform of this system. So, China and India have common interests on many global issues, such as the reform of the international financial system, climate change, and the WTO negotiations. China, India, Brazil and South Africa have organised the BRICS and BASIC groups, which promote the reform of the international order. If China, India and other countries cannot consolidate their views on these global issues, they could be crushed one by one by the dominant power in the system and lose forever the chance to rise again.

Secondly, in the trilateral relations between China, India and the United States, India's status will benefit from China's rise. China's growth is a prerequisite for India's rise. If India really becomes embroiled in conflicts with China, it's hard to say whether the US will stretch out a hand to help it. But if India surpasses China, it will definitely replace its neighbour as the target of the US.

Thirdly, as two neighbouring powers in Asia, both China and India need a peaceful and stable periphery to develop their economies. Statesmen in both countries know clearly that development is their primary task, and that development needs stable circumstances. So, China and India have a common task to maintain the stability of the region. This is the determining factor that encourages China and India to keep their border areas stable for at least 10 years.

At least, the Chinese and Indian economies are complementary. Since they are in symbiosis, they could, theoretically, nourish and assist each other's survival and development. Sino-Indian bilateral trade has developed quickly in the past ten years, and the trade volume has risen 20 fold. Although India complains that there are some problems in the bilateral trade structure, and the Indian trade deficit is too large, it is evident that Chinese goods, which are of good quality and cheap, raise Indian people's living standards. China and India have ample room to cooperate, especially in infrastructure construction. China has large amounts of capital and extensive experience in the construction of infrastructure; India on the other hand needs to improve its infrastructure facilities, but lacks finance. Sino-Indian cooperation in this field will benefit both sides.

Within India, the so-called "China threat" is a trick of Indian political figures to pull the wool over the eyes of their people and Western countries. From the aspect of domestic politics, by making waves in relations with China, Indian politicians can obscure domestic contradictions, bolster up national morale, pull votes, and the military can get an increasing budget. From the aspect of international politics, India can obtain advanced weaponry and technologies from Western countries. In fact, the major direction of Indian military expansion is the Indian Ocean - the Navy received the largest part of India's rapidly growing defence budget. India's military strategy on land is defensive in nature but in the Indian Ocean, India has another competitor that is much stronger than China. The so-called "China threat" is just a cover.

The direction of Sino-Indian relations is determined for the medium-term at least, but the border issue is still a hindrance to bilateral relations. India did undertake some domestic reflection on the Sino-Indian conflict of 1962 and Nehru's policy towards China at that time, but no consensus was achieved. The Indian government never released publicly the Henderson-Brooks report that summarised the reasons why India was defeated. Taking a coherent view of this history will play a decisive role in the peaceful resolution of the Sino-Indian border problem. We should not neglect the negative role of the Indian multiparty system, in which foreign policy is often hijacked by domestic affairs. The role of the opposition parties and mass media in the Sino-Indian border conflict of 1962 is a case in point. It is necessary for the Indian government to reveal the truth about the Sino-Indian boundary conflict to the Indian people, and for Chinese and Indian scholars to conduct joint research projects on some historical problems, to alter the longstanding misconceptions held by both sides.

INDIA-CHINA RELATIONS: HOW CAN THEY BE IMPROVED?

Multi-Sector Co-operation

The development of economic co-operation is the main pillar of India-China relations. The volume of India-China trade increased from US$100 million in 1988, to US$73.9 billion in 2011. China has become India's biggest trading partner and India is China's seventh largest trading partner. The two governments have set the goal of increasing their trade volume to US$100 billion by 2015. With increasingly closer trade relations, mutual investment has developed quickly as well. By December 2011, China's accumulated investment in India had reached US$57.6 million and India's investment in China had reached US$44.2 million. Their mutual investment is still booming.

In their political interaction, a multi-channel and multi-level political dialogue platform has been set up, with frequent bilateral visits for in-depth discussions to resolve difficult issues and problems. On 26 September 2011, the first Sino-Indian Strategic and Economic Dialogue was launched, in which Chinese and Indian economic and foreign affairs policymakers began frank and direct discussions. National leaders of the two countries have frequent meetings in bilateral, regional and global forums. Taking 2012 as an example, in March President Hu Jintao travelled to India to take part in a joint Brazil, Russia, India and China meeting and spoke with Prime Minister Manmohan Singh of India. Then, in June, Premier Wen Jiabao met with Prime Minister Singh at the "Rio+20" United Nations Conference on Sustainable Development in Brazil. In November, Premier Wen again met with Prime Minister Singh in Cambodia, during the East Asia Summit. The leaders' diplomacy strongly promotes the development of the relationship between their countries.

China and India have also begun co-operating on security issues, particularly on border and non-traditional security issues. In January 2012, State Councillor Dai Bingguo and Indian National Security Advisor Shivshankar Menon met to discuss border issues; this was the fifteenth meeting of its kind. The two parties agreed to build a mechanism for consultation and co-ordination on border affairs. The first meeting of the mechanism was held in March 2012. China and India have also reached a basic consensus on strengthening maritime security co-operation and a maritime affairs dialogue is currently being planned. Cultural exchanges and co-operation between China and India continue to expand. This has become an important driving force for promoting the development and deepening of relations between the two countries. For example, in 2011 and 2012, 500 Indian and 500 Chinese young people were invited to visit the other country and to participate in cultural activities. That same year, 606,000 people travelled from India to China and 118,000 travelled from China to India, illustrating how frequently the people of the two countries interact.

Economic Constraints

Despite the development that has occurred so far, however, there are still many constraints in bilateral relations between China and India, affecting political, economic and security co-operation. In economic relations, the current status of India-China co-operation does not match the economic scales of the two countries. There is a huge opportunity for them to expand the size of their markets and deepen their economic interdependence. In 2011, the trade volume between China and India was only equal to one-sixth of that between China and the United States and one-third of that between China and South Korea. Given the large populations in each of these countries, it is obvious thatneither country has fully explored the market opportunities available in the other. Moreover, India has been worried about a trade deficit with China; for instance, India had a US$27 billion deficit with China in 2011. Such a trade imbalance could lead to nervousness in the bilateral relationship. According to the *Wall Street Journal*, India has been putting pressure on the Chinese Government to import more Indian products and has set high tariffs to protect Indian industries. Further, the relative backwardness of the domestic infrastructure in India is another constraint on co-operation that restricts deeper economic collaboration and personnel exchanges.

Border Issues

The India-China border and other territorial disputes, along with the issue of Tibet, restrict the establishment of political trust. Such a bilateral security dilemma is difficult to solve and is not conducive to co-operation. India has been concerned with China's infrastructure building in Tibet, which it views as a strengthening of China's strategic advantage in the region. According to the Indian media, Prime Minister Singh agreed to station an additional

90,000 troops along India's border with China in 2012. Although India has officially recognised that Tibet is part of China, it still hosts the Tibetan independence force. Moreover, given that China and Pakistan maintain a quasi-alliance, while India and Pakistan are still hostile to each other, the power-balance game is still being played in the region. China is also very sensitive about India's recent involvement in oil exploration in the South China Sea and its actions to strengthen maritime co-operation with Japan, which has disputes with China over islands in the region. The so-called "String of Pearls" strategy, which suggests that China is constraining India by constructing ports and bases in the Indian Ocean region, has been heavily covered by the Indian media.

Perception Problems

Finally, the peoples of China and India lack a comprehensive and rational understanding of each other. In India, China is often viewed as a dangerous competitor; the media particularly portrays China this way. In China, a few nationalists tend to express a strong dislike of India and do not recognise that the country should be viewed as a regional and global power. A recent poll showed that two-thirds of Chinese respondents had negative views of India and only 23 per cent of Indian interviewees believed that the relationship between China and India was co-operative. The mutual distrust between the two peoples has undoubtedly affected the development of the relationship between their countries and may continue to do so.

Future Prospects

Although these constraints exist, we still believe there is a positive future for the bilateral relationship, because the two countries share many common interests in a wide variety of areas. For example, their economic structures are complementary. Further, China is a manufacturing power and India is a major worldwide player in the service industry. Both countries face similar problems in domestic economic and social development and can share their experiences and support each other in approaching these. Regarding security, from China's point of view, if China cannot handle its relationship with India effectively, it will not be able to shape an ideal security environment, which is crucial for its domestic development. For India, a good relationship with China will not only benefit India's development but also be an important way to enhance its international influence.

On the regional level, China and India actively participate in multilateral co-operation processes, such as the free-trade schemes in South-East Asia. Both countries have concluded a free-trade agreement with the Association of South-East Asian Nations.

The recently launched negotiations for the Regional Comprehensive Economic Partnership also include them. If concluded by 2015, as intended, this partnership will become one of the world's largest free-trade areas. Moreover, both countries recognise that non-traditional security issues in the region, such as terrorism, transnational crime, piracy, natural disasters and other challenges, can only be tackled through joint efforts and regional co-operation. One example is the sub-regional co-operation between China, India, Burma and Bangladesh, which focuses on economic co-operation, as well as non-traditional security issues, such as narcotics. On a global level, broad common interests exist between China and India, such as reform of international financial institutions, maintenance of an open international trade system and tackling the challenge of climate change. As developing countries, China and India can strengthen coordination in global institutions to protect their national interests. China and India's strategic partnership has already had a great impact, especially in dealing with North-South relations. This is why, worldwide, an increasing number of people are beginning to talk about a possible future for "Chindia".

True Strategic Partners

We believe that China and India should become strategic partners in the true sense, rather than viewing each other as hostile competitors. Currently, it seems that a certain degree of asymmetry exists in China's and India's perceptions of each other. In particular, India does not trust China politically and views it as a competitor. In contrast, to the extent that India features in Chinese strategic thinking, it is viewed more as a development partner, rather than a competitor. These different views affect the efficiency of cooperation, which has already led to misunderstandings between the two and some estrangement. Therefore, to achieve fully the goal of co-operation based on common interests, China and India should first adjust their view of each other's role in their foreign policy, by viewing each other as real strategic partners, beyond mere rhetoric. On the regional level, China and India are stakeholders in maintaining regional peace, stability and prosperity. They should go beyond zero-sum thinking and employ a co-operative attitude to resolve their differences and address common regional challenges. Globally, they should play a greater role in the process of reforming global governance.

Prerequisites for Success

The key to achieving this partnership is to abolish both the Cold War mentality and the concept of "sphere of influence". India and China should not see South Asia or East Asia as being solely under their respective spheres of influence. For its part, India should understand that China respects the special role that India plays in South Asia and work with Beijing to promote the development and stability of the region. China's active approach in South Asia and the South Asian Association for Regional Co-operation does not aim at eliminating the influence of India; its involvement concerns the fact that it shares borders with South Asian countries. If we judge a country geographically, China could also be seen as a South Asian country, in the sense that the South Asian-influenced Tibetan Plateau comprises a quarter of China's overall territory. Historically, culturally and geographically, China has had close ties with South Asian countries and India does not need to be nervous about China's engagement with the region. Taking economic development as an example, China's south-western provinces, such as Sichuan and Yunnan, have strong interests in promoting business connections with South Asia, as they see this region as a major market and investment destination. China's investment in the ports of the region ispurely for commercial purposes. This investment is important because China needs commercial ports on the Indian Ocean for transportation across the region, which is very important for China's trade and its energy supplies.

In turn, China should also accept the reality that India is an important player in East Asia. India, as an emerging power, has been seen as an economic opportunity by many regional countries. For example, the prime minister of Singapore, Lee Hsien Loong, once commented that the historical origin of Singapore was due to trade between China and India. It now seems that history is repeating itself, as an opportunity exists for Singapore in linking the two countries. It is natural for India to pursue its interests in the region, as East Asia is the most robust economy in the world, particularly since the Global Financial Crisis.

Some Chinese intellectuals have expressed concern that India could ally with the US to constrain China. Judging from developments since 2010, however, there is no evidence that India has formed a strong alliance with the US to compete with China. For example, India refused to join in the proposed quadrilateral security mechanism comprising the US, Japan, India and Australia.

Regardless of the effort the US has put into trying to draw India closer by emphasising shared values and democratic institutions, Indian policymakers have remained as neutral as possible and developed foreign policy based on India's own national interests.

India has its own goal of great power status and understands that a good relationship with China is the key to achieving it. Both countries are latecomers to the international system and passive receivers of the existing international norms and rules. Hostility between these two countries will only weaken the alliance between the emerging countries in attempting to reform the global order. Based on the above, the authors recommend following measures to improve India-China relations:

- Upgrading the current Sino-Indian Strategic and Economic Dialogue meetings to a higher level – for example, by having future dialogues led by the Chinese State Councillor and Indian National Security Advisor, with the full participation of diplomatic, economic and military policymakers;
- Strengthening co-ordination and communication in regional and global institutions;

- Nurturing a more positive image of each other, both in government and society;
- Working on non-traditional security issues, such as the maritime security co-operation, and making it a basis for better mutual understanding;
- Careful handling of sensitive issues – particularly such issues as the Tibetan independence movement, the South China Sea and the so-called "String of Pearls"; and,
- Promoting open regionalism and rejecting the idea that East Asia and South Asia should be viewed as separate blocs and defined regions.

3

China's Unsolved Territorial Disputes

IMPLICATIONS FOR ITS TIES WITH NEIGHBOURS

China's unresolved land and maritime border disputes with its neighbours continue to be a negative factor in bilateral relations among them; undeniably they also complicate the regional situation. What are the root causes of China's territorial positions? Why certain disputes remain unsettled? Can such situation lead to future conflicts? Has China begun to work towards implementing an economic interests based foreign policy and if so, how that may impact on the country's so far adopted core-interest based foreign policy resulting in its territorial assertiveness? These are some of the questions the following study attempts to address.

China, like India, has five thousand years of civilization and history; in both the countries, the roots of the present can always be traced to the past; a prominent instance in the case of China is the influence of China's founding Emperor Qin Shihuang, on the thinking of the country's architect, Mao Zedong. Similar is the linkage seen between China's traditional " Tian Xia" (Under the Heaven) concept and its current stand on 'territorial sovereignty'. The concept considers that all the people and areas where they lived belong to the Chinese Emperor, the Son of God, who is in possession of mandate of heaven; regarding areas which are not under the control of the Emperor, their rulers derived their power from the Emperor. It holds that the biggest political unit for the Chinese is the framework of 'world/society', not the 'country or nation state'.

One can clearly see the connection of the Tian Xia concept with the current sense of the People's Republic of China (PRC) on borders ; China has been "grading all other states at various levels of tributaries based on their approximation to Chinese cultural and political forms and treating the borders between it and surrounding peoples as not so much political and territorial demarcations, but as cultural differentiations". Reflecting Chinese sense of territories, quite different from those of other civilizations, are authoritative maps published by the PRC in end eighties and in first decade of the current century which, while defining China's modern borders as that existed during the Qing Dynasty period (1644-1911), described the extent of the country's "historically lost" territories; they encompassed vast areas belonging to neighbouring countries, including parts of India's Northeast and Andamans. At the same time, clarifications that the PRC has no claims to these territories in a contemporary sense, accompanied the maps (The Historical Atlas of China, 1982-1987 and History of China's Modern Borders, vol. 1, 2007). Worth mentioning in the context of historical boundaries, is also Mao's description of Tibet as China's "palm" and of Nepal, Sikkim, Bhutan, NEFA and Ladakh as China's "five fingers".

China's penchant to compare its modern borders with those existed prior to the perceived 'historical losses' of territories is significant to understanding of the PRC's current boundary issues. An authoritative article (in Chinese language), noticed in 2005 is a case in point. It reiterated what the Historical Atlas of China mentioned above said about China's modern borders as that existed during the Qing Dynasty period (1644-1911) and affirmed that borders of contemporary China must be seen as a continuity and succession from historic borders of the country. It further stated that the evolution of the country's land and sea border areas was due to a multiplicity of factors like politics, military, geography, history, economy and culture. "Unless a composite view based on all factors, is taken, it may not be possible to correctly comprehend the nature of China's borders", it asserted. Notable also is the article's contention that the central government had exercised absolute control over certain border territories though they had enjoyed political autonomy some times and that the border areas are of strategic importance to China, especially to counter military threat or armed aggression from abroad; this may go to justify China's current stand on Tibet and Xinjiang, which were not formally a part of imperial China at times. With respect to sea boundaries, the article recognized the existence now of differing viewpoints internationally, but argued that it is necessary for the concerned nations to recognize China's historical sea boundary in the background of its traditionally advanced coastal areas; this position may have a meaning with respect to China's continuing claims over islands under dispute in South China Sea and East China Sea.

The PRC shares 22000 km land borders with 13 neighbouring nations - the Democratic People's Republic of Korea (DPRK), Russia, Mongolia, Kazakhstan, Kyrgyzstan, Tajikistan, Afghanistan, India, Nepal, Bhutan, Myanmar, Laos and Vietnam (India's contention is that China and Pakistan have no common border; China's border is with a part of India's Kashmir which is occupied by Pakistan). In this background, deserving focus are the following four key questions - why China is still unable to resolve land border issues with two of its neighbours- India and Bhutan (the PRC is not making the border with the DPRK an issue which needs to be understood in the context of special but complex ties existing between the two communist states), while it has been successful in settling disputes with others? Which of the contending neighbours gave border concessions to China during negotiations and why they did so? What are the cases when China had to yield to territorial demands from others during talks and what was its motivation in doing so? Lastly, why China has, in recent years, chosen a line of assertiveness towards its territorial claims and how that line is impacting on the regional security?

To examine why China still has unresolved territorial issues- three land borders with respect to India, Bhutan and the DPRK and the fourth one concerning sovereignty claims relating to maritime borders in East China Sea and South China Sea, a comprehension of relevant data would be necessary. Taking the Sino-Indian boundary problem first, a comparison of the positions of India and the PRC would be in order. India's official stand is as under: *"In the Eastern Sector, China claims approximately 90,000 square kilometres of Indian Territory in the State of Arunachal Pradesh. Indian Territory under the occupation of China in Jammu & Kashmir is approximately 38,000 sq. kms. In addition, under the so-called China-Pakistan Boundary Agreement signed between China and Pakistan on 2 March 1963, Pakistan illegally ceded 5,180 sq. kms. of Indian territory in Pakistan Occupied Kashmir to China. India and China are engaged in discussions to arrive at a fair, reasonable and mutually acceptable solution to the boundary question at an early date".* India holds that "there is no commonly delineated Line of Actual Control (LAC) between India and China. There are areas along the border where India and China have differing perceptions of the LAC. Due to both sides undertaking patrolling as per their respective perceptions of the LAC, transgressions do occur. The Indian government regularly takes up any transgression with the Chinese side through established mechanisms.

China's official border position is as follows: *"The China-India border has never been demarcated and that the Chinese government does not recognize the illegal 1914 Simla Convention agreement over McMahon line, reached by the British, Indian and the local Tibetan representatives behind the back of the Chinese government. Following independence, India inherited the British colonial legacy and in 1950s, advanced its border line with China to the McMahon line. In 1959, India also put forward its territorial claim on the Akssai Chin region of China's Xinjiang, in the Western part of China-India border. After the China-India border war in 1962, the two countries formed the current line of control in their respective borders. The total length of China-India border is about 2000 kms. The border falls into three sectors- Eastern, Middle and Western. The total area of the region disputed by the two sides is about 125,000 sq.kms; about 90,000 sq.kms in the Eastern sector, about 2000 sq.kms in the Middle sector and about 33,000 sq.kms in the Western sector. In February 1987, India established the so called Arunachal Pradesh state largely on the three areas south of the so called McMahon line of China's Tibet- Monyul, Loyul and Lower Tsayul, which are currently under Indian illegal occupation. These three areas located between the illegal McMahon line and the traditional customary boundary between China and India,, have always been Chinese territories. The Chinese side many times made solemn and just statements that it absolutely does not recognize the illegal McMahon line and the so-called Arunachal Pradesh state".* China also points *to the "consensus reached with India for a fair, reasonable and mutually acceptable solution of the border issue through negotiation as well as to the two sides making up the principle of resolving the problem eventually as a package rather than step by step".*

One can easily see in what has been said above the deep positional differences between India and China on the border issue. They are the main reason for the issue remaining alive with no immediate prospects for a solution. Admittedly, negotiations held so far between the two sides could lead to some progress; important bilateral agreements signed by them include those on "Maintenance of Peace and Tranquility along the Line of Actual Control in the India-China Border Areas (1993),, " Agreement on Political Parameters and Guiding Principles for Settling Border Question (2005), " Working Mechanism for Consultation and Coordination on India-China Border Affairs" (2012) and "Border Defence Cooperation Agreement" (2013). The two sides have agreed on a three-step strategy for border settlement – making the guiding principle, then setting up a frame work agreement to implement the guiding principle and lastly, solving the border issue. Regarding the first, they have already reached the 2005 agreement mentioned above. There is still no consensus on the second. There have so far been eighteen meetings of Special Representatives of the two countries to discuss the disputed border - last one in New Delhi in March 2015.

In general, deserving recognition are the efforts being taken by India and China to diffuse the border tension; they need to be understood in the context of an apparent China-India understanding that the boundary problem is complicated, requiring a long time to solve and that in the meanwhile, bilateral ties should be promoted in other fields, particularly in the economic front. Tibet issue is indirectly related to India-China boundary issue. If China is able to effectively deal with the question of the Dalai Lama, who is in exile in India with a large Tibetan ethnic refugee population, the atmosphere can perhaps ultimately become conducive to a resolution of China-India border issue; that looks difficult at this stage.

The unresolved China –Bhutan border issue, also requires attention. The two nations have no diplomatic ties, but bilateral negotiations to settle the nearly 470 km border shared by them are in progress since the 1980s, under the guidance of the agreed Guiding Principles of 1988 and the Agreement on the Maintenance of Peace and Tranquility in the Bhutan-China border of 1998. The last 22nd round of negotiations was held in Beijing in July 2014. Between China and Bhutan, there are three territorial areas of dispute - The Jakarlung and Pasamlung valleys,in the north-central border, and the Doklam plateau in Eastern Bhutan. While the two territories to the north are of interest to China due to their proximity to Tibet, as well as what it perceives as its "historic claims" to the areas, the Doklam Plateau is important to it strategically.

If China establishes control over Doklam plateau, it can challenge India as that region lies immediately east of Indian defences in Sikkim. This piece of dominating ground not only has a commanding view of the Chumbi Valley but also overlooks the Silguri Corridor further to the east." Reports suggest that China has proposed to Bhutan to cede to it the area close to Chumbi valley, a tri-junction abutting Bhutan, Tibet and the Indian state of Sikkim in lieu of which Beijing would give up its claim over Bhutan's central areas. Chumbi valley is of geostrategic importance to China because of its shared borders with Tibet and Sikkim. The North-Western areas of Bhutan which China wants in exchange for the Central areas lie next to the Chumbi Valley tri-junction. If Bhutan cedes areas to China as mentioned above, there will be strategic implications for India's defence of its Siliguri corridor— the chicken neck which connects India to North East India and Nepal.

The PRC visualizes occurrence of 'local wars under informatisation conditions'. The belief is that such wars can be short and happen in China's periphery, enabling China to realize limited political objectives. Can China use force to settle borders with India? The answer is affirmative considering that China's 'Active Defence' strategy does not rule out the military resorting to 'offensive operational postures'. Forceful recovery of 'Southern Tibet' (as China calls Arunachal) and fighting a 'partial war' with

India were topics in the Chinese blogs not very long ago. China's use of force to turn territorial conditions in its favour has precedence. Beijing launched 'counter attacks in self-defence' against Vietnam, India and former Soviet Union in 1979, 1962 and 1969 respectively. In the current period, China is indulging in a show of force in East and South China seas.

China's third unresolved border is with the DPRK; for reasons quoted in Para 3 above, the two sides are not making it a bilateral issue. Their disputes concern the area surrounding Mount Paektu (referred to as Changbai Mountain in China), islands and rights of navigation in Yalu and Tumen rivers, and access to the East Sea or Sea of Japan. This is so despite their agreement to split the land surrounding Paektu in 1962 and current sharing of administration over the mountain and the lake surrounding it. In recent years, China has been rapidly developing the area including building an airport and ski resort; some believe that these steps of China are aimed at bolstering its claims of sovereignty over the area. The PRC created further controversy in 2008 when it applied for the region to be considered a UN Educational, Scientific, and Cultural Organization (UNESCO) World Heritage Site. There are other reports on the DPRK's bid to host the 2018 Winter Olympics on the contested Paektu area.

The unsolved maritime border issues are most serious for China as against competing claims of several littoral nations and the emerging regional order. Conditions in this regard put China against 8 littoral parties - Japan, South Korea, the Philippines, Vietnam, Malaysia, Brunei and Indonesia, as well as Taiwan. The PRC shares maritime borders with four countries, Japan and South Korea in the East China Sea and with the Philippines and Vietnam in the South China Sea.

In the East China Sea (1,249,000 sq-km), China is currently in disputes with Japan over Senkakus chain of islands (called Diao Yu by the Chinese) and with South Korea (Socotra rock, a submerged rock in the Yellow Sea). The disputes are over the extent of their respective exclusive economic zones, each resorting to different parts of the UN Conventions on the Law of the Sea. The eight uninhabited islands and rocks in the Senkakus chain have a total area of about 7 sq km and lie north-east of Taiwan, east of the Chinese mainland and south-west of Japan's southernmost prefecture, Okinawa. They, controlled by Japan, provide rich fishing grounds and lie near potential oil and gas reserves. The islands are also in a strategically significant position, amid rising competition between the US and China for military primacy in the Asia-Pacific region. China's creation of a new air-defence identification zone (ADIZ) in November 2013, which would require any aircraft in the zone - which covers the Senkakus chain of islands - to comply with rules laid down by Beijing, assumes significance in this context. The move is being seen as one meant for China's assertion of sovereignty over the Senkakus chain.

In the South China Sea (3,500,000 sq-km), one of the world's busiest waterways with huge potential oil and gas fields to be exploited, China claims most of the water 'based on historical facts and international law' and shows them in its maps within its 'nine dotted' imaginary line. All littoral nations - Vietnam, the Philippines, Malaysia, Brunei and Indonesia have officially challenged the Chinese South China Sea claims including on the Paracel Islands, known as Xisha in Chinese and Hoàng Sa in Vietnamese, Spratly islands (Nansha in Chinese, Truongsa in Vietnamese) and the Macclesfield Bank (Zhongsha islands in Chinese). The ASEAN has attempted to resolve the disputes through multilateral talks but China prefers to deal with each country on a bilateral basis. China has expressed concern at the US Asia-Pivot policy and questions the latter's intentions behind its call for freedom of navigation in the South China Sea. China has constructed an island with room for an airstrip at Fiery Cross Reef, West of Spratlys. There is a belief that the proposed air strip is symbolic of China's plan to create an ADIZ in South China Sea also.

Conclusions that can be drawn from what has been said above on China's land and sea boundary disputes, are given below:

- The total number of countries/ territory with which China has territorial disputes as of now is 11 (India, Bhutan and the DPRK through land; Japan, South Korea, the Philippines, Vietnam, Malaysia, Brunei and Indonesia, as well as Taiwan through sea).

- China in recent years has not resorted to wars to settle disputes; its last wars were with India in 1962 and with Vietnam in 1979. Beijing's ongoing assertive land actions (intrusions into Indian border) and sea skirmishes do not come under the category of wars.
- Ethnic issues are indirectly involved in China's border problems relating to Tibet and Xinjiang. But China's handling of such issues has been different in each of these cases. On Tibet ethnic issue, China considers it as an internal matter, not related to Sino-Indian border question as India recognizes Tibet as part of the PRC. It has established full control over Tibet and does not find the exiled Tibetan community in India as a threat to its sovereignty over Tibet. Its only demand to India is on not allowing any anti-Chinese activities of exiled Tibetans. Coming to the ethnic issue concerning Xinjiang Uighurs, it also does not have a direct role in the PRC's settlement of borders with Central Asian nations. China however seems to consider the ethnic separatism factor in Xinjiang serious unlike the case in Tibet; this is because of its finding that Xinjiang independence activists are getting support from bases across the borders. This has motivated China in seeking support from the concerned governments for combating the perceived security threat to Xinjiang coming from the exiled Uighur separatist groups abroad; in return, China either made territorial concessions or provided economic benefits to its Central Asian neighbours.
- China had other motives for realizing settlement of border issues. They include the need for the PRC to gain access to Central Asia energy resources. For this purpose, China realized the importance of offering a quid pro quo to the concerned regional governments. For e.g., it dropped its claim over 80% of the disputed land with Kazakhstan, invested in the 3000 km long gas pipeline project across Kazakhstan and gave up claims over 70% and around 95% respectively of the disputed territories with Kyrgyzstan

and Tajikistan. On the reverse, Tajikistan ceded 386 sq kms of Pamir mountain range to China.

- With their own strategic interests in mind, nations like Russia offered border concessions to China. Russia reached an agreement with China in July 2008 after about 40 years of border talks. Earlier, it returned to China (2004) two territories stretching 174 sq kms, located at the confluence of the rivers, Ussuri in Russia and Heilong in China, under Russian occupation since 1929; the two were Tarabarov island, called Yinlong by the Chinese and half of Bolshoy Ussuriysky island, called Heixiazi by the Chinese. (Chinese scholars feel that the issue of 'Southern Tibet', called Arunachal by India, can be solved through a "Heixiazi'-type formula which settled the Sino-Russian border).

A new dimension to unresolved land and sea territorial disputes is being noticed ever since national security interests began to dominate China's external line in 2008; the demands on China imposed by this 'core interest'-based foreign policy course for making no compromises on all issues concerning the country's territorial sovereignty, have resulted in the PRC's territorial assertiveness which is giving rise to fears among the neighbouring nations about the intentions of the former. In this regard, what the Chinese Communist Party (CCP) leader Xi Jinping has said (Speech delivered at a party Politburo Study session convened on 28 January 2013) are important in this connection. He declared that "China will never pursue its development at the cost of sacrificing interests of other countries .... We will never give up our legitimate rights and will never sacrifice our national core interests. No country should presume that we will engage in trade involving our core interests or that we will swallow the 'bitter fruit' of harming our sovereignty, security or development interests".

The 18th CCP Congress document echoed the same spirit. It proclaimed that China's 'banner is to forge a win-win international cooperation'; at the same time it laid emphasis on making 'no compromises' on issues concerning 'national sovereignty and security of core interests'. Most significant has been the document's clarification that "the two aspects are pillars of Chinese diplomacy and do not conflict with each other" (People's Daily, 16 November 2013); the mention in the document that China "will never yield to outside pressure" and "will protect legitimate rights and interests overseas', has been noticed for the first time in a CCP congress material. On his part, the Chinese Foreign Minister explained his country's new foreign policy direction by saying (Beijing, 8.3.2014) that the PRC "will play the international role of a responsible, big country". This signaled a firm shift in the direction so far existed of the PRC's external course - 'hiding one's capacities and biding one's time' (veteran leader Deng Xiaoping's famous 24-character maxim of tao guang yang hui).

The post-2008 assertive international behaviour of China can be attributed to a variety of factors. The change seems to have come about mainly due to (i) China's confidence gained through its ability to achieve a sustained growth leading to a build-up of the country's 'comprehensive national strength', (ii) China's feeling that an opportunity has arisen for itself to increase its influence globally as the world balance of power shifts from the West to East and a multi-polar world gradually emerges, (iii) the PRC's growing need to protect land and sea trade routes in the interest of the much needed import of resources from abroad and (iv) deepening Chinese fears concerning sovereignty over Tibet and Xinjiang and (v) rising suspicions on the purpose of the US Asia-Pacific strategy.

China's introduction of certain new foreign policy formulations at this juncture, looks significant diplomatically as they seem to symbolize some efforts on its part to correct the existing unfavorable image for the country internationally, which obviously resulted from an assertive external approach.

The first new formulation is now known as *"New Type of Great Power Relations'*. It was promoted by the PRC President Xi Jinping in his meetings with US counterpart Barack Obama in June 2013, July 2014 and November 2014, primarily addresses Sino-US ties. It had three points – major powers should have no conflict or confrontation, should emphasize dialogue and should treat each other's strategic intentions objectively; they should have mutual respect, including for each other's core interests and major concerns;

and they should conduct mutually beneficial cooperation, abandon the zero-sum game mentality and advance areas of mutual interest. The US is reluctant to endorse the proposal; because it feels that such endorsement would imply its recognition to China's 'core interests', which case will not be in its strategic interests.

The second is the *"Community of Shared Destiny"* concept, which figured in the address of the CCP chief Xi Jinping at the aforesaid Foreign Affairs Work conference. The concept, providing for realizing Asia's economic potential and durable security, stipulated that community of destiny will be based on deep economic integration, but going beyond trade. It will be a vision of a political and security community in which economically integrated countries in the region support and defend one another from outside threats and intruders, as well as manage internal threats together through collaborative and cooperative mechanisms.. Echoing the vision in the concept are China's two mega proposals for establishing regional connectivity - the Silk Road Economic Belt (SREB) that would be established along the Eurasian land corridor from the Pacific coast to the Baltic Sea, and the 21st century Maritime Silk Road (MSR) connecting Asia and Europe through sea route.

The outside world watched with lot of interest the elevation in status by China of its relations with neighbours during the Conference on Foreign Relations, mentioned above. Ties with periphery, was brought to No.1 position, followed by those with Great Powers and Developing countries ranking No.2 and No.3 respectively. The priority shift reflected Beijing's assessment that relations with Asian nations and with rising powers are becoming more and more important to it, than ties with the developed countries. Confirming the new Chinese thinking is Xi Jinping's declaration that "Asians have the capacity to manage security in Asia by themselves". Experts assess that the first priority to periphery reflect the Chinese perceived long-term economic and geo-political trends. Beijing has come to recognize that the periphery is becoming increasingly vital to China's future. China's Vice Foreign Minister stated in April 2014 that the country's trade with East and Southeast Asia totaled "$1.4 trillion, more than

China's trade with the United States and European Union combined." He noted "half of China's top ten trade partners are in Asia." Moreover, China realizes it must secure its geostrategic flanks to prepare the country's ascent into the upper echelons of global power.

Xi Jinping's new foreign policy formulations, new Silk Road initiative and priority to China's ties with neighbours, taken together, could be indicators that China has begun to accord primacy to economic interests in its foreign policy; this may mean emerging intention on the part of China to make adjustments to its hitherto adopted assertive core-interest based foreign policy approach. One has however to wait further for a full picture in this regard.

INDIA SCALES UP MILITARY FORCES ON DISPUTED CHINA BORDER

India is creating a mountain strike corps of 90,000 soldiers along the 2,000-mile stretch. Just last year Chinese troops entered territory claimed by India, sparking a three-week standoff.

India is raising a new mountain strike corps of nearly 90,000 soldiers to strengthen its defense along its disputed border with China in the high reaches of the Himalayas.

China will be a top foreign policy challenge for Narendra Modi, the incoming prime minister who won a landslide victory last week. Business ties between India and China are booming. But despite rounds of talks, the two countries have yet to resolve their decades-old dispute over the 2,000-mile border between the two countries. It remains one of the most militarized borders in the world.

The strike corps will have its own mountain artillery, combat engineers, anti-aircraft guns, and radio equipment. Over 35,000 soldiers have already been raised in new infantry units in India's northeastern state of Assam. The entire corps will be fully raised over the next five years with 90,274 troops at a cost of $10.6 billion. The proposal to raise a new strike corps was recommended last year by India's China Study Group, a government body that considers all strategic issues related to China.

The strike corps signals a new assertiveness in New Delhi and will provide an additional defense capability to India, which for a long time focused on the land borders with Pakistan. While the decision predated Mr. Modi, he is likely to further strengthen India's military modernization which is one of his party's top agenda items.

"China has made frequent border transgressions into Indian border," says retired Lieutenant General Prakash Katoch, who formerly commanded the Indian Army's Special Forces wing. "The new prime minister has to ensure that our borders are well protected. It cannot be business as usual."

He predicts that as both countries are growing and keen to increase their influence, China and India will increasingly step on each other's areas of interest and importance.

LINGERING GRIEVANCES

India and China fought a brief border war in 1962. Ever since, the relationship between the neighbouring Asian countries has been mired in distrust, although business ties between India and China are robust: they share over $70 billion in annual bilateral trade, a figure that's projected to rise in the next decade.

China lays claims to more than 35,000 square miles of land in the eastern sector of the Himalayas, while India says China occupies 14,600 square miles of its territory on the Aksai Chin plateau in the west. Last year in May the two armies ended a three-week standoff in the Ladakh region after Chinese troops entered at least six miles into territory claimed by India. China denied that troops had crossed into Indian territory. Since then both the countries have taken a number of steps to reduce border tension including prior notice of military patrols along the ill-defined border.

Yet both countries are building roads, railroads, and airfields along the border, which would facilitate the rapid movement of troops and artillery to the border zone. Having seen the massive improvements China has made in its border infrastructure, India is now building roads and upgrading its airfields along China's border and deploying attack helicopters and fighters jets to them.

Eventually, C-130J planes, bought by the Indian Air Force from the US, will be deployed in the eastern command. The multi-tasking C-130J is the most advanced special operations aircraft in the world that can transport troops to remote places.

"We lost the war in 1962 [with China] because we had no connectivity to our borders," says Maj. General P.L. Kher (ret.), a veteran of 1962 war. "We lost the war because we were poorly trained and equipped. We want friendship with China but there is no reason that we should not strengthen our military capability."

At one of the Indian border posts during the 1962 war, out of 60 Indian soldiers who were guarding the post only 14 survived, including Kher.

The 1962 war and India's defeat remains a subject many within the Indian military establishment do not like to discuss. The inquiry report about why India lost the war remains a top secret. India's traditional policy has been not to build any offensive military formations along the China border, fearing it might provoke Beijing.

SINO-INDIAN BORDER DISPUTE

Sovereignty over two large and various smaller separated pieces of territory are contested between China and India. The westernmost, Aksai Chin, is claimed by India as part of the state of Jammu and Kashmir and region of Ladakh but is controlled and administered as part of the Chinese autonomous region of Xinjiang. It is a virtually uninhabited high altitude wasteland crossed by the Xinjiang-Tibet Highway. The other large disputed territory, the easternmost, lies south of the McMahon Line. It was formerly referred to as the North East Frontier Agency, and is now called Arunachal Pradesh. The McMahon Line was part of the 1914 Simla Convention between British India and Tibet, an agreement rejected by China. The 1962 Sino-Indian War was fought in both of these areas. An agreement to resolve the dispute was concluded in 1996, including "confidence-building measures" and a mutually agreed Line of Actual Control. In 2006, the Chinese ambassador to India claimed that all of Arunachal Pradesh is Chinese territory amidst a military build up. At the time, both countries claimed incursions as much as a kilometre at the northern tip of Sikkim. In 2009, India announced it would deploy additional military forces along the border.

Aksai Chin

From the area's lowest point (on the Karakash River at about 14,000 feet (4,300 m) to the glaciated peaks up to 22,500 feet (6,900 m) above sea level, this is a desolate, largely uninhabited area. It covers an area of about 37,244 square kilometres (14,380 sq mi). The desolation of Aksai Chin meant that it had no significant human importance other than ancient trade routes crossing it, providing brief passage during summer for caravans of yaks from Xinjiang and Tibet.

One of the earliest treaties regarding the boundaries in the western sector was issued in 1842. The Sikh Confederacy of the Punjab region in India had annexed Ladakh into the state of Jammu in 1834. In 1841, they invaded Tibet with an army. Chinese forces defeated the Sikh army and in turn entered Ladakh and besieged Leh. After being checked by the Sikh forces, the Chinese and the Sikhs signed a treaty in September 1842, which stipulated no transgressions or interference in the other country's frontiers. The British defeat of the Sikhs in 1846 resulted in transfer of sovereignty over Ladakh to the British, and British commissioners attempted to meet with Chinese officials to discuss the border they now shared. However, both sides were apparently sufficiently satisfied that a traditional border was recognised and defined by natural elements, and the border was not demarcated. The boundaries at the two extremities, Pangong Lakeand Karakoram Pass, were reasonably well-defined, but the Aksai Chin area in between lay largely undefined.

The Johnson Line

W. H. Johnson, a civil servant with the Survey of India proposed the "Johnson Line" in 1865, which put Aksai Chin in Jammu and Kashmir. This was the time of the Dungan revolt, when China did not control Xinjiang, so this line was never presented to the Chinese. Johnson presented this line to the Maharaja of Jammu and Kashmir, who then claimed the 18,000 square kilometres contained within his territory and by some accounts he claimed territory further north as far as the Sanju Pass in the Kun Lun Mountains. Johnson's work was severely criticised for gross inaccuracies, with description of his boundary as "patently absurd", and he was reprimanded by the British Government and resigned from the Survey. The Maharajah of Jammu and Kashmir apparently sent a few soldiers to man the abandoned fort at Shahidulla (modern-day Xaidulla) at one point, by the time most sources placed Shahidulla and the upper Karakash River firmly within the territory of Xinjiang (see accompanying map). According toFrancis Younghusband, who explored the region in the late 1880s, there was only an abandoned fort and not one inhabited house at Shahidulla when he was there – it was just a convenient staging post and a convenient headquarters for the nomadic Kirghiz. The abandoned fort had apparently been built a few years earlier by the Dogras. In 1878 the Chinese had reconquered Xinjiang, and by 1890 they already had Shahidulla before the issue was decided. By 1892, China had erected boundary markers at Karakoram Pass.

In 1897 a British military officer, Sir John Ardagh, proposed a boundary line along the crest of the Kun Lun Mountainsnorth of the Yarkand River. At the time Britain was concerned at the danger of Russian expansion as China weakened, and Ardagh argued that his line was more defensible. The Ardagh line was effectively a modification of the Johnson line, and became known as the "Johnson-Ardagh Line".

The Macartney-Macdonald Line

In 1893, Hung Ta-chen, a senior Chinese official at Kashgar, handed a map of the boundary proposed by China toGeorge Macartney, the British consul-general at Kashgar. This boundary placed the Lingzi Tang plains, which are south of the Laktsang range, in India, and Aksai Chin proper, which is north of the Laktsang range, in China. Macartney agreed with the proposal and forwarded it to the British Indian government. This border, along theKarakoram Mountains, was proposed and supported by British officials for a number of reasons. The Karakoram Mountains formed a natural boundary, which would set the British borders up to the Indus River watershed while leaving the Tarim River watershed in Chinese control, and Chinese control of this tract would present a further obstacle to Russian advance in Central Asia. The British presented this line, known as the Macartney-MacDonald Line, to the Chinese in 1899 in a note by Sir Claude MacDonald. The Qing government did not respond to the note, and the British took that as Chinese acquiescence. Although no official boundary had ever been negotiated, China believed that this had been the accepted boundary.

1899 to 1947

Both the Johnson-Ardagh and the Macartney-MacDonald lines were used on British maps of India. Until at least 1908, the British took the Macdonald line to be the boundary, but in 1911, the Xinhai Revolution resulted in the collapse of central power in China, and by the end of World War I, the British officially used the Johnson Line. However they took no steps to establish outposts or assert actual control on the ground. In 1927, the line was adjusted again as the government of British India abandoned the Johnson line in favour of a line along the Karakoram range further south. However, the maps were not updated and still showed the Johnson Line.

From 1917 to 1933, the "Postal Atlas of China", published by the Government of China in Peking had shown the boundary in Aksai Chin as per the Johnson line, which runs along the Kunlun mountains. When British officials learned of Soviet officials surveying the Aksai Chin for Sheng Shicai, warlord of Xinjiang in 1940–1941, they again advocated the Johnson Line. At this point the British had still made no attempts to establish outposts or control over the Aksai Chin, nor was the issue ever discussed with the governments of China or Tibet, and the boundary remained undemarcated at India's independence.

Since 1947

Upon independence in 1947, the government of India used the Johnson Line as the basis for its official boundary in the west, encompassing Aksai Chin. However, India did not claim the northern areas nearShahidulla and Khotan, for including which in Indian territory, among other things, Johnson had been criticised.

From the Karakoram Pass (which is not under dispute), the Indian claim line extends northeast of the Karakoram Mountains north of the salt flats of the Aksai Chin, to set a boundary at the Kunlun Mountains, and incorporating part of the Karakash River and Yarkand River watersheds. From there, it runs east along the Kunlun Mountains, before turning southwest through the Aksai Chin salt flats, through the Karakoram Mountains, and then to Pangong Lake.

On 1 July 1954 Prime Minister Nehru wrote a memo directing that the maps of India be revised to show definite boundaries on all frontiers. Up to this point, the boundary in the Aksai Chin sector, based on the Johnson Line, had been described as "undemarcated."

During the 1950s, the People's Republic of China built a 1,200 kilometres (750 mi) road connecting Xinjiang and western Tibet, of which 179 kilometres (111 mi) ran south of the Johnson Line through the Aksai Chin region claimed by India. Aksai Chin was easily accessible from China, but was more difficult for the Indians on the other side of the Karakorams to reach. The Indians did not learn of the existence of the road until 1957, which was confirmed when the road was shown in Chinese maps published in 1958.

The Indian position, as stated by prime minister Jawaharlal Nehru, was that the Aksai Chin was "part of the Ladakh region of India for centuries" and that this northern border was a "firm and definite one which was not open to discussion with anybody".

The Chinese minister, Zhou Enlai argued that the western border had never been delimited, that the Macartney-MacDonald Line, which left the Aksai Chin within Chinese borders was the only line ever proposed to a Chinese government, and that the Aksai Chin was already under Chinese jurisdiction, and that negotiations should take into account the status quo.

In April 2013 India claimed, referencing their own perception of the Line of Actual Control (LAC) location, that Chinese troops hadestablished a camp in the Daulat Beg Oldi sector, 10 km on their side of the Line of Actual Control. This figure was later revised to a 19 km claim. According to Indian media, the incursion included Chinese military helicopters entering Indian airspace to drop supplies to the troops. However, Chinese officials denied any trespassing having taken place. Soldiers from both countries briefly set up camps on the ill-defined frontier facing each other, but the tension was defused when both sides pulled back soldiers in early May.

Trans Karakoram Tract

The Johnson Line is not used west of the Karakoram Pass, where China adjoins Pakistan-administered Gilgit–Baltistan. On 13 October 1962, China and Pakistan began negotiations over the boundary west of the Karakoram Pass. In 1963, the two countries settled their boundaries largely on the basis of the Macartney-MacDonald Line, which left the Trans Karakoram Tract in China, although the agreement provided for renegotiation in the event of a settlement of the Kashmir dispute. India does not recognise that Pakistan and China have a common border, and claims the tract as part of the domains of the pre-1947 state of Kashmir and Jammu. However, India's claim line in that area does not extend as far north of the Karakoram Mountains as the Johnson Line

The McMahon Line

British India and China gained a common border in 1826, with British annexation of Assam in the Treaty of Yandabo at the conclusion of the First Anglo-Burmese War (1824–1826). Subsequent annexations in further Anglo-Burmese Wars expanded China's borders with British India eastwards, to include the border with what is now Myanmar.

In 1913–14, representatives of Britain, China, and Tibet attended a conference in Simla, India and drew up an agreement concerning Tibet's status and borders. The McMahon Line, a proposed boundary between Tibet and India for the eastern sector, was drawn by British negotiator Henry McMahon on a map attached to the agreement. All three representatives initiated the agreement, but Beijing soon objected to the proposed Sino-Tibet boundary and repudiated the agreement, refusing to sign the final, more detailed map. After approving a note which stated that China could not enjoy rights under the agreement unless she ratified it, the British and Tibetan negotiators signed the Simla Convention and more detailed map as a bilateral accord. Neville Maxwell states that McMahon had been instructed not to sign bilaterally with Tibetans if China refused, but he did so without the Chinese representative present and then kept the declaration secret.

V.K. Singh argues that the basis of these boundaries, accepted by British India and Tibet, were that the historical boundaries of India were the Himalayas and the areas south of the Himalayas were traditionally Indian and associated with India. The high watershed of the Himalayas was proposed as the border between India and its northern neighbours. India's government held the view that the Himalayas were the ancient boundaries of the Indian subcontinent and thus should be the modern boundaries of British India and later the Republic of India.

Chinese boundary markers, including one set up by the newly created Chinese Republic, stood near Walong until January 1914, when T. O'Callaghan, an assistant administrator of North East Frontier Agency (NEFA)'s eastern sector, relocated them north to locations closer to the McMahon Line (albeit still South of the Line). He then went to Rima, met with Tibetan officials, and saw no Chinese influence in the area.

By signing the Simla Agreement with Tibet, the British had violated the Anglo-Russian Convention of 1907, in which both parties were not to negotiate with Tibet, "except through the intermediary of the Chinese Government", as well as the Anglo-Chinese Convention of 1906, which bound the British government "not to annex Tibetan territory." Because of doubts concerning the legal status of the accord, the British did not put the McMahon Line on their maps until 1937, nor did they publish the Simla Convention in the treaty record until 1938. Rejecting Tibet's 1913 declaration of independence, China argued that the Simla Convention and McMahon Line were illegal and that Tibetan government was merely a local government without treaty-making powers. In 1947, Tibet requested that India recognise Tibetan authority in the trading town of Tawang, south of the McMahon Line. Tibet did not object to any other portion of the McMahon line. In reply, the Indians asked Tibet to continue the relationship on the basis of the previous British Government.

Tibetan officials continued to administer Tawang and refused to concede territory during negotiations in 1938. The governor of Assam asserted that Tawang was "undoubtedly British" but noted that it was "controlled by Tibet, and none of its inhabitants have any idea that they are not Tibetan." During World War II, with India's east threatened by Japanese troops and with the threat of Chinese expansionism, British troops secured Tawang for extra defence.

China's claim on areas south of the McMahon Line, encompassed in the NEFA, were based on the traditional boundaries. India believes that the boundaries China proposed in Ladakh and Arunachal Pradesh have no written basis and no documentation of acceptance by anyone apart from China. Indians argue that China claims the territory on the basis that it was under Chinese imperial control in the past, while Chinese argue that India claims the territory on the basis that it was under British imperial control in the past. The last Qing emperor's 1912 edict of abdication authorised its succeeding republican government to form a union of "five peoples, namely, Manchus, Han Chinese,Mongols, Muslims, and Tibetans *together with their territory in its integrity*" However, V.K. Singh cites the presence of the Mauryan Empire and Chola Dynasty in regions India does not place a claim to but which were heavily influenced by Indian culture.

India's claim line in the eastern sector follows the McMahon Line. The line drawn by McMahon on the detailed 24–25 March 1914 Simla Treaty maps clearly starts at 27°45′40"N, a trijunction between Bhutan, China, and India, and from there, extends eastwards. Most of the fighting in the eastern sector before the start of the war would take place immediately north of this line. However, India claimed that the *intent* of the treaty was to follow the main watershed ridge divide of the Himalayas based on memos from McMahon and the fact that over 90% of the McMahon Line does in fact follow the main watershed ridge divide of the Himalayas. They claimed that territory south of the high ridges here near Bhutan (as elsewhere along most of the McMahon Line) should be Indian territory and north of the high ridges should be

Chinese territory. In the Indian claim, the two armies would be separated from each other by the highest mountains in the world.

During and after the 1950s, when India began patrolling this area and mapping in greater detail, they confirmed what the 1914 Simla agreement map depicted: six river crossings that interrupted the main Himalayan watershed ridge. At the westernmost location near Bhutan north of Tawang, they modified their maps to extend their claim line northwards to include features such as Thag La ridge, Longju, and Khinzemane as Indian territory. Thus, the Indian version of the McMahon Line moves the Bhutan-China-India trijunction north to 27°51′30"N. India would claim that the treaty map ran along features such as Thag La ridge, though the actual treaty map itself is topographically vague (as the treaty was not accompanied with demarcation) in places, shows a straight line (not a watershed ridge) near Bhutan and near Thag La, and the treaty includes no verbal description of geographic features nor description of the highest ridges.

Sikkim

India's annexation of Sikkim in 1975 was rejected by China at the time. The Sino-Indian Memorandum of 2003 was hailed as a *de facto* Chinese acceptance of the annexation. China published a map showing Sikkim as a part of India and the Foreign Ministry deleted it from the list of China's "countries and regions". However, the Sikkim-China border's northernmost point, "The Finger", continues to be the subject of dispute and military activity.

FACTS BEHIND CHINA-INDIA BORDER DISPUTE

If a general of the Chinese imperial government representing the Manchu dynasty had, by force of arms, pillage and plunder, succeeded in subjugating the North American continent and on that basis had artificially created a border line between the United States and Canada called, let us say, The Manchu Line, would a sovereign U.S. government abide by thus border line?

Let us suppose further that the boundary line demarcated by this general included, for the Canadian side, parts of Buffalo, Detroit, Seattle and Duluth. Let us suppose again that the treaty between Canada and the U.S. dictated by this general had never been accepted by any government of the United States, and that in truth the people of the U.S. regarded this treaty and its boundary line as illegal, null and void, and as the imposition of a foreign power at a time when the U.S. was weak, divided and under the domination of a foreign imperialist power.

All we have to do with this analogy is to just change the name — Canada to India, United States to China and China to Great Britain — and the picture becomes immeasurably clearer than it is represented in the U.S. press.

The Mcmahon Line

It is the position of the Chinese People's Republic that the so-called McMahon Line — named after the British General McMahon — is illegal, null and void, and the result of a predatory, imperialist imposition of the British government in the year 1914.

No Chinese government ever accepted the McMahon Line. Neither did the Imperial Government of China in 1914, nor the Chiang Kai-Shek government ever agree to it. The very fact that even the Chiang Kai-Shek clique, which is nothing but a tool of U.S. imperialism, has not dared to dispute the Chinese People's Republic's position of the China-India border dispute, it in itself the most eloquent testimony to the correctness of the Chinese position. Nevertheless, the Chinese People's Republic has made every effort to achieve a reasonable and just settlement of the territory in dispute. It has consistently shunned the use of arms.

Proposals For Negotiations

Although the border dispute is almost three years old now, and the Chinese have made innumerable other approaches to the Indian government to settle it on some amicable and acceptable basis the Nehru government has invariably turned them down. In the past two months alone the Chinese government made several proposals for negotiations.

It made a notable effort on August 4, and another one on September 13. In neither of these proposals did the Chinese government lay down any preconditions for the negotiations. Nor did the Chinese government resort to the type of language which could in any way be construed as a threat to India.

On the contrary, the diplomatic notes directed to the Indian government were couched in the most conciliatory language, and were calculated to effectuate a reasonable settlement which would safeguard the territorial integrity of China as well as India.

As a matter of fact, the London Times, certainly no friend of the Chinese revolutionary government, had to publicly admit on October 8 that if military operations were resumed on the Sino-Indian border, "onlookers will have to note that it was New Dehli.., that declined to embark upon them (talks)..."

The position of the London Times is of exceptional importance because it has always sided with India as against China. The London Times was obliged to make the above statement only after the Indian paper, Tribune, had reported that at a cabinet meeting the Indian government had decided to use armed force to deal with China.

Nehru's "Limited Offensive"

It was also reported in the world press on October 8, that Nehru had authorized India's new commander-in chief of the eastern border area to "fight a limited offensive operation."

These are the incontrovertible facts. As to what lies behind the aggressive attitude of the Nehru government, it must be borne in mind first of all that the imperialist world, particularly the U.S. would like nothing better than to see the two principal Asiatic powers, the two powers which hold the greatest revolutionary promise for mankind in the east, locked in military combat, shedding the blood of thousands, absorbing the resources and energies of millions of people, which should be used to construct a revolutionary way of life. The efforts of the U.S. government, it must be noted, have been directed, insofar as India is concerned, not only to make it economically and financially dependent upon U.S. monopoly interests, but also to inflame the Indian bourgeoisie, particularly its right-wing extremist elements, against the Chinese People's Republic.

Four Billion U.S. Aid

According to The New York Times of October 22(1969), the U.S. has poured into India more than four billion dollars. A substantial section of this money has gone to line the pockets of Indian businessmen, government officials, and especially the extremist elements who are interested in diverting the mass discontent of the Indian peasants and workers into other channels. U.S. diplomats, State Department planners, and military figures in the Pentagon have for a long time felt that the biggest diversionary tactic that imperialism could employ to disrupt the revolutionary anti-imperialist front was to continually stir up, bribe and corrupt as many of the representatives of the Indian bourgeoisie as it could to fan the flames of an India-China war.

Nehru himself was subjected to unremitting pressure when he was in the U.S. More U.S. aid was used as bait to lure Nehru into the trap of a protracted India-China war, which can only result in further detriment to India, China and the cause of all oppressed people.

Since Nehru's Visit

Since the Indian Prime Minister left the shores of the U.S. there have been only rare intervals in which there has been a let up in the war fever fanned by the Indian bourgeoisie and its agent Nehru. For a long time Nehru played the role of moderator between left and right in the Indian-China border dispute, cautioning the extremist elements of the bourgeoisie in Parliament, and repudiating suggestions for offensive operations by his military advisers.

But his October 4 decision, taken after a cabinet meeting, made it clear beyond any shadow of a doubt that he had completely capitulated to the right wing on this issue and was kowtowing to U.S. imperialist interests. The present military efforts of the Chinese are merely a response to the offensive action taken after the Indian cabinet session.

A Defensive Battle

The Chinese government is fighting a defensive battle. It is only too well aware that U.S. imperialism is ready at all times to take advantage of any preoccupation that China may have with India to open another front against China wherever and whenever it finds it feasible, whether it be in the Pescadores, the Taiwan strait or new harassments over the air space of China. There are those who say China should give in — give up what belongs to China in the interest of peace. These are the people who are always ready to give, especially things that do not belong to them.

When to give — or whether to give — is a question which only the Chinese can decide, as it as *their* territory. Surely the Chinese, who have gone through hell and fire in the course of 22 years of civil war, in which they have had to trade many times — space for time — and in fact have endured many retreats, need no reminders on this score.

Solidarity Of Asian People

The workers of the world and the progressive anti-imperialist countries in particular, are most deeply concerned in a speedy, reasonable and honorable settlement on the part of China and India. Such a settlement can only be arrived at if the ruling group in New Delhi accepts China's offer for the resumption of talks on a high level between the two governments without any pre conditions. A border settlement would remove a tremendous obstacle to the solidarity of the Asian people who are struggling for a new life, and would be a tremendous rebuff to imperialism and its servants and underlings.

INDIA-CHINA RIVALRY EXPOSED IN ONGOING BORDER DISPUTES

As a consequence, the 4,056-kilometer (2,520 miles) frontier between India and China, one of the longest inter-state borders in the world, remains the only one of China's land borders not defined, let alone demarcated, on maps or delineated on the ground. While Indians doubt China's sincerity in border negotiations, Chinese question India's leaders' will and capacity to settle the dispute in a "give-and-take" spirit.

Up until 2005, there was a great deal of optimism about a possible breakthrough. Evidence of this came during Prime Minister Vajpayee's China visit in June 2003 when New Delhi's readiness to address Chinese concerns on Tibet was matched by Beijing's willingness to resolve the Sikkim issue by recognizing the trade route through the Nathu La Pass on the China-Sikkim frontier with India and later showing Sikkim as part of India in its maps.

For its fraction, New Delhi reiterated its stance on the Tibetan Autonomous Region as part of China. This visit also paved the way for border talks to be held through special representatives of the leaders to find an early "political solution" to the boundary question, rather than going only by the legal and historical claims of the two sides. India indicated its willingness to settle for the territorial status quo by giving up claims to the Aksai Chin in Ladakh and hoped China would give up its claims to Arunachal Pradesh in the eastern sector and recognize the McMahon Line just as Beijing had accepted Tibet's British-drawn boundaries with Afghanistan and Myanmar (formerly known as Burma).

In order to give a new thrust to the ongoing border negotiations, an "Agreement on the Political Parameters and Guiding Principles for the Settlement of the Boundary Question" was signed during Chinese Prime Minister Wen Jiabao's visit to India in April 2005. The joint statement issued at the end of the visit talked of a "Strategic and Cooperative Partnership" between India and China.

No Group

Since then, though, Beijing has upped the ante by demanding major territorial concessions in populated areas of Arunachal Pradesh on terms that many in New Delhi see as "humiliating and non-negotiable." Tawang, in particular, has emerged as a sticking point since the Chinese claim it to be central to Tibetan Buddhism given that the sixth Dalai Lama was born there. Ties between China and India were strained even further in May 2007 when the Chinese government refused a visa to an Indian official from disputed Arunachal Pradesh to visit China, and the Indian government's invitation soon thereafter to Taiwan's opposition Kuomintang (K.M.T.) party presidential candidate, Ma Ying-jeou, to visit India in June 2007 to hold talks with senior Indian officials. China voiced its opposition to Ma's visit and called on India to abide by the "One China policy."

Thereafter came media reports of the People's Liberation Army (P.L.A.) encroachments across the Line of Actual Control (L.A.C.)

and Chinese small arms supplies to insurgents in India's volatile northeast via Bangladesh and Myanmar. Then, in August 2007, Beijing demanded the removal of two old Indian Army bunkers near the tri-junction of Sikkim, Bhutan and Tibet, claiming that these were located on their territory. This move raised questions about China's declared policy of treating Sikkim as part of Indian territory. Not surprisingly, China's increasing assertiveness over the disputed borders has led to a rapid meltdown in the Sino-Indian border talks and a "mini-Cold War" has quietly taken hold at the diplomatic level during the past two years, despite public protestations of amity.

Some observers argue that Hu Jintao's desire to control the choice of the next Dalai Lama has led to pressuring India to concede access to the Tawang Monastery, which is crucial to this choice. The deterioration in Sino-Indian relations under Hu, however, should not have come as a surprise given his reputation as a hardliner over Tibet. (After all, Deng Xiaoping had groomed him for the Chinese Communist Party leadership because of his prominent role in the successful suppression of the Tibetan revolt in 1988.) In this context, the rapid pace development of road, rail and military infrastructure in Tibet close to its borders with India and Nepal is seen as preempting any possible destabilization of Tibet post-Dalai Lama.

Others, however, do not see any sinister designs in western China's development. Instead, they attribute the recent downturn in Sino-Indian relations more to domestic power struggles within the Chinese Communist Party (C.C.P.) than to the Dalai Lama succession issue or to Chinese concerns about India's growing tilt toward the United States. While there may be an element of truth in all these arguments, there are other more fundamental reasons behind the recent chill in Sino-Indian relations. Apparently, the strategic consequences of India's economic resurgence coupled with U.S. Secretary of State Condoleezza Rice's offer in March 2005 to "help make India a major world power in the 21st century" have greatly bothered the Chinese. This offer, and the long-term India-U.S. defense cooperation framework and the July 2005 U.S.-India nuclear energy deal that followed soon after, have been compared by Chinese strategic analysts to "the strategic tilt" toward China executed by former U.S. President Richard Nixon in 1971 to contain the common Soviet threat. Claiming that these developments have "destabilizing" and "negative implications" for their country's future, China's India-watchers have started warning their government that Beijing "should not take India lightly any longer."

Chinese leaders be led to believe that China's growing economic and military might would eventually enable Beijing to re-establish the Sino-centric hierarchy of Asia's past as the U.S. saps its energies in fighting small wars in the Islamic world, Japan shrinks economically and demographically while India remains subdued by virtue of Beijing's "special relationships" with its South Asian neighbours. However, a number of "negative developments," from Beijing's perspective, since early 2005 — the Indian and Japanese bids for permanent seats on the U.N. Security Council, the formation of the East Asia Summit that includes India, Australia and New Zealand, the Indo-U.S. nuclear deal, India's ability to sustain a high economic growth rate of eight to nine percent and the strategic implications of India's "Look East" policy — have apparently upset Chinese calculations.

Therefore, after a hiatus of a few years, Chinese media commentaries have resumed their criticism of Washington's "hegemonic ideas" and for drawing "India in as a tool for its global strategic pattern." Some Chinese analysts express serious reservations about U.S. efforts to draw "India in as a tool for its global strategic pattern," arguing that "India's DNA doesn't allow itself to become an ally subordinate to the U.S., like Japan or Britain." Nonetheless, most see India as a "future strategic competitor" that would be an active member of an anti-China grouping due to the structural power shifts in the international system and advocate putting together a comprehensive "contain India" strategy based on both economic tools (aid, trade, infrastructural development) and enhanced military cooperation with "pro-China" countries.

4

Revisiting Sino-Indian Confidence Building Measures

First of all let me briefly delve into the basics of CBMs per se before going into the contours of India-China relations in terms of disputes, divergences and CBMs. CBMs are arrangements designed to enhance assurance of mind and belief in the trustworthiness of states. Confidence is the product of much broader patterns of relations than those which relate to military strategy. These patterns encompass economic, cultural, technical and social relationships. Thus military and non-military initiatives have to be undertaken by antagonistic states to reduce tensions and enhance mutual confidence. CBMs are designed to increase understanding by reducing suspicions. They are separable into military and non-military CBMs and into those having unilateral, bilateral or international content. Military CBMs are also classifiable into transparency, communications and constraint measures to perform the related functions of information, notification, observation and stabilization. CBMs can further be catalogued into provisions enabling exchange of information, mutual access to observation or arrangements to handle incidents and crises.

Now coming to the Sino-Indian relations, even though more than fifty years had passed since the outbreak of the Sino-Indian war, the present regional and bilateral conditions are still far from congenial. India and China display a peculiar case of "constrained cooperation," with economically convergent interests tending to artificially overshadow prevailing strategic differences. China acknowledges that it shares an interest in a peaceful and stable South Asia. Nevertheless, strengthened Indo-U.S. ties are widely perceived in Beijing as an attempt by Washington to enlist India as a counterweight to China. This situation is despite the fact that India and China are among the world's great civilizations.

BACKGROUND

The new governments of independent India and communist China showed a natural desire to assert their authority in all the territories, however remote and inhospitable, to which they believed they had a just claim. Given the nature of the terrain and troubled history of the border regions, it was almost inevitable that there should be uncertainty and disagreements about the exact course of the boundaries between the two countries. In October and November 1962, India and China fought a two-front war along the eastern and western sectors of their Himalayas border. After pushing Indian forces back and occupying a large portion of territory, China unilaterally called for a ceasefire and offered to withdraw its forces twenty kilometres from the Line of Actual Control without a demilitarized zone. Both countries understood that these arrangements were not to prejudice any future settlement of the border dispute. However, China knows that India is no longer a push-over of the 1962 variety because of the growing strength of the Indian armed forces.

BORDER DISPUTE AN OBSTACLE TO BUILDING TRUST BETWEEN CHINA AND INDIA

The then Indian chargé d'affaires Brajesh Mishra couldn't believe his ears at Chairman Mao Zedong's cue as they shook hands at a May Day parade on the Tiananmen rostrum in 1970. The wounds of the 1962 border war, in which India suffered a humiliating defeat, were still raw. Pointedly, Mishra was placed at the end of the line-up of diplomats arranged in order of precedence to meet Mao - after the British chargé d'affaires - making the gesture all the more dramatic.

Mishra immediately saw the opening Mao was creating for ties to resume, and was relieved it meshed with his own brief. Before he left for Beijing, then prime minister Indira Gandhi had laid it out for him in one sentence: "I am in a box so far as relations with China are concerned, and I want us to get out of that box." Despite this common yearning for détente, China and India would soon drift further apart - this time over the Bangladesh liberation war in 1971. While India backed the Bengali freedom fighters, Beijing threw its lot behind its "all-weather friend" Islamabad - a relationship that would dog Sino-Indian relations for decades.

It wasn't until the 1990s that China and India would finally start a structured process of normalising ties. Economic relations have since gone from strength to strength, with China now India's largest trading partner. But as the recent three-week Himalayan stand-off brought home, the undercurrent of animosity still runs deep, and the possibility of unfriending each other all over again is never far away.

Arcing a curious trajectory, India and China's modern history would easily qualify for an "it's complicated" relationship status: active courting, followed by demonstrative friendship, violent break-up and now cautious reconciliation. It is this pull of a volatile past and the prospect of profitable cohabitation that Premier Li Keqiang will negotiate as he starts his India visit on Sunday. Li has already had a foretaste of the job at hand. His goodwill gesture of picking India as his first foreign destination on assuming power almost came undone with last month's border crisis. Even though both sides agreed to stand down, the episode will continue to hang heavy when Li lands in New Delhi.

According to Neville Maxwell, author of the seminal *India's China War*, such run-ins are natural as history shows an undefined border acts as a running sore between even the least bellicose of neighbours and can quickly turn malignant. "However much the neighbours may try to develop cordial relations in other aspects, the territorial dispute lurks in the background, making full trust unattainable," he says.

Not that the "other aspects", notably economic engagement, are insignificant. Chinese goods have flooded Indian markets and Indian companies routinely raise yuan debt from Chinese banks. As the two sides have set a goal of US$100 billion trade by 2015, Li's visit is likely to see a raft of billion-dollar deals, with the attendant fanfare and boilerplate diplomatese on "strategic partnership".

But Professor Ma Jiali, executive deputy director of the Strategy Study Centre at the Beijing think tank China Reform Forum, points out: "The border dispute is the biggest obstacle to building strategic trust between China and India. It is directly related to the territorial sovereignty, core interests and national sentiment of the people of both countries." The dispute is over two separate territories, one in the western sector of the border and the other in the east. In the west, both China and India lay claim to 38,000 square kilometres of snowy wastelands known as Aksai Chin.

There is no demarcated border there, only a Line of Actual Control that fuzzily separates the territories controlled by them. And, each side has its own perception of where that line lies. It was in these icy heights that the recent stand-off took place. In the eastern sector, China claims some 90,000 square kilometres to the south of the McMahon Line, which was agreed to by Britain and Tibet in a secret deal in 1914 and not recognised by China. While China calls the region South Tibet, for India it is its Arunachal Pradesh state. The McMahon Line is the de facto border in this sector.

Although China never accepted the McMahon Line, it was open to a land swap, under which India could keep what it claims on the eastern border while China would keep Aksai Chin in the west. Providing the best route into Tibet from the rest of China, Aksai Chin was non-negotiable for Beijing. For Delhi, both territories were off the table as inviolable flanks of national identity.

India and China have held 15 rounds of border talks at the special representative level since the mid-1990s but the gains have been limited. The border is remarkably well managed, with not a shot fired across it in over 20 years, but it's far from being settled, meaning the pre-1962 claims still hold for both sides. Half a century later, the border war today is seen largely as a dispute over land in the high mountains. But for a long time, India's first prime minister, Jawaharlal Nehru, who invested, and lost, substantial political capital in a policy of friendship with China (embodied in the early 1950s Indian slogan of*Hindi-Chini bhai bhai*, or India and China are brothers), would describe Aksai Chin as a place "where not a blade of grass grows".

And, in the course of the 1962 war, Chinese troops swept towards the plains as Indian forces retreated. Rather than holding on to their gains, China called a ceasefire and the troops returned to their old positions. Land was not the only thing the war was about. Far deeper factors were at play. The war coincided with the Sino-Soviet split. Declassified documents show Soviet leader Nikita Krushchev's irritation with China's handling of the border tension, and the Chinese leadership's anger at the Soviet backing of Nehru. For China, showing India its place was also a loaded message for the Soviet Union.

In India, Nehru was being squeezed between a rising left movement and the ascent of the right. In China, Mao was trying to reassert power within the party as the voices against the Great Leap Forward grew louder.

And then there was Tibet. Nehru, while accepting China's sovereignty over Tibet, sought greater autonomy for it to act as a buffer between the two Asian giants. For him, Sino-Indian friendship was the cornerstone of Asia's rise, and for the relationship to work, China and India needed some space. Tibet would give them that space and guarantee the two armies would never come face to face. But for China, as Ma puts it, Tibet is a "core national interest". It is just as central to China's national pride as the border lands are for India's, with or without grass.

Dibyesh Anand, an associate professor at London's Westminster University, says: "There is a nationalist-security dissonance at the heart of how China and India approach Tibet and the border dispute. For China, Tibet is a nationalist issue and the border is a strategic issue, while for India, Tibet is a strategic issue and the border is a nationalist issue. The difference is, you can bargain over a strategic issue but not over a nationalist one." In *Protracted Contest: Sino-Indian Rivalry in the Twentieth Century*, sinologist John Garver notes the "brief period of Sino-India friendship from 1954 to 1958 coincided with a limited but genuine degree of Tibetan autonomy". India interpreted a 1954 pact signed with China on Tibetan border trade as an implicit guarantee of Tibet's relative autonomy while China read it as India's promise to keep its hands off Tibet. The honeymoon ended when they started blaming each other for breaking the deal.

Things came to a head when the Dalai Lama fled to India following the Lhasa revolt of March 1959. China was furious that India provided him refuge and allowed him to set up a government-in-exile. Nehru was peeved that China wasn't cutting him any slack on Tibet, weakening his position at home. Mao was convinced India was colluding with the Americans to incite Tibetan refugees and India started patrolling the far-flung borders more aggressively under a "forward policy". From there on, war was but a matter of time.

Many of the anxieties of 1962 linger. China still feels encircled by hostile powers and is as insecure over Tibet. "India uses the special status of Dalai to allow Tibetan refugees to launch separatist activities for creating trouble to resolve the border problem in the future. Indian politicians also interact with officials of the government-in-exile and Dalai," complains Ma. But Professor Susan Shirk, author of *China: Fragile Superpower*, believes that for the Chinese, it should be possible to shelve the territorial dispute. "This is because the media and the nationalist public don't pay much attention to it," says Shirk.

China sees India as one of the possible sources of trouble. For India, China*is* the trouble. India's sense of betrayal, at what it sees as a sudden and unwarranted land grab by a trusted friend, has festered with time, with China's rise and its proximity to Pakistan only fuelling its own fears of encirclement.

"Tibet and the border dispute can take them back to a 1962-like situation. Economic interdependence should not be seen as replacing political negotiation," warns Anand. Unless, of course, they find a way to live with their differences and yet profit from each other.

Mishra, the chargé d'affaires in Beijing who went on to become India's national security adviser, would later recall in *Across the Himalayan Gap* that during his stint in China, he would attend the regulation diplomatic banquets but never actually got to eat anything. This was because the speeches would start during the second course and since the Chinese hosts would invariably lay into India and praise Pakistan, Mishra and his wife would have to walk out in protest. This went on for a while until Mishra noticed the speeches weren't starting until after the cakes and ice cream came out. A Pakistani diplomat told him the Chinese had noticed the Mishras were missing out on the food and decided to hold the speeches until after dessert.

THEORETICAL FRAMEWORK OF THE CBMS

At the outset of this section it is desirable to define CBMs. Confidence Building Measures (CBMs) are regarded as "diverse arrangements that can help reduce tensions and promote good neighborly relations. Traditionally they are designed to make the behaviour of states more predictable by facilitating communication among or between states and establishing rules or patterns of behaviour for state's military forces." Succinctly CBMs can be defined as broader concept to defuse tension and increase the possibilities of peace among the hostile nations by concerted efforts. It has been fashionable in much of the English literature on the subject to visualize confidence building measures (CBMs) essentially in their Western framework. However, the CBMs in the Asian context have preceded all these Western models, most of which owe their origins to the Final Act of the Helsinki process of the Conference on Security and Cooperation in Europe (CSCE) that was concluded in 1975. Besides, the Asian CBMs have also been far more broad based than even those Western mechanisms that were launched later under the Document of the Conference on Disarmament in Europe held in 1986 at Stockholm (Sweden). Similar arrangements had been for long experimented amongst various Asian nations, including both China and India. There are propositions saying that India-China CBMs were borrowed from the western literature which is not true. The truth of the matter is that the CBMs had been institutionalized in Asia much earlier the Helsinki Accord of 1975. The peace process consists of three stages namely Conflict Avoidance Measures (CAMs), Confidence Building Measures (CBMs) and Peace Building Measures (PBMs).

Conflict Avoidance Measures (CAMs)

It means the avoidance of unwanted and unintended conflicts or wars arising particularly from miscalculations or misinterpretations. To start the peace process, we need here a minimum political will to stop wars. This is workable especially in the nuclear era. These initial steps like the establishment of hotlines between two countries' military, or even between Prime Ministers or Presidents but cannot solve underlying political and territorial disputes. Nevertheless, it has enormous worth in the context of nuclearisation of both India and China. CBMs have been particularly ineffective, if not absent, during times of conflict, because despite declarations to the effect, neither country has moved beyond the point of 'conflict avoidance', towards actual confidence building measures, and finally, towards strengthening peace. One thing you have to keep in the mind that to start negotiations between adversaries especially one whom you consider as someone stabbed in the back is very very difficult. Whereas which is not so in the case of parties where no prior enmities exist. Of course if you see Henderson Brooks Report it says it is India which started war than the normal perception in India looking at China as aggressor.

Confidence Building Measures (CBMs)

The second stage of this process is far more difficult as it requires far more political capital to resolve the deep-seated grievances or core issues. In the case of Sino-Indian conflict, the transition phase from conflict avoidance to confidence building is extremely difficult, because of the persistence of irritants between India and China. Probably this transition might be easier if there are no core issues blocking the way. The 1954 Sino-Indian Agreement on Trade and Intercourse between India and the Tibet Region, the 1962 Colombo Power Proposals, various Border Talks, the 1993 Agreement on Maintaining Peace and Stability in the Region in the Vicinity of the Actual Control Line were some of the examples of confidence building measures. Probably this transition might be easier if there are no core issues blocking the way. However, following the June 1989 Tiananmen Square incident, while most world powers had imposed sanctions, thus, completely isolating China, the relations between China and India not only continued to be smooth but experienced a greater momentum: the period between the second half of 1989 and 1990 saw ten high-level visits between the two countries that included visits to New Delhi by Vice Premier Wu Xueguian in October 1989 and Foreign Minister Qian Qichen in March 1990. This bonhomie can be attributed to the mutual goodwill of India and China which is essential for the success of CBMs.

Peace-Building Measures (PBMs)

This last stage requires enormous amount of political will for conflict reconciliation and resolution, where the peace process have to encounter with vested interests, hardliners. It is here the role of leadership is put to test as leaders must be able to take risk taking efforts for peace against their own constituencies. If formidable hurdles like the 1962 aggression, sporadic border skirmishes can be crossed to avoid war and to negotiate a fragile peace, national leaders can go ahead with further broadening and deepening existing patterns of co-operation and making positive developments as irreversible as possible. It is here the role of people to people contacts must also be emphasized. Perhaps if we all made a conscious effort to ignore our preconceptions and be more optimistic, the road to peace would be smoother.

MAIN DEVELOPMENTS: SINO-INDIAN CBMS PROCESS

In this chapter we will be seeing the various CBMs between India and China and will be delved the most important agreements among them. There was no improvement in bilateral relations until the reestablishment of full diplomatic ties in 1976. In 1986-87 India and China were involved in a crisis in the Sumdorong Chu area of Arunachal Pradesh where a Chinese incursion had taken place. This led to the mobilization of both Indian and Chinese forces and something of a stand-off ensued. This tension lasted over twelve to eighteen months. At least one lesson relevant to CBMs was that even in a period of relative calm things can veer out of control to the detriment of both sides. Relations began to improve after the then Indian Prime Minister Rajiv Gandhi, visited

China in December 1988. The border question still remains unresolved. However, even in the absence of a formal settlement, both countries have been willing to negotiate CBMs to avoid conflict and to provide the basis for increased cooperation. In 1981 for example, China unilaterally allowed Indian pilgrims access to pilgrimage sites in Tibet. Between 1981 and 1988 a series of eight official discussions on the border issues and Sino-Indian relations took place. Following Rajiv Gandhi's visit, an India –China joint working Group (JWG) was established to go into the boundary dispute. Relations improved markedly with the visit of the then Indian Prime Minister Narasimha Rao, to Beijing in September 1993.

The mandate of the JWG is to settle the border issue and to promote peace and tranquility along the frontier. Some of the measures negotiated by the JWG include:

1) Military-to-military meetings to be held twice a year, in June and October, along both the eastern and western sectors of the border at Bum La Pass and Spanggur Gap.
2) Military-to-military communication links to be installed at key points along both the eastern and western sectors of the border.
3) An agreement was reached on the establishment of dedicated communication links, or "hotlines," between military headquarters.
4) Local commanders are to be encouraged to conduct meetings, as needed, using color-coded flags to initiate contact.
5) Exchanges between defence educational institutions and between Strategic Studies Research Institutes were to be arranged.
6) An agreement was reached regarding prior notification of military maneuvers and troop movements along the border.
7) An agreement on the prevention of airspace violations was arrived at.
8) Exchanges between defence educational institutions and between strategic studies research institutes wee to be arranged.

9) Exchanges between high-level defence officials began with Sharad Pawar, the then Indian Defence Minister, who visited Beijing in July 1992.
10) Another working group was established in 1988 to cover issues relating to economic cooperation, trade, science and technology.

In addition to progress on border issues through the JWG, India and China have begun to explore other areas of cooperation. The Sino-Indian rapprochement that began with the Narasimha Rao–Li Peng Summit in Beijing in September 1993 led to what has been an epoch-making agreement on the Maintenance of peace and Tranquility along the Line of Actual Control in the India-China border Areas. This agreement begins by reiterating the five principles of peaceful coexistence mutually agreed upon by the two countries in the April 1954 agreement on trade between India and the Tibet Region of China. This Sino-Indian rapprochement culminated in a historic visit by the then Chinese President Jiang Zemin to New Delhi in December 1996. During his visit, the two countries signed the agreement on CBMs in the military field along the line of actual control in the china-India border Areas.

Thanks to the joint efforts, China and India have established following CBMs:

1) In 1990, China and India decided to establish the meetings between the soldiers on both sides of the actual control lines on an unfixed basis.
2) In 1992, the two countries established a hotline between the meeting stations on both sides of the actual control line.
3) In September 1993, China and India signed the Agreement on Maintaining Peace and Stability in the Region in the Vicinity of the Actual Control Line. The agreement stipulates that the two sides should seek solutions to the border disputes through peaceful means: the two sides do not use force or threaten to use force; before the final solution to the border issue, two sides strictly respect and obey the actual control line; the military strength of reach side in the respective area of actual control line should be

kept at minimum size, which serves to match the relationship of friendly neighbourhood between the two countries; the two sides should reduce the armed forces to the limit reached between them in the areas along the actual control line etc.

4) In 1993, for the implementation of the afore-mentioned agreement, a special working group composed of diplomats and military experts was established.
5) In 1995, China and India agreed to withdraw from the two confronting outposts near the actual control line and agreed that they would never enter them.
6) Also in 1995, China and India agreed to carry out mutual visits by the personnel from the military agencies, organize joint expeditionary part for exploration of ventures; the two sides also agreed to forbid hunting, firing guns and explosion in the area near the actual control line.
7) In 2005, an agreement on 'political parameters and guiding principles for settlement of the boundary dispute' was signed when the then Chinese Premier Wen Jiabao was in Delhi.
8) Hand-in-Hand 2008: The India-China Joint Military Exercise
9) In 2010, India and China signed an agreement to establish a hotline between the Prime Ministers or heads of the two countries.
10) In 2013, India and China signed set of CBMs called Border Defence Cooperation Agreement (BDCA).

Of all these agreements, the author thinks that only two agreements are significant.

They are the 1993 and the 1995 agreements because these agreements were actually responsible for paving the way for the institutionalization of the subsequent CBMs.

AGREEMENT ON MAINTENANCE OF PEACE AND TRANQUILLITY, 1993

This Agreement on Maintenance of Peace and Tranquillity along the Line of Actual Control" (henceforth MPTA) which is widely considered as the first CBMs was signed between the then Prime Ministers Narasimha Rao and Li Peng at Beijing's Great Hall of the People on September 7, 1993 which was rightly hailed as the first major conventional arms control agreement between two Asian countries without any role played by third countries.

As the first thing, it reiterates its faith in Panchsheel and asserts that these Five Principles of Peaceful Coexistence should be revived to form the basis of inter-state relations. But far from the earlier Sino-India Panchsheel Agreement of April 1954 where only India made major concessions, this clearly represents the equality of the two nations and lays out various CBMs that should further buttress Sino-India understanding and mutual confidence. This spirit and sincerity is crystal clear throughout its concise text that details on a number of CBMs.

Article I of the MPTA starts by highlighting the consensus where both sides wish to resolve the boundary question "through peaceful and friendly consultations" and both undertake to "strictly respect and observe the line of actual control" and never to "use or threaten to use force" and whenever necessary "jointly check and determine the segments" of their borders. Article II makes a far more concrete recommendation asking the two sides to keep their border military presence "to a minimum level compatible with the friendly and good neighbourly relations" and in fact to further agree "to reduce" them "in conformity with the requirements of the principle of mutual and equal security." Taking off from here, Article III talks of evolving "effective CBMs" and asks each side to not "undertake specified levels of military exercises in mutually identified zones" and to "give the other notification of military exercises" along the border. Then Articles IV and V speak about their agreement to create mechanisms for dealing with intrusions and other exigencies while in Article VI both sides clarify that despite these resolutions, nothing in this treaty shall "prejudice their respective positions on the boundary question."

To actually kick off initiatives, Article VII asks both sides to start by specifically defining the "form, method, scale and content of effective verification measures," and Article VIII initiates this process by asking each side to "appoint diplomats and military experts to formulate, through mutual consultations, implementation measures for the present agreement," and this setting up of an Expert Group can be easily described as the greatest achievement of this pact in terms of building Sino-Indian CBMs. Finally, Article IX gives its date of coming into effect and declares all its versions–Hindi, Chinese, and English–as equally valid.

CBMS FOR LINE FOR ACTUAL CONTROL, 1996

This second CBMs is the twelve-Article agreement on CBMs was signed during President Jiang Zemin's November 1996 visit to New Delhi. Amongst some new initiatives, this treaty is primarily geared to fulfil the agenda of their first such agreement of 1993 and it seeks to further extend their existing CBMs to more specific and sensitive areas in the military field.

Going by its first Article that reads, "Neither side shall use its military capability against the other side," it virtually stands out as a no-war pact and both sides have also projected it in that spirit. The agreement once again affirms their commitment to the LOAC (Article II) while this time fully recognizing that both have "different perceptions" on certain segments for which the two agree "to speed up process of clarification" and start "to exchange maps indicating their respective perceptions…as soon as possible" (Article X). It in this businesslike approach to these sensitive questions that gives hope for the future as it depicts their mutual confidence in the current state of their rapprochement. Besides, all these years there had been major confusion as China does not consider its deployments in Tibet as being open for mutual reductions and India believes that Chinese forces on the Tibetan plateau have a clear one-to-ten advantage against Indian forces who will have to operate from below.

Accordingly, Article III of this agreement provides that in keeping with "the principle of mutual and equal security" all future ceilings are expected to be based on "parameters such as the nature of terrain, road communications and other infrastructure and time taken to induct/deinduct troops and armaments." Article IV clearly categorizes certain types of offensive weapons, withdrawal of which will be given priority. These include combat tanks, infantry combat vehicles, guns (including howitzers) with 75 mm or bigger calibre, mortars with 120 mm or bigger calibre, surface-to-surface missiles, surface-to-air missiles, and to start with, the two sides will "exchange data on the military forces and armaments" that are to be reduced. It also exhorts the two to "avoid holding large scale military exercises involving more than one division (15,000 troops) in close proximity to the LOAC" and to inform the other side on "type, level, planned duration and areas of exercise" in case it involves more than a brigade (5,000 troops), and about deinduction "within five days of completion," and the other side shall be free to seek any number of clarifications as it deems necessary.

Taking a major step forward, the two agree that no combat aircraft which "include fighter, bomber, reconnaissance, military trainer, armed helicopter and other armed aircraft" shall be allowed to fly "within ten kilometres" of the LOAC "except by prior permission" from the other side (Article V). Similarly, Article VI prohibits any use of "hazardous chemicals, conduct blast operations or hunt with guns or explosives within two kilometres" of the LOAC unless it is "part of developmental activities" in which case the other side shall be informed "through diplomatic channels or by convening a border personnel meeting, preferably five days in advance." Then to "strengthen exchanges and cooperation between their military personnel and establishments," Article VII provides that the two sides shall expand (a) "meetings between their border representatives at designated places; (b) "telecommunication links" between these border points; and (c) establish "step-by-step medium and high-level contacts between the border authorities" of the two sides. Should any land or air intrusions take place "because of unavoidable circumstances like natural disasters," the other side is expected under Article VIII to "extend all possible assistance to them" and the two shall exchange information and have consultations to work out "modalities of return of the concerned personnel."

And finally, as under Article XI the Sino-Indian Joint Working Group on Boundary Question starts "mutual consultations" for "detailed implementation measures", once again under Article IX each side shall have "the right to seek clarification" regarding the "manner in which the other side is observing the agreement" or on any "doubtful situation" in the border region, and under Article XII, though all Hindi, Chinese and English versions are "equally authentic," but "in case of divergence, the English text shall prevail" and like most other agreements, it is also subject to ratification and "shall enter into force on the date of exchange of instruments of ratification."

Other CBMs

Apart from being a major take-off point for many fresh initiatives, these two agreements also provide a major boost for their other existing channels for Sino-Indian border related CBMs. Within less than two months of the MPTA, for example, a Chinese ship, Zheng He, made a port visit to Bombay, which was the first of its kind in the last 35 years. Before this only the INS Mysur had visited Shanghai in 1958. This was followed by these important visits to New Delhi: Li Ruihuan (Chairman of the National Committee of the Chinese People's Consultative Committee), Wen Jiao (an alternate member of the Central Politburo), Wu Yi (Foreign Trade and Economic Cooperation Minister) and Chi Haotian (Defence Minister) respectively in December 1993 and January, June and September 1994. Qiao Shi, Chairman of the Standing Committee of the National People's Congress (NPC) came to India in November 1995 and finally President Jiang Zemin (who is also Chairman of the Central Military Commission) paid a three-day visit to New Delhi in November 1996.

Also working on the basis of the Chinese guanxi (personal contacts), principle, exchanges between other opinion makers and members of strategic research institutions (like the Institute for Defence Studies and Analyses, United Services Institution of India, Centre for Policy Research, and Rajiv Gandhi Foundation from India and China Institute for Contemporary International Relations, China Association for Friendly International Contact, Fudan University, etc from China) have also been increasingly formalized. Similarly, Xinhua, People's Daily and Beijing Review have their accredited correspondents in India and India's Press Trust of India has a resident reporter in Beijing. The agreements on exchange of scholars (between the Indian Council for Social Science Research and Chinese Academy of Social Sciences signed at New Delhi in January 1992) and their Agreement on Radio and Television Cooperation (signed in Beijing on September 7, 1993) have also contributed to expanding mutual awareness. Contacts have also evolved between various non-governmental organisations (NGOs) like trade unions and women's organizations, stimulating a great deal of interest and goodwill. The Festival of China was staged in India in 1992 and the Festival of India was held in China in April 1994. In fact, the Communist Party of China now has direct links with the Indian National Congress, the Bhartiya Janata Party and the Communist Party of India (Marxist). The two countries had also opened up direct flights between New Delhi and Beijing and now have telecom lines between various cities of the two countries.

The Joint Working Group (JWG) on Boundary Question has been a most effective and generic forum for implementing Sino-Indian CBMs. To begin with, the JWG has institutionalized regular meetings of military commanders from both sides at Bumla and Dichu in the eastern sector, Lipulekh near Pithoragarh (U.P.) in the middle sector and Spanggur near Chushul in the western sector. These meetings are organised and conducted by the area commanders from the two sides to establish facts on the ground and can also be held more than once or in case of any exigencies. Besides, commanders on both sides are provided with "hotline" links to ensure consultations in case of any intrusions or other emergencies.

Advance notice of proposed military maneuvers on one side is provided to the other and mechanisms for handling possible intrusions on either side are put in place. The high point of these JWG meetings occurred during its eighth meeting during August 1995 at New Delhi where the two sides agreed to actually disengage their troops from four border posts in the Wangdong tract where they had been deployed at an alarming proximity to each other. Apart from their land borders, the two Air Forces have also been building ties and officers of the People's Liberation Army-Air Force (PLAAF) have already visited India's Air Force bases in 1995.

Similarly, the two Navies have also been working together, allaying each other's doubts about the Chinese naval presence in Myanmar or India's maritime capabilities at its Fortress Andaman. India has suggested that China's envoy visit the Indian naval base at Port Blair in Andaman and Nicobar. At a certain stage there were even reports of China and India preparing for joint military and naval exercises which, however, was soon denied by the Chinese officials.

STUMBLING BLOCKS IN THE NORMALIZATION PROCESS

These CBMs though good per se could not take the peace process to its logical conclusion in spite of the consent of both the parties. Notwithstanding the progress in certain directions, there have been some problems which the author views as stumbling blocks in the developing relations between India and China.

The Nuclear Factor

The Sino-Indian rapprochement had got stalled due to Pokharan II. But it is only a matter of time before the process comes back to its normal equilibrium. Looking at China's own example, India can perhaps afford to wait or even ignore China's criticism. In the face of China's own nuclear explosions in October 1964, the Kennedy Administration had even thought of physically eliminating China's nuclear facilities. In such adversity, Beiujing had, however, continued to denounce American reactions to its nuclear weapons and Washington had to finally give up its policies and build détente with the Chinese. During the 1990s, the two countries had intimate interaction in the economic sphere and the two sides have since evolved into the economic sphere and the two sides have since evolved into strategic partners.

It is the sovereign right of India to determine whether or not its security compulsions require it to go in for nuclear weapons as an ultimate shield, notwithstanding the opinion of the western nations. One example in this context would suffice. After the North Korean missile test in August 1998, the U.S. and Japan decided to conduct joint research on a missile defence system to protect Japan and US troops in Korea. It was argued that in the absence of this, despite possessing nearly 10,000 nuclear weapons, the U.S. needs a new system of missile defence to protect its troops abroad, then surely India can have a small number of nuclear weapons to protect itself from any country in the neighbourhood truing to blackmail it. This is bound to have its impact on Indian decision making as well.

Cartographic Aggression

It has become the habit of Chinese to commit cartographic aggression very often without the feeling of guilty. The Chinese maps continue to show large tracts of Indian Territory (particularly Arunachal Pradesh) as belonging to China. When these in accuracies are pointed out to China, it tries and wishes them away as errors in map making.

This typoe of aggression is always a serious matter and cannot be countenanced as it had led to the 1962 war with China. Further, China and India had agreed under Article X of the 1996 Agreements to exchange maps of the entire LAC an important CBM for the two countries-but China did not do so. Since 1996 the CBMs have not made the progress they should have.

Territorial Claims

The border and territorial disputes remain one of the biggest sticking points in Sino-Indian relations. On the border issue it needs to be recognized that the 4,000 km long border has been tranquil over the last several years.

It is only last year that the 19 kilometres deep intrusion by an armed patrol of China's People's Liberation Army (PLA) into the strategically sensitive area around Daulet Beg Oldi in the Aksai Chin region occurred, and detected by India on 16 April 2013, which has been unprovoked.

Despite years of high-level special representative talks, India's border with China remains largely undefined. China also claims sovereignty over the northeastern Indian state of Arunachal Pradesh, and tensions have flared in recent years over Beijing's refusal to grant Chinese visas to residents of the disputed state, on the grounds that Arunachal Pradesh's residents are, in their eyes, already Chinese citizens.

The Sino-Pakistani Relationship

China's security relationship with Pakistan can be characterized as enduring and strengthening, a dynamic that gives pause to many in New Delhi. The increased presence of Chinese military engineers in the border flashpoint of Pakistani-controlled Kashmir has Indian defense experts especially concerned. The PRC sees Pakistan as a strategic surrogate against India. China's military, missiles and nuclear assistance to Pakistan continue. There is no guarantee that Pakistan will not use Chinese supplied arms against India.

The Tibet and Tibetan Diaspora

Tibet is another issue that is significant source of friction between the two countries. Relations between India and China took a nose-dive with the flight of His Holiness Dali Lama to India in 1959. Over 100,000 Tibetan exiles currently live in India, but Beijing and New Delhi have done little to formalize their status. The author is of the opinion that this issue could become more pressing in the coming years, especially if the youngest generation of Tibetans proves more assertive in its dispute with China. Despite New Delhi's assurance that the spiritual leader would not be allowed to engage in any anti-China activity from India's soil, Chinese suspicions in this regard remain strong. Authoritative views in China allege that India wants to play the Tibet card against the PRC and as examples, point to India's not banning Tibet government in exile and continuing support to the Dalai Lama coming from eminent Indian personalities.

IMPACT OF THESE DISPUTES ON SINO-INDIAN RELATIONS OR CBMS

Given these disputes and divergences, bilateral relations between Asia's giants remain, in the words of Zhang Yan, China's ambassador to India, "very fragile, very easy to be damaged, and very difficult to repair." Both have massive manpower resources, a scientific and industrial base, and million-plus militaries. For the first time in more than fifty years, both are moving upward simultaneously on their relative power trajectories. As the pivotal power in South Asia, India perceives itself much as China has traditionally perceived itself in relation to East Asia. Both desire a peaceful security environment to focus on economic development and avoid overt rivalry or conflict. Still, the volatile agents of nationalism, history, ambition, strength, and size produce a mysterious chemistry. Neither power is comfortable with the rise of the other. Both seek to envelop neighbours with their national economies. Both are nuclear and space powers with growing ambitions. Both yearn for a multi-polar world that will provide them the space for growth and freedom of action. Both vie for leadership positions in global and regional organizations and have attempted to establish a sort of Monroe Doctrine in their respective neighborhoods without much success.

And both remain suspicious of each other's long-term agenda and intentions. Perception has been one of the major problems of international relations. And India and China is not an exception to this trend. Each perceives the other as pursuing hegemony and entertaining imperial ambitions. Both are non–status quo powers: China in terms of territory, power, and influence; India in terms of status, power, and influence. Both seek to expand their power and influence in and beyond their regions at each other's expense. China's "Malacca paranoia" is matched by India's "Hormuz dilemma." If China's navy is going south to the Indian Ocean, India's navy is going east to the Pacific Ocean. Both suffer from a siege mentality born out of their elites' acute consciousness of the divisive tendencies that make their countries' present political unity so fragile. After all, much of Chinese and Indian history is made up of long periods of internal disunity and turmoil, when centrifugal forces brought down even the most powerful empires. Each has its vulnerabilities—regional conflicts, poverty, and religious divisions for India; the contradiction between a market economy and Leninist politics for China. Both are plagued with domestic linguistic, ethno-religious, and politico-economic fault lines that could be their undoing if not managed properly.

In other words, China and India are locked in a classic security dilemma: one country sees its actions as defensive, but the same actions appear aggressive to the other. Beijing fears that an unrestrained Indian power—particularly one that is backed by the

West and Japan—would not only threaten China's security along its restive southwestern frontiers (Tibet and Xinjiang) but also obstruct China's expansion southwards. Faced with exponential growth in China's power and influence, India feels the need to take counterbalancing measures and launch strategic initiatives to emerge as a great power, but these are perceived as challenging and threatening in China. As a result of all these power struggle the ultimate victim is the CBMs which remain a half-hearted measures which sarcastically described by some as conflict building measures.

What India must do?

In view of the above disputes and divergences in perceptions and approaches, a vital question arises over what are the options for India to pursue? How then do we deal with China's growing strength and assertive attitude on issues or core interests for India?

First, we need to increase our own defensive capabilities particularly in the border areas.

Secondly, it will be useful for decisions and policy makers to consider the possibility of bringing the Tibet issue with China with frank and direct conversation.

Thirdly, we need to consider whether we could apply pressure on China by enhancing our official and non-official contacts with Taiwan.

Fourthly, we need to strengthen our capacity and capabilities in the Indian Ocean region and not to allow China to enhance its presence there.

Last but not the least we need to establish strong and active relations with like-minded countries like USA, Japan, Germany, Britain and Australia to put a psychological balancer in the minds of our adversaries.

Conclusions

Both have gained nothing in pursuing the course of confrontation so far. Both sides have realized that the peaceful relations between India and China are in the interests of both the countries. This can happen only if there is agreement on the terms of coexistence-equality, a fair and early settlement of the border dispute, appreciating each other's security concerns, an agreement on nuclear security, good neighbourly relations without ulterior aims, and expanding economic, political and security cooperation. Only then can the two states shed their legacy of mistrust. Just like in the international relations people generally say that nothing is permanent except national interests, let us hope that Sino-Indian rivalry too is not permanent.

The above discussed CBMs have been reached on the basis of political trust than any international thrust. They in turn advanced the political trust between the two countries. Since early 1990s when China and India began to establish the CBMs, politicians and scholars in the two countries have understood the importance to improve the relations between them. Both sides saw that only the constructive relationship can be materialized on the basis of political trust.

Furthermore these two big powers have a lot of similarities and common in the changing world. These again prompt them to have better mutual understanding and wider and closer cooperation in international affairs. Therefore they joined their efforts, the relations between the two. Thanks to their efforts, the relations between the two countries have been steadily improving and the situation in the border areas have been kept peaceful and stable, although there have been minor setbacks, such as the accusations by some politicians that China poses a threat.

To sum up, though there are disputes and divergences that prevent them from reaching a compromise to all these problems, there is no denying of the fact that the CBMs between the two countries have played a very important role in the development of the bilateral relations. Specifically speaking, CBMs between China and India have contributed positively in the following ways:

- the hotline liaison between the meeting situations;
- the reduction of the armed forces in the disputed area;
- the diminishing of the armed conflict in the border regions;
- the exchange of visits by the top military leaders;
- the relaxation of tensions in the border region;

- the increase of mutual understanding and trust;
- the stability and development of the bilateral relations.

This kind of contributions in the face of long and severe disputes and crises are worth accomplishing. The existing CBMs have brought about an atmosphere for further CBMs in the future and in wider areas. In the future, the CBMs between China and India can be expanded to the following areas-limiting the activities which may lead hostilities; limiting the military activities which may lead to confrontation; carrying out dialogues in the military conversions; carrying out cooperation in the non-operational and non-sensitive areas, such as military medicine, military sports, military arts, military history, exchange of military students. There is a realization in both the countries of late that the only way to reduce the potential friction between them is to go for new confidence-building measures (CBMs) between India and China. Barring the exceptional skirmishes, by and large the Sino-Indian border has not suffered any major disruptions during these last ten years thanks to this process of evolving CBMs. This, when compared to India's experience of incessant firing incidents and infiltration on its borders with Pakistan, makes the Sino-Indian border look almost peaceful.

Therefore considering the above benefits of CBMs on the Sino-Indian relations, it can be said that its role has been significant in moulding the course of the India-China relations, though at times not up to the mark. It is ironically found during the course of the study that the Sino-India CBMs were effective in the peace times rather than in the war times. This irony certainly defeats the very purpose for which CBMs are forged that is good neighbourly relations and reduction of tensions. This is the reason why in spite of so many treaties, India and China could not resolve tensions that erupts occasionally. It is this increasing realization and understanding on the part of India and China of late that they lack political will in executing CBMs in letter and spirit, that gives hope that this complicated boundary question can be resolved in the course of time. Sometimes some commentators negate these Sino-Indian CBMs citing that they have not resulted in resolving the Sino-Indian boundary question. But keeping in mind the complexities involved, the gradual evolution of CBMs has not only preserved peace between these two Asian giants but also generated a great deal of mutual trust and understanding giving hope towards eventually resolving their border dispute. Keeping in the mind of the Chinese President Xi Jinping's statement that he considered the improvement of relations with India as his 'historic mission', I would like to end this article with the positive note that there is bright future for the CBMs as far as the India-China relation is concerned because of the following factors which gives hope that all the disputes may be solved. The factors having potentiality for facilitating the Confidence-Building Measures are as follows:

A Good First Step: CBMs on certain mutually important issues say border skirmishes may sow the seeds for broader Sino-Indian cooperation, no matter whether the disputes between the two powers are too significant for such an approach. In this regard, it is a welcoming fact that both the countries had already opened the telephone hotline between the Prime Minister of India and the Chinese Premier. This can be extended to the levels of sector headquarters and the Director General Military Operations (DGMOs) so as to have a strategic communication between India and China. Such a hotline is expected to help in early resolution of situations like the one which happened in Depsang Valley in Ladakh on April 16 2013, when Chinese troops intruded 19 km into Indian Territory crossing the Line of Actual Control.

A Shared Enemy: Both China and India have confronted and fallen victim to terrorist violence and there is common ground for CBMs to combat this threat. Beijing and New Delhi have already taken steps to collaborate on counterterrorism, coordinating joint military exercises and setting up a high-level policy dialogue.

Nuclear Perspectives: In my view, Chinese and Indian philosophies on nuclear weapons have much in common—both favor disarmament and No First Use policies—which creates room for agreements on how best to develop a stable nuclear balance in the region. In my opinion this convergence may lead to a wide range of nuclear CBMs, from joint advocacy of global disarmament to the separation of land-based nuclear warheads from their delivery systems.

STRATEGIC ENCIRCLEMENT OF INDIA

When Asia's leaders meet at the annual East Asia summit to discuss geo-strategic and economic issues of common interest, most of the discussions on the sidelines of the summit are centred on China's aggressive posturing in its area of influence. China's recent assertiveness in the South China Sea and its belligerence on the Senkaku/ Diaoyu islands are indicators of its growing proclivity to settle territorial and boundary disputes by force rather than through diplomatic negotiations.

India's unresolved territorial and boundary dispute with China and an un-demarcated Line of Actual Control (LAC) on the Indo-Tibetan border do not augur well for long-term peace and stability between these two Asian giants. Territorial and boundary disputes that are carried over from history and left unresolved carry within them the seeds of future conflict. The next major transgression on the LAC could possibly lead to a localised border conflict as either Indian patience with Chinese intransigence wears thin or the Chinese view Indian attempts to build infrastructure and develop the border areas as the adoption of an aggressive forward posture.

Hence, the possibility of a limited border war between the two Asian giants cannot be entirely ruled out even though the probability is low. China's continuing opposition to India's nuclear weapons programme; its nuclear and missile collusion and intimate defence cooperation with Pakistan; its support to the military-backed regime in Myanmar; efforts at making inroads into Nepal; increasing activities in the Bay of Bengal; its relentless efforts to increase its influence in Bhutan and Bangladesh; and, its attempts to isolate India in the ASEAN Regional Forum (ARF) and keep India out of the Shanghai Cooperation Organisation; are all pointers to a carefully orchestrated plan aimed at the strategic encirclement of India.

MILITARY DOCTRINE: ACTIVE DEFENCE AND LOCAL WARS UNDER CONDITIONS OF INFORMATIONISATION

The People's Liberation Army (PLA) is rapidly modernising itself and is known to be preparing to fight a "limited border war under hi-tech conditions". According to several White Papers on China's National Defence, China is engaged in developing a "revolutionised, modernised and regularised people's army with Chinese characteristics. (It is) endeavouring to transform its armed forces from a numerically superior to a qualitatively superior type and from a manpower-intensive to a technology-intensive type, as well as to train high-quality personnel and improve the modernisation of weaponry in order to comprehensively enhance the armed forces combat effectiveness."

Since China's ill-conceived incursion into Vietnam in 1979, PLA doctrine has evolved from Mao's "people's war" to "people's war under modern conditions" through a "limited/local war" phase to the current doctrine introduced in 1993. The new doctrine is more assertive than ever before and is not bound by any restrictions to confine and limit future conflict to within China's national boundaries. Underpinning the new professionalism of the PLA is the basic doctrine of "active defence" *(jiji fangyu)* that seeks to conduct "people's war under modern conditions" (better understood as "local wars under hi-tech conditions" – *gaojishu tiaojian xia de jubu zhanzheng).*

The active defence doctrine calls for integrated deep strikes – a concentration of superior firepower that is to be utilised to destroy the opponent's retaliatory capabilities through pre-emptive strikes employing long-range artillery, short-range ballistic missiles (SRBMs) and precision guided munitions. David Shambaugh, a well-known China scholar in the US has written: "Rather than conducting a 'people's war' (a strategy to 'lure the enemy in deep' into one's own territory), the PLA doctrine of 'active defence' calls for forward positioning, frontier defence, engagement of the enemy at or over the border and potential engagement in conflict beyond China's immediate periphery... this doctrine is essentially pro-active and seeks to take the battle into enemy territory."

Beijing has identified the following five limited war scenarios as likely scenarios during future conflict: military conflict with neighbouring countries in a limited region; military conflict on territorial waters; undeclared air attack by enemy countries; territorial defence in a limited military operation; and, punitive offensive with a minor incursion into a neighbouring country.

The new doctrine and the strategy and tactics associated with it have been influenced by the lessons of Gulf War I in 1991 and the Iraq War of 2003, both of which have been extensively studied by Chinese scholars. The doctrine requires the creation of a capability to project force across China's borders through rapid deployment, conventional SRBMs and cruise missiles, information warfare, electronic warfare, precision-guided munitions, enhanced night fighting capabilities and other advanced military technologies.

China also follows 'anti-access and area denial' (A2AD) strategies to deny the adversary access to his planned launch pads in an endeavour to prevent build-up of forces for a war against China. Planning for A2AD strategies flows from the apprehension that if superior, well-equipped forces (like the US and its allies) are allowed to arrive in the war zone with the force levels and in the time frame planned by them, they are bound to prevail. The Chinese calculate that "by mounting a credible threat to do so, they will be able to deter the United States from intervening in the first place, or at least limit the scale and scope of that intervention." The Chinese aim to deter a conflict or at least delay the opponent's preparation till the PLA is better prepared to react. The PLA seeks to achieve this aim through attacks against air bases and ports and other elements of the logistics chain and against information systems so as to disrupt command and control during build-up. While A2AD strategies are unlikely to succeed in preventing conflict completely, these could impose considerable delay and caution during build-up and cause attrition.

MODERNISATION OF THE PLA: RMA WITH CHINESE CHARACTERISTICS

The PLA expects to fight the next war under conditions of what it calls "informationisation" or "informationalisation". In the 2004 White Paper on National Defence, informationisation was explained in the following terms: "To adapt itself to the changes both in the international strategic situation and the national security environment and rise to the challenges presented by the RMA worldwide, China adheres to the military strategy of active defence and works to speed up the RMA with Chinese characteristics:

- To take the road of composite and leapfrog development.
- To build a strong military by means of science and technology.
- To deepen the reform of the armed forces.
- To step up preparations for military struggle.

PLA analysts have called the ongoing RMA an "informationised military revolution". It emerges that informationisation "clearly relates to the PLA's ability to adopt information technologies to command, intelligence, training and weapon systems. This would include broad investment in new automated command systems linked by fibre-optic Internet, satellite and new high-frequency digital radio systems… The PLA can also contest the information battle space with its new space-based, airborne, naval and ground-based surveillance and intelligence gathering systems and its new anti-satellite, anti-radar, electronic warfare and information warfare systems… there is increasing 'information content' for new PLA weapons as it moves to link new space, airborne and ELINT sensors to missile, air, naval and ground-based 'shooters' to enable all its services to better use new precision-strike weapons."

According to General Liu Huaqing, former Vice Chairman of the Central Military Commission, "Information warfare and electronic warfare are of key importance, while fighting on the ground can only exploit the victory. Hence, China is more convinced (than ever) that as far as the PLA is concerned, a military revolution with information warfare as the core has reached the stage where efforts must be made to catch up and overtake rivals." According to the 2004 White Paper, "In its modernisation drive, the PLA takes informationalisation as its orientation and strategic focus." The PLA has adopted what it calls a "double historical mission" and a "leapfrog development strategy" – accelerating military informationisation while still undergoing mechanisation.

Developing cyber warfare capabilities is seen as presenting a level playing field in an otherwise David versus Goliath scenario as Chinese hardware is no match for the weapons technology fielded today by the US and its allies. Recent cyber attacks directed against Taiwan and the US are indicative of the efforts to develop new techniques, viruses and logic bombs. Information warfare will be crucial in the opening phases of a war aimed at the re-unification of Taiwan or a border conflict with India as it will be important to knock out the adversary's communications infrastructure by cyber as well as physical means. A private army of "laptop warriors" – young civilian hackers on whom the state can bank during crises – is being developed for this purpose besides the employment of regular PLA personnel.

Conclusion

Compared with China's historically reactive stance of luring the enemy in deep and destroying him through strategic defence, the present doctrine is essentially pro-active and seeks to take the battle into enemy territory. It also strives to achieve surprise in a pro-active manner that is demonstrated by new "quick-strike" tactics. The aim is to catch the enemy unprepared in order to inflict substantial damage on strategic targets and disrupt logistics to gain psychological ascendancy. While the land frontier is expected to continue to generate some local tensions, the CMC has identified space and the oceans as the new areas where future conflict might take place.

China is modernising rapidly and steadily enhancing its military capabilities. The military gap between China and India is growing as India's military modernisation is constrained by its low defence expenditure, which is now 1.78 per cent of the GDP, while China's defence budget has kept up a steady double-digit growth rate for over a decade. At present there is a quantitative gap between the PLA and the Indian armed forces. If Indian military modernisation continues to stagnate, this will soon become a qualitative gap as well. With the rapid modernisation of the PLA, China will soon be in a position to dictate terms to India on the settlement of the territorial dispute. Hence, while China poses a long-term strategic challenge to India as a competing regional power in Asia, it will remain a major military threat till the territorial dispute is resolved.

India needs to take this reality into account and distinguish between what China professes, that is peaceful co-existence, and what it actually does and plan accordingly. In the near future, a situation of tenuous peace and tranquility is likely to continue to prevail along India's Himalayan frontier. It will be punctuated increasingly by patrol face-offs, Chinese transgressions like those at Depsang in 2013 and Chumar in 2014 across the LAC, perhaps even incursions and intrusions, and new claims on Indian territory such as the Tawang Tract.

CHINA'S CLAIM TO TIBET IS FACTOR IN BORDER DISPUTE

This is perhaps the most militarized Buddhist enclave in the world. Perched above 10,000 feet in the icy reaches of the eastern Himalayas, the town of Tawang is not only home to one of Tibetan Buddhism's most sacred monasteries but also the site of a massive Indian military buildup. Convoys of army trucks haul howitzers along rutted mountain roads. Soldiers drill in muddy fields. Military bases appear every half-mile in the countryside, with watchtowers rising behind concertina wire.

A road sign on the northern edge of town helps explain the reason for all the fear and the fury: The border with China is just 23 miles away; Lhasa, the Tibetan capital, 316 miles; and Beijing 2,676 miles. "The Chinese army has a big deployment at the border, at Bumla," said Madan Singh, a junior commissioned officer who sat with a half-dozen soldiers one afternoon sipping tea beside a fog-cloaked road. "That's why we're here." Though little known to the outside world, Tawang is a flashpoint in relations between the world's two most populous nations. It is the focus of China's most delicate land-border dispute, a conflict rooted in Chinese claims of sovereignty over all of historical Tibet.

In recent months, both countries have stepped up efforts to secure their rights over this rugged patch of land. China tried to block a $2.9 billion loan to India from the Asian Development Bank on the grounds that part of the loan was slated for water projects in Arunachal Pradesh, the state that includes Tawang. It was the first time China had sought to influence the territorial dispute through a multilateral institution. Then an Indian general announced that the Indian military was deploying extra troops and fighter jets in the area. The growing belligerence has soured relations between the two Asian giants and has prompted one

Indian military leader to declare that China has replaced Pakistan as India's biggest threat.

Economic progress might be expected to bring the countries closer. China and India did $52 billion of trade last year, a 34 percent increase over 2007. But businesspeople say that border tensions have infused official deliberations over business deals, dampening the willingness of Chinese and Indian companies to invest in each other's countries. "Officials start taking more time, scrutinizing things more carefully, and all that means more delays and ultimately more denials," said Ravi Bhoothalingam, a former president of the Oberoi Group, the luxury hotel chain, and a member of the Institute of Chinese Studies in New Delhi. "That's not good for business."

The roots of the conflict go back to China's territorial claims to Tibet. Not only does the Dalai Lama, the exiled spiritual leader of the Tibetans, live in the foothills of the western Himalayas with the blessing of the Indian government, but China insists that this swath of northeast India has historically been part of Tibet, and thus should be part of China. Tawang is a thickly forested area of white stupas and steep, terraced hillsides that is home to the ethnic Monpa people, who practice Tibetan Buddhism, speak a language similar to Tibetan and once paid tribute to rulers in Lhasa. The 6th Dalai Lama was born here in the 17th century.

The Chinese army occupied Tawang briefly in 1962, during a war with India fought over this and other territories along the 2,521-mile border. More than 3,100 Indian soldiers and 700 Chinese soldiers were killed and thousands wounded in the border war. War memorials highlighting China's aggressions in Tawang here are big draws for Indian tourists. "The entire border is disputed," said Ma Jiali, an India scholar at the China Institutes of Contemporary International Relations, a government-supported think tank in Beijing. "This problem hasn't been solved, and it's a huge barrier to China-India relations."

In some ways, Tawang has become a proxy battleground, too, between China and the Dalai Lama, who passed through this valley when he fled into exile in 1959. From his home in the distant hill town of Dharamsala, he wields enormous influence over

Tawang. He appoints the abbot of the powerful monastery and gives financial support to institutions throughout the area. Last year, the Dalai Lama announced for the first time that Tawang is a part of India, bolstering the Indian government's territorial claims and infuriating China.

Traditional Tibetan culture runs strong in Tawang. At the Tawang monastery, an important centre of Tibetan learning, monks express apprehension about China's rule over Tibet, which the Chinese army seized in 1951. "I hate the Chinese government," said Gombu Tsering, 70, a senior monk who watches over the monastery's museum. "Tibet wasn't even a part of China. Lhasa wasn't a part of China." Few expect China to try to forcefully annex Tawang, but military skirmishes are a real danger, analysts say. The Indian military recorded 270 border violations and nearly 2,300 instances of "aggressive border patrolling" by Chinese soldiers last year, said Brahma Chellaney, a professor of strategic studies at the Centre for Policy Research, a research organization in New Delhi. Mr. Chellaney has advised the Indian government's National Security Council.

"The India-China frontier has become more 'hot' than the India-Pakistan border," he said in an e-mail. China has grown increasingly hostile to the Dalai Lama after a severe outbreak of ethnic unrest in Tibet. This year, it turned its diplomatic guns on India. China moved in March to block a $2.9 billion loan to India from the Asian Development Bank, a multi-nation group based in Manila that has China on its board, because $60 million of the loan had been earmarked for flood-control projects in Arunachal Pradesh, the state that includes Tawang. The loan was approved in mid-June over China's heated objections.

Weeks after China first tried to block the loan, the chief of the Indian air force, now retired, told a prominent Indian newspaper that China posed a greater threat than Pakistan. Another official, J.J. Singh, the governor of Arunachal Pradesh and retired chief of the Indian army, said the next month that the Indian military was adding two divisions of troops, totalling 50,000 to 60,000 soldiers, to the border region over the next several years. Four Sukhoi fighter jets were immediately deployed to a nearby air base. Since

2005, when Chinese Prime Minister Wen Jiabao visited India, the two countries have gone through 13 rounds of bilateral negotiations over the issue. A last round was just held last month, with no results. Though China has actually resolved many of its border disputes in recent years, India remains a glaring exception.

The Government of Tibet in Exile

From July 20 to 23, 1994, Beijing staged the Third Forum on Work in Tibet which recommended the total destruction of an entire civilization flourishing on the Tibetan Plateau for thousands of years. This cultural "empire" once encompassed far-flung areas like Buryatia, Tuva and Kalmykia in Russia; Mongolia; Laddakh, Lahaul-Spiti, Sikkim, and Arunachal Pradesh in India; Mustang, Dolpo and Solo Khumbu in Nepal; Bhutan and parts of western China.

The policy formulated in 1994 in Beijing-and these days pursued with Cultural Revolutionary zeal in Tibet-will mean the annihilation of the spiritual homeland of this shared culture. Implementation of the Third Work Forum is thus having a crippling impact on the traditional culture of millions of non-Tibetans as the well-spring of their cultural inspiration is forcibly drained and there is nothing to replenish the continuous growth and development of this distinct and highly evolved civilization.

Losing Hearts and Minds

The decisions made at the Third Forum rest on two fundamental conclusions which Beijing drew. It realized it was losing out in two vital fields-ideology and propaganda. For a state whose existence is justified by its ideological superiority and the power of its propaganda to shape the thinking of the masses, the implications of this for the future was at best uncertain, at worst dangerous. Beijing concluded it was losing the ideological war because, despite the unrelenting assault on Tibetan Buddhism, Tibetans were as devoted to their traditional beliefs as ever. Beijing has succeeded in physically enslaving the country but it has not won over the hearts, minds and loyalty of the Tibetan populace.

Communist ideology, enforced by the military might of China, had failed to dent the heart of Buddhism. Added to this was the communist authorities' total bafflement at the non-violent policy underpinning the Middle Way Approach advocated by His Holiness the Dalai Lama to resolve the issue of Tibet's future status. For a regime which is based on Mao's dictum that political power grows out of the barrel of a gun, this supposedly eccentric philosophy which says victory lies in capturing the hearts and minds of people by the power of ideas rather than killing by the power of the gun comes as a bolt from the blue. Much of Beijing's knee-jerk reaction to, and its bafflement at, His Holiness the Dalai Lama's new policy of rapprochement lies at the heart of its new hardline policy.

Beijing considered it was losing the propaganda war because, for one reason or the other, the world's media and its pop culture considered-at least for the moment-Tibet and Tibetan Buddhism their very own cuddly pandas. Despite its financial might China found it extremely difficult to exterminate this image of Tibet and get its voice heard on the Tibetan issue in the court of the international media. In order to address these weaknesses the Third Forum concentrated on two issues. One was to focus on Tibet's economic development in the hope that this would keep Tibetan demonstrations off the streets. This was tantamount to bribing the Tibetans with promises of riches to come if they toed the party line. The other concern was to win the coming and new generations of Tibetans over to the Chinese viewpoint.

Beijing has given up on the present generation of Tibetans as a lost cause. If the coming generations of Tibetans were also lost to the 'Dalai Clique' this, the Chinese concluded, would have dangerous consequences for Chinese rule in Tibet. The 15-year-old Gyalwa Karmapa's dramatic escape from Tibet in January 2000 was a warning to the Beijing authorities of the erosion of loyalty to China. The Karmapa's flight, and the earlier escape of Agya Rinpoche, the abbot of Kumbum Monastery, came as a huge embarrassment for China, because retaining these high lamas gave China a degree of legitimacy for its rule in Tibet. This is the reason why Beijing is enforcing with greater strictness its 1993 instruction of recalling young Tibetans studying in schools and monasteries run by Dharmasala in India. This is also the rationale for Beijing closing down schools in Tibet which are privately run by Tibetans.

For these reasons Tibet today is in the throes of a second Cultural Revolution as the Chinese authorities step up their long-term strategy to exterminate Tibet's distinct cultural and ethnic identity. The authorities are pursuing a four-pronged strategy to achieve their final objective. They have stepped up repression while employing their huge propaganda machine to paint a rosy picture of Tibet. They have quickened the pace of economic development to dampen Tibetan nationalism and are simultaneously moving more Chinese settlers onto the Tibetan Plateau to change Tibet's demographic composition and to ease social unrest because of mounting unemployment back in China.

The Third Work Forum on Tibet was convened by the top Chinese leadership and was presided over by President Jiang Zemin. The authorities have now enshrined this Work Forum as the most "important strategic policy to rejuvenate Tibet" and have hailed its directives as the new manifesto for party work on the plateau. The significance of the Third Work Forum lies in the fact that it overturned the more liberal policies laid out for Tibet's "development" by the First and Second Work Forums held in 1980 and 1984. The first two work forums were initiated by the late Hu Yaobang, then Secretary General of the Chinese Communist Party.

This liberal and somewhat maverick leader is credited with masterminding a series of measures to improve the social, economic and political conditions in Tibet. The brief spell of liberalization markedly improved the living conditions of the majority of Tibetans and contributed to a more relaxed intellectual and social climate.

The Third Work Forum reversed these policies and reinstated hardline measures under which Tibet is still reeling today. The Tibetans in Tibet perceive the current repressive policies as a second Cultural Revolution. The question is why did China choose to jettison its earlier more liberal policies and adopt a manifesto which is leading to the systematic destruction of Tibet's distinct culture. The answer lies in domestic and international events which forced China to formulate a series of hardline policies on Tibet which eventually crystallized into the Third Work Forum for Tibet. The world which confronted China in the late 1980s and early 1990s was a frightening one.

Starting from 1987, Tibet was rocked by a string of protest demonstrations, which called for Tibetan independence. One of the largest demonstrations which erupted on March 5, 1989 in Lhasa, forced the authorities to impose martial law on the city. These demonstrations are now seen to have been an inspiration behind the outburst of Chinese students' pro-democracy uprisings. The authorities saw the series of Tiananmen Square demonstrations as a sign of their Central Government losing control, and in an attempt to regain supremacy, the authorities slaughtered-perhaps hundreds if not thousands of students on June 4, 1989. These demonstrations were a chilling replay to the authorities of the May 4, 1919 student demonstrations in Beijing which signalled a political and cultural awakening across the erstwhile Middle Kingdom.

Bejing's fears of losing control were exacerbated by external events which saw the unraveling of the communist world. The Solidarity Movement in Poland, the fall of the Berlin Wall, and the implosion of the Soviet Union fed Beijing's paranoia over threats to the Chinese Communist Party hold on power. Official China's fears were further inflamed by the rapidly changing attitude of the broad masses as they turned back from communism to traditional beliefs like Confucionism, Buddhism, Islam, Christianity and indigenous folk cults. In the eyes of ordinary citizens communism was becoming totally discredited and this, more than anything else, was the biggest nightmare for China's leadership. The leadership's justification for staying in power was being disavowed by the masses. For a one-party dictatorship this historically indicates the first step along the slippery road to dissolution and removal of power.

For these reasons the Chinese leadership then reverted to its earlier view that traditional beliefs were its real enemy. In competing with Buddhism, Confucionism, Islam, Christianity and other isms, communism was losing out in terms of its ability to retain the loyalty and allegiance of the masses. The leadership revived the old aphorisms once served up to the Tibetan people to justify their policies to destroy Tibetan Buddhism during the Cultural Revolution. Bewildered Tibetans were then told that just as there cannot be two suns in the sky, so there cannot be both Buddhism and socialism in Tibet. Inevitably Buddhism then had to give way to socialism. And again, today, religion is being blatantly sublimated to Chinese state power.

These were the fears of the Chinese leaders when they met in Beijing in 1994 to hammer out their new Tibet initiatives. For the Chinese authorities Tibet is an especially sensitive issue because of their conviction that hostile Western forces are using the issue of Tibet to "westernize" China and to lead to its territorial fragmentation. The third generation Chinese leaders came to the conclusion that stability in Tibet was vital to the stability of China as a whole. Earlier, Tibet was merely of peripheral concern to the vital interests of China's sprawling communist empire. Now, with the Third Work Forum, the authorities were saying, "We must clearly understand that we must do our work in Tibet not only for the sake our of own region's stability and development, not only for the interests of our people, but also for the sake of the whole nation's stability and development."

In Tibet, China faced peculiar problems because of the inherent strength of Tibetan Buddhism and the depth of devotion of the populace to His Holiness the Dalai Lama. The sustained burst of religious revival that followed in the wake of the brief spell of liberalization in Tibet confirmed the leadership's worst fears that decades of concerted assault on Tibetan culture and religion had not extinguished the people's traditional beliefs and values. From merely nuisance value, the Chinese leadership now viewed Tibetan Buddhism as a very real and imminent threat to the stability of Chinese rule in Tibet.

At the same time the Chinese leadership's attitude towards His Holiness the Dalai Lama changed. From being an uncertain ally in the peace process in Tibet, the current Chinese leadership now saw him as a full-blown "enemy". A top-level conclave held in Beijing on March 10, 1993 concluded that, "There are different factions within the Dalai Clique; they are, however, unanimous in their political nature and position. They differ from each other in ideological viewpoints and ways of expressing them. Different strategies must be adopted to use their differences, to deal with them differently in order to divide and destroy them."

Repeated statements by high-level officials describe the struggle against "splittism", the official term for Tibetan independence, as a "life-and-death struggle". At the 1994 annual meeting of the "TAR" Communist Party Committee to brief members on the policy thrust of the Third Work Forum on Tibet, Raidi, deputy Secretary of the Committee said, "Up to now, his (the Dalai Lama's) standpoint on Tibet's independence has never changed, and we must reveal his double-faced true colour. The focal point in our region in the struggle against splittism is to oppose the Dalai Clique. As the saying goes, to kill a serpent, one must first cut off its head."

In short, the Third Work Forum decided that Beijing was in a position to solve the Tibet issue without the Dalai Lama's involvement. It abandoned the earlier liberal policy of including His Holiness the Dalai Lama in any future settlement of Tibet's status. His Holiness the Dalai Lama was clearly singled out as the cause of China's "Tibet problem".

The Third Work Forum also abandoned the policy of granting concessions to Tibet because of the plateau's "special characteristics". This policy had been the cornerstone of recommendations made by the First and Second Tibet Work Forums.

To carry out its new hardline policies in Tibet, Beijing appointed Chen Kuiyuan as the "TAR" Party Secretary in 1992. Chen Kuiyuan's appointment is significant because he had a track record for being a tough and ruthless administrator. He had already served as the First Secretary of the Chinese Communist Party in Inner Mongolia and is credited with repressing the rebellious Mongols, many of whom refer to him as "the butcher". Chen Kuiyuan was especially recommended to the post by Hu Jintao, the current Vice-President of China, who was then the First Secretary of the Chinese Communist Party in Tibet.

Tackling Tibetan Nationalism

The Third Work Forum policies chalked out for Tibet contained four key elements. China stepped up the scale of repression in Tibet. External propaganda work was escalated. The pace of economic development in Tibet-and its corollary of encouraging more Chinese settlers and businessmen to take advantage of the economic boom on the "roof of the world"-was also increased. In short, Beijing had decided to tackle Tibetan nationalism head-on and observers are still assessing the consequences on both Chinese rule in Tibet and on the populace.

Beijing remains convinced that these key components of its current policy will stabilize Chinese rule over Tibet and solve once and for all, the vexed problem of its negative image over the way Tibet has been handled. One main target of the current policy of repression is Tibetan Buddhism. Chinese leaders are increasingly alarmed by the proliferation of monasteries and temples which the period of liberalization spawned throughout Tibet: they are seen as the bastions of Tibetan nationalism. The authorities have set up "Democratic Management Committees" to control monasteries and nunneries and created "Work Inspection Teams" to supervise the "education" of monks and nuns.

A major thrust is underway to break the bond of loyalty between the clergy in Tibet and His Holiness the Dalai Lama in India. Campaigns like "Strike Hard" and "Patriotic Re-education", unleashed in 1996, are aimed at crippling the rise of Tibetan Buddhism which the authorities suspect is weaning the loyalty of the Tibetan people away from the communist party and towards His Holiness the Dalai Lama. One salient feature of the "Strike Hard" campaign is how differently it is interpreted in China and Tibet. China's "Strike Hard" campaign was started to weed out corruption. Tibet's version is used as a political tool to eliminate those whom the authorities label "splittists". In Tibet, rather than striking at corruption, the authorities turn a blind eye to this social disease in the hope that it will erode the traditional morality of Tibetans and undermine Tibetan Buddhism.

In fact, at a secret meeting held in December 1999 in Chengdu, capital of Sichuan province, Chen Kuiyuan, the hardline Party Secretary of "TAR" recommended to the Central Chinese Government that an all-out effort must be made to eradicate Tibetan Buddhism and culture from the face of the earth so that no memory of them will be left in the minds of coming generations of Tibetans-except as museum pieces.

Chen Kuiyuan stated that the main cause of instability is the existence of the Dalai Lama and his Government-in-Exile in Dharamsala and these must be "uprooted". He recommended that Tibet, Tibetan people and Tibetan Buddhism-in other words the very name of Tibet-must be destroyed and the "Tibet Autonomous Region" be merged with provinces like Sichuan. While treating Tibetans to boot-heel subjugation at home, internationally China was on an overdrive propaganda blitz. At a brainstorming conclave held on March 10, 1993, Zeng Jian-hui, Vice-Minister of the Propaganda Ministry, told participants, "The propaganda work on the question of Tibet is one of the focal points of the entire external propaganda work...With regard to attacks by the West and the Dalai Clique and their frequent activities, our external propaganda should launch offensive. We should expand our spheres of influence; in particular, we should infiltrate our propaganda into the mainstream life of the West.

"Firstly we should continue to send Tibetan scholars and Tibetan singing and dancing troupes abroad to lecture and perform. Secondly, relevant embassies and consulates should aim at the public opinion and the activities of the Dalai Clique in the countries where they are stationed and utilize speeches, picture exhibitions, special articles and other forms to carry out propaganda work, so as to win over officials and people of those countries... We should reinforce the work of utilizing the power of foreign propaganda. A few years ago, in the light of the situation of that time, we made arrangements for foreign journalists to visit Tibet."

The September 3, 2000 edition of *People's Daily* carried a story headlined "Tibet Welcomes Foreign Journalists for Objective Reporting". It stated that "A senior Tibetan official said Sunday that Tibet welcomes foreign journalists to come for objective and just reporting, but not those who take distorted views. Raidi, Deputy Secretary of the Tibet Autonomous Regional Committee of the Communist Party of China and Chairman of the Standing Committee of the Tibetan Autonomous Regional People's Congress, made the remarks at a meeting here with a press delegation of Thailand." In this context, it is interesting to note that N. Ram, the editor of India's *Frontline* magazine, devoted 36 pages of the

September 15, 2000 issue to promote the Chinese line and recommended that the Indian Government expel the Central Tibetan Administration from Indian soil for being the main stumbling block to normal relations between India and China. It is difficult to assess to what extent the views contained in his stupendous reporting marathon are his own.

These editorial outbursts are in line with policy decisions outlined in the early nineties. During a two-day secret conclave in March 1993 in Chengdu, Vice-Minister Zeng Jian-hui, told participants, "All foreigners that we entertain and send to Tibet must have a relatively objective opinion of Tibet. We should use people from abroad to carry out the propaganda on Tibet for us, which is more powerful than if we do it."

Along with its external public relations strategy, China is presently carrying out a potentially much more dangerous policy of speeding up the pace of Tibet's economic development and its related drive to bring more Chinese settlers onto the Tibetan Plateau. Beijing's Western China Development Programme, which incorporates Tibet in its ambit, is devised to shift the focus of China's economic activities from Coastal China to the interior-both to narrow the imbalance in the level of economic development between the two regions and to ease population pressure on the coastal areas which attract millions of migrant workers. The focus of Beijing's Western China Economic Development Programme in Tibet is to exploit the plateau's still untapped minerals and other natural resources and to upgrade Tibet's infrastructure-like roads and telecommunications-to facilitate transportation of these resources to China. The other purpose of the heightened level of economic activity is to divert the Tibetans' attention from their political fate to focus on their livelihood-thus undermining Tibetan nationalism. The Chinese authorities aim to manipulate the situation in Tibet still further by bringing in more Chinese settlers who would then demographically cement Chinese rule once and for all. These current hardline policies and their implementation in Tibet are impacting the stalled Sino-Tibetan Dialogue and will vitally affect the ability of Tibetans to survive as a distinct people and culture.

Beijing's Flawed Perceptions

The basic flaws in China's new policy in its search to resolve the problem of Tibet is thinking the solution can exclude the involvement of His Holiness the Dalai Lama. The other is in attempting to solve the problem over the heads of Tibet's citizens.

These two fundamental mistakes will exacerbate China's Tibet problem, not solve it. The reason lies in the history of Tibet and in the sentiments of the people. The institution of the Dalai Lamas of Tibet is more than 600 years old, if we start from the birth of the first Dalai Lama in 1391. In the course of its growth and development, the very institution itself came to symbolize fundamental beliefs and the political destiny of the nation. The bond between the Dalai Lamas and the Tibetan people is fundamental and unbreakable; any attempt, however sustained, will never succeed in driving a wedge between the two.

Consequently, China's current policy of forcing Tibetans-especially monks and nuns-to denounce His Holiness the Dalai Lama and pledge loyalty to the Chinese Communist Party will prove counterproductive.

In view of this the Third Work Forum's basic assumption that in the case of Tibet time is on the side of China, and that Beijing can stall the problem of Tibet till the demise of the present Dalai Lama whereupon the issue of Tibet will solve itself, is fatally flawed-based as it is on a mistaken perception of the role played by the institution of the Dalai Lamas in the development of Tibetan history.

This assumption, if not reviewed, revised and abandoned, will prove catastrophic for the Chinese leadership and for those who chose to turn their whimsical personal analysis into state policy. The reason is simple. The Chinese Communist Party was founded in the 1920s and came to power in 1949. Within this short span of time the masses have lost faith in communist ideology, and members of the party these days pay mere lip service to the ideological justifications of the party. Conversely, the institution of the Dalai Lamas as a political force is more than 300 years old. These days the Dalai Lama is recognized by Tibetans throughout the world as the heart of Tibetan nationalism. How can a party which has lost its soul outlast an institution which symbolizes the very soul of a people? For these reasons it is imperative for China to review and re-assess its current hardline stance towards Tibet. China must re-start its stalled peace process over Tibet and consider His Holiness the Dalai Lama as a vital and active partner in the procedures. If China does this it will have won a powerful ally and companion along the road to peace, stability and continued prosperity.

5

Look Beyond the Sino-Indian Border Dispute

The Sino-Indian border dispute originated from the British and Russian expansion in Central Asia in the early 20th century. Since the 1950s, the border dispute has always shadowed the ebb and flow of the Sino-Indian relations. The simmering border dispute erupted after the revolt the Dalai Lama clique engineered in 1959. The CIA-supported revolt in Tibet, India-embraced the Dalai Lama, and India-hosted Tibetan Government-in-exile turned out to be one of the causes of the border war in 1962. Nehru's policy of no-dispute and no-negotiation and his forward policy became a direct cause of the border war. Then the China-India relationship dramatically moved toward hostility and confrontation from brotherhood and friendship and entered an era of cold war which lasted nearly two decades.

The Chinese and Indian governments have attempted to resolve the border dispute through diplomatic negotiations since the1980s. The border negotiations have been institutionalized and generated several meaningful documents. However, each other's position on the border disputes themselves has never been changed.

To accelerate and intensify the boundary negotiations, the two governments have agreed to appoint the two Special Representatives. They have periodically met and conducted an in-depth exchange of views on resolving the boundary question. Both sides have agreed to press ahead with the framework negotiations in accordance with the agreed political parameters and guiding principles so as to seek for a fair and reasonable solution acceptable to both. Prior to that, both sides should work together to maintain peace and tranquility in the border areas. Although the border dispute remains unresolved in all the sectors, peace, stability, and tranquility have been maintained by the joint efforts of the two governments.

While we are cautiously optimistic about the steady improvement of the bilateral relations between the two rising Asian giants, we are increasingly concerned about the consequences of their geopolitical rhetoric and strategic suspicion originated primarily from the unresolved border dispute.

A BRIEF REVIEW OF THE CHINA-INDIA BORDER DISPUTE

The entire China-India boundary has never been formally delimited by any mutually-accepted treaty. There has existed a boundary line of actual control between the two countries. It took shape on the basis of the extent of each other's administrative jurisdiction over a long course of time. The entire boundary has been traditionally divided into three sectors—the eastern sector, the middle sector, and the western sector with all in dispute. The western sector involves the dispute over the Aksai Chin area India claims as part of Latah and China claims as part of Xinjiang. The middle sector involves a dispute over various points between the Tibet-Kashmir- Punjab border junction and the Nepal-Tibet-Uttar Pradesh border junction. The eastern sector involves a dispute over the area between the pre-1914 Outer Line and the McMahon Line.

In the eastern sector, the British–Indian government had observed the foothills of the Himalayas as the "Outer Line" of its administrative jurisdiction by 1914. Although the Chinese-Tibetan authorities had claimed the tribal areas beyond the British Outer Line within the Tibetan jurisdiction, their administrative jurisdiction actually covered only Tawang tract, the Walong area along the Lohit valley, and some other scattered enclaves in the tribal areas.

Today the line of actual control observed by both sides conforms to the McMahon Line. The disputed area between the pre-1914

Outer Line and the McMahon Line covers a total area of 90,000 square kilometres. According to China, this area is composed of Tibet's three districts of Monyul, Loyul and lower Zayul. According to India, this area is its Arunachal Pradesh, formerly the North-East Frontier Agency of Assam State.

In the western sector, the line of actual control runs roughly along the Karakoram range, conforming to the Chinese claim. The Indian government claims that the boundary runs along the Kunlun range from the Karakoram Pass. The disputed Area is the Aksai Chin region between the two ranges, covering a total area of about 33,000 square kilometres. This area falls mainly in China's Xinjiang and part of it belongs to the Ari District of Tibet. India claims that it is part of its Ladakh area of the State of Jammu and Kashmir. This area, sparsely inhabited, serves as the traffic artery linking Xinjiang and Tibet.

Therefore, in terms of the general China-India border dispute, the McMahon Line in the eastern sector and Aksai Chin in the western sector have been central to the negotiations on the settlement of the border dispute.

The Mystery of the McMahan Line

After Russia successfully divided Mongolia into Outer and Inner Mogolia with the Outer Mongolia as a buffer zone between China and Russia, the British- Indian authorities dreamed the same dream and tried to divide Tibet into Outer Tibet and Inner Tibet and made the Outer Tibet as a buffer zone between British India and China. To achieve such a objective, the Simla conference was held in 1914,with British Henry McMahon, Chinese Chen Ivan, and Tibetan Lonchen shatra as representatives.

There were actually two parallel conferences at Simla, the tripartite conference focusing on the division of Tibet, and the other was the secret one, keeping Chen Ivan out of their negotiations on the Indian-Tibetan boundary. In early 1914, Henry McMahon and Lonchen Shatra secretly negotiated on the division of Tibet and the boundary between Assam and Tibet as a package deal. An agreement was reached through a secret exchange of notes in Delhi on March 24 and 25, 1914. This boundary line, later known as the McMahon line, was shown on a map in two sheets.

The tripartite conference focused on McMahon's proposal referring to China's suzerainty over Tibet and the outer-inner division of Tibet. On the map attached to the draft convention of the conference, two lines were drawn, one red and the other blue. The red line showed Tibet as a geographical and political unit, and the blue line divided Inner from Outer Tibet. In its southern extension, the red line curves around along the crest of the Himalayas, roughly conforming to the McMahon Line except in the Tawang tract where the McMahon Line reached short of the Tawang tract, implying that the Tawang tract remained part of Tibetan territory. On this map, the Tawang tract was not put within the British-Indian territory.

Without the consent of the Chinese government, Chen Ivan, under McMahon's threat and pressure, initiated the draft convention on April 27, 1914, but with the clear understanding that "to initial and to sign are two different actions," and that his initials would not bind his government, whose views he would immediately seek. The next day, the Chinese government instructed Chen Ivan that "The Chinese representative was forced to initial the draft convention. The Chinese government cannot accept it. You should declare it invalid." Since Chen Ivan refused to sign the draft convention, it was then amended and initialed by McMahon and Lonchen Shatra on July 3, 1914. On the map attached to the draft convention, the McMahon Line was marked just across the town of Tawang, indicating that the area to the north of Tawang would fall within the Tibetan territory.

The British-Indian government did not accept the Simla convention. Viceroy Hardinge forwarded McMahon's report on the Simla conference to London on July 23, 1914, stating that the Indian government recognized that a consideration of the northeastern frontier did not form part of the functions of the conference, and the views and proposal put forward might be regarded as personal to Henry McMahon, not carrying the endorsement of the Government of India. Chen was also instructed to declare that the Chinese government "would not recognize any treaty or similar document that might now or hereafter be signed between Great Britain and Tibet." The Tibetan authorities understood that without securing the Sino-Tibetan boundary, they could not accept the Indo-Tibetan boundary.

The Dalai Lama even recognized the logic relationship between the status of Tibet and the legality of the McMahon Line. In his 1959 address to the Indian Council of World Affairs, he contended that if Tibet had no sovereignty when the Simla convention laid down the McMahon Line, that line was invalid. He challenged Nehru that if you deny the sovereign status to Tibet, you deny the validity of the McMahon Line."

Three maps are related to the Simla conference. One is attached to the March 24 notes; one to the April 27 convention, and the third to the July 3 convention. As far as the Tawang Tract is concerned, the three maps show the McMahon line quite differently. On the first map, the McMahon Line was shown running alng south of the Thagla range far north of Tawang; on the second map, it is not shown in the Tawang tract; and on the third one, it is superimposed on the word " Tawang".

In 1936, Basil Gould, Political Officer in Sikkim, was dispatched to Lhasa and discussed the Tawang issue with the Tibetan government. The Tibetan attitude was Tawang had been Tibetan up to 1914 and they regarded the adjustment of the Tibet-Indian boundary as part and parcel of the general adjustment and determination of boundaries contemplated in the 1914 convention. If they could, with British help, secure a definite Sino-Tibetan boundary, they would observe the Indo-Tibetan border as defined in 1914.

In 1944, just before the British quit from India, basil Gould informed the Tibetan authorities that the Bitish-Indian government was willing to modify the McMahon Line soas to exclude Tawang from the territory it claimed. He also proposed that the Se La range should be a new boundary line. However, The Tibetan authorities did not accepted it and continued to collect revenues in the Tawang tract and remained administrative control over the Tawang tract.

It was in February1951 that the Indian government took over the Tawang tract by force before the PLA entered and liberated Tibet. The Tibetan authorities organized protest demonstrations in Tawang and Lhasa against India's occupation of the Tawang tract, but no avail.

As far as the objective of the Simla conference was concerned, it certainly aborted. The McMahon Line was not even accepted by the British-Indian government. After the Simla conference, from 1914 to 1935, on the official maps published by the Survey of India, the McMahon Line was not shown, but instead the Outer Line along the foothills of the Himalayas was shown. The Tibetan authorities continued to exercise administrative jurisdiction in the tribal areas as they did before. The Simla conference went down in history as an unaccomplished cause.

As to the Simla conference, the first official record appeared in Volume XIV of the 1929 edition of Aichison'sTreaties. It did not refer to the McMahon Line, but to the discussion on the Sino-Tibetan frontier. It was stated that a tripartite convention was drawn up and initialed in 1914, but the Chinese government refused to permit its representative to proceed to full signature.

In 1935, Olaf Caroe, deputy secretary of the Foreign and Political Department of the British-Indian Government discovered the secret documents of the Simla conference in dealing with a case involving the illegal entry into Tibet through the Tawang tract. He realized that the northeastern frontier might be a matter of dispute with the Chinese in the future. He proposed to revise the official record of the Simla conference in the Aichison's Treaties and show the McMahon Line on the official maps. The British government approved his proposal.

This original 1929 edition was soon withdrawn from circulation and replaced by a spurious edition, actually printed in 1938, but with an imprint of 1929. However, at least three copies of the original 1929 edition survived, one in Peking Library, one in Harvard University library, and one in the India Office. In the revised edition, it was stated that the Simla conference negotiated an agreement on the status of Tibet and the boundary of Tibet with both China and India. Such a revision was nothing but scandalous diplomatic forgery. Then the McMahon Line began to appear o the Indian official maps. However, it was still marked as "Undemarcated Boundary."

The Puzzle of Aksai Chin

In the western sector of the China-India border, the dispute has centered on the Aksai Chin area. The British left Aksai Chin area as "undefined" at the time of their transfer of power in 1947.nehru himself once stated that " it is a matter of argument as to what art of it (Aksai Chin) belongs to us and what part of it belongs to somebody else.... The point is, there has never been any delimitation there in that area and it has been a challenged area."

Before the British left India, the British-Indian government had shown no boundary at all in that area on its official maps. In Volume XII of Aichison'd Treaties published in 1931, it was stated that"The northern as well as the eastern boundary of the Kashmir state is still undefined." The Survey of India maps published in the 190s and 1930s did not indicate any boundary alignment or show any color difference inthis are, and wide spaces between Kashmir and Xinjiang and between Kashmir and Tbet were shown blank. 95[8] Louis Dane, Indian Foreign Secretry, stated clearly in a letter to the Indian office that Aksai Chin was I Chinese Xinjiag. The neighborhood of the Lanak Pass at the head of the Changchenmo valley was supposed to be the most northerly boundary point on the Kashmir-Tibet border.

In 1945, guided by Olaf Caroe, then foreign secretary of India, on new Survey of India maps the Aksai Chin area bgan to be shown by a color-wash with the words"Boundary Undefined" marked on it.

In 1947, the Indian Army in its "top secret" m submitted to the British Cabinet Mission accepted the Karakoram range as the northern boundary of India in the western sector.

However, after the signing of the trade agreement concerning Tibet in 1954, following Nehru's instructions, new Survey of India maps began to show an international boundary in the western sector running along the crest of the Kunlun range, which for the first time placed the whole Aksai Chin area within the Indian territory.

According to Sir H.A.F. Rumbold, an official in the Indian Office, the Simon Commission wished to include a map of India in Volume I of their report in 1929. Rumbold found nothing in the India office to justify the line on the Kunlun range shown on some maps. The Commission accordingly adopted a line roughly along the crest of the Karakoram range, excluding the Aksai Chin area. Nehru, even on August 28, 1959, stated in the Lok Sabha that "This was the boundary of the old Kashmir statewith Tibet and Chinese Turkestan. Nobody had marked it." On the other hand, Chinese maps have shown the Karakoram range as its boundary in the western sector at least since the 1920s. There was no evidence that the British-Indian authorities ever disputed this with the Chinese government before they left India in 1947.

The widely accepted modern concept of boundary marking involes three steps: delimitation, delineation and demarcation. Delimitation involves defining the boundary in written terms through treaties and agreements. Delineation involves sketching the boundary in maps through joint boundary surveys. Demarcation involves marking the boundary line on the ground through pillars, chains and other markers.

Reviewing the historic facts for the entire China-India border, such a China-India boundary has never existed, though each side has made its own territorial claims. Historical facts have also showed that, in the old days, wide desolate tracts in the remote high mountains between the two countries were physically inaccessible. Therefore, the China-India border dispute has been the dispute on the "zone" rather than the " line" in the eastern and western sectors. Mutual understanding and recognition of such historical evolution of the China-India border should become the starting point for the future border deliberations.

INDIA-CHINA BORDER DISPUTE

The continuing (since April 15,2013) Chinese troop intrusion (about 20 troops) 10 kms into Indian territory near Burthe in the Daulat Beg Oldi (DBO) area of Eastern Ladakh in the western sector of the Sino-Indian border should be a matter for careful analysis and concern, but not alarm.

A spokesman of the Chinese Foreign Office has denied any Chinese intrusion into Indian territory in this area. The Government of India, for the present, has been treating it as one of those intrusions which take place sometimes due to differing perceptions of the Line of Actual Control (LAC) in this area and trying to deal with it through the normal mechanism for handling such issues without disturbing peace and tranquillity across the border.

There is no evidence to show that this could be a prelude to a major Chinese assertion of territorial sovereignty in this area. The Chinese aim seems to be to re-assert their claim of sovereignty over this area without disturbing peace and tranquillity. The Chinese troops are presently camping in the area in a tent. We will have reasons to be more than concerned only if they stay put there and construct permanent defences as they often do in the uninhabited islands of the South China Sea.

Since last year, the Chinese have been a little more assertive of their sovereignty claims over the islands of the South and East China Seas. They have reportedly constructed permanent defensive and administrative structures on some of the islands over which they have disputes with Vietnam and the Philippines. In the East China Sea, where they have sovereignty disputes with Japan, they have avoided any such construction, but stepped up seemingly aggressive air and naval patrols of the areas in the vicinity of these islands. The Chinese Navy has also stepped up its visits to the islands in the South China Sea claimed by Beijing.

Till now we have seen greater Chinese activism in the enforcement of their sovereignty claims only in the South and East China seas, but not across the Sino-Indian border. If the Chinese troops stay put in the Burthe area and construct defensive structures in the area, that will be an indicator of their deciding to follow a similar policy of activism across the Sino-Indian border too. That should add to our border concerns. We may have to revisit our peace and tranquillity strategy and think of a more activist policy to face the Chinese activism.

In the Western sector of the border, which is largely unpopulated, the status quo favours the Chinese. Since 1962, they are already in occupation of whatever territory they have claimed. We have very few options to re-assert our sovereignty in any area of this sector which is under Chinese control. In the Eastern sector

(Arunachal Pradesh, which the Chinese call Southern Tibet), the area is populated and the status quo favours India. Even though our defensive and administrative infrastructure in the Arunachal Pradesh area is not comparable with the Chinese infrastructure in the Tibet Autonomous Region (TAR), we are in a much stronger position in the Eastern sector than in the Western.

While the Chinese continue to repeat from time to time their claims to the Arunachal Pradesh area, they have avoided in the Eastern sector the kind of ground activism that one comes across in the Western sector. There is a noticeable keenness on the part of both China and India to avoid any provocative incident either in the Eastern or Western sector. The Chinese are unlikely to relent in their claims to Indian territory in the Eastern sector till after they have succeeded in imposing on the Tibetans a Dalai Lama chosen by the Communist Party of China (CPC) with the help of the Panchen Lama chosen by the CPC.

The wave of self-immolations (115 incidents so far) in the Tibetan areas of China since March 2009 has created concerns in Chinese mind of possible political instability in the Tibetan areas after His Holiness the Dalai Lama when the CPC imposes its nominee on the Tibetans.

The older generation of Tibetans continues to abide by His Holiness' exhortations for peaceful means of protest. The Chinese are worried that the GenNext of Tibetans represented by organisations such as the Tibetan Youth Congress (TYC) may take to violent means to resist the imposition of a Dalai Lama chosen by the CPC. In their calculation, this may necessitate action by the PLA in the populated areas of Arunachal Pradesh. Till Tibet is pacified without fears of any further trouble and the Chinese have forced the Tibetans to accept their nominee as the Dalai Lama, Beijing would like to maintain its claim to Arunachal Pradesh to justify action by the PLA in that area to contain trouble, if need be.

If they now make a deal with India recognising Arunachal Pradesh as an integral part of India, they will not be able to act in that area. By recognising Tibet as an integral part of China we have given up our options for action in Tibet. The Chinese would not want to commit the same mistake by recognising Arunachal Pradesh as an integral part of India. They will, therefore, keep the Arunachal Pradesh issue alive till they have forced the Tibetans to accept their decision regarding succession of His Holiness. We should factor this into our border strategies relating to China.

THE SINO/INDIAN DISPUTE

Ever since its establishment in 1949, the attitude of the Communist Chinese Government towards India has been bound up with the Tibetan issue. India had, on gaining independence in 1947, inherited the British "special position" in Tibet, along with the Mission in Lhasa and trade agencies in larger towns. It had retained the services of British officials stationed in Tibet. When, in 1949, Tibetan leaders made their bid to contact foreign Governments, they first contacted these officials, and it was only a short step for the suspicious minded Chinese to regard this as evidence of Indian collusion with the British.

The Communist Chinese also had ideological reasons for believing that such collusion existed. At the time of their coming to power, Moscow was propagating the line of a world divided into two camps, with the Indian Government depicted as a tool of British imperialism and firmly situated in the opposing camp. The Communist Chinese leaders, who previously had had little contact with the outside world, faithfully repeated these accusations against Nehru and his Government.

Following the Chinese occupation of Tibet in late 1950, Peking's suspicions of the Indians were further aroused when Nehru, in notes to the Chinese Government, expressed the "surprise and regret" of his Government at the Chinese action. He described as "deplorable" the Chinese use of force in Tibet.

Standard diplomatic practice stipulates that a state does not criticise the behaviour of another state acting within its own territorial boundaries unless there are special reasons for so doing. The Indians justified their criticism of the Chinese on the ground of their special interest in Tibet, from which the Chinese inferred that the Indians were implying some restriction on Chinese sovereignty. A sharp reply was received from the Chinese accusing the Indians of unwarranted interference and claiming that the policy of the Indian Government was "affected by foreign influences hostile to China in Tibet".

Nevertheless, whatever suspicions the Chinese may have felt about the Indians in 1949-50 must to some extent have been allayed by subsequent developments. India opposed the 1950 Tibetan appeal to the United Nations; it was one of the few non-communist countries not to condemn China's intervention in the Korean War; it sought to have China seated an the United Nations. The culmination of these moves to improve relations with China was the signing, in April 1954, of an agreement by which India recognised without qualification China's sovereignty over Tibet and conceded many of India's former rights there. A few months later the Chinese Premier, Chou En-lai, paid a successful visit to India, and in October of the same year Nehru visited Peking.

The very considerable improvement in Sino/Indian relations from 1950 to 1954 was on the Indian side almost entirely the result of efforts by Nehru, who saw friendship between China and India as the starting point of a new order in world affairs. It must have been obvious to the Chinese that considerable opposition to Nehru's pro-China policies, at least as far as Tibet was concerned, existed both within and outside the Indian Government. It should also have been clear that problems were going to arise over wide discrepancies in the claimed Sino/Indian border, as shown in maps published by both sides.

However, as long as Nehru's China policy appeared to produce results, his opposition in India remained silent. It was important for both Nehru and the Chinese that this policy continued to appear to give results, and hence the efforts made by both sides to keep intact the edifice of good relations. The Chinese, under the 1954 agreement, allowed India to maintain certain trade and pilgrimage rights in Tibet. They sought to play down the significance of border differences, stating that they had simply inherited their claimed Sino/Indian frontier from the pre-1949 Nationalist Government and that it would be "revised" in due course. Nehru, for his part, avoided public mention of the reality and extent of border differences, and it seemed that both sides were moving towards a compromise settlement of the question.

What were these differences, and what evidence was there that both sides were in fact prepared to compromise?

The Sino/Indian border can be divided into three sectors:

(i)an eastern sector where 99,000 square kilometres of territory described by the Indians as the Northeast Frontier Agency, or N.E.F.A is in dispute: (ii) a middle sector where some 2.000 square kilometres of territory on either side of the main Himalayan passes is disputed: and (iii) a western sector where the Indian province of Ladakh borders on Tibet and Sinkiang and where both the Indian/Tibet and Indian/Sinkiang borders are disputed, in particular the ownership of some 30,000 square kilometres of high plateau country known as the Aksai Chin.

To an outside observer looking at the frontier as it stands, an apparent basis for a compromise settlement would be for China to drop its claim to the N.E.F.A. in exchange for India dropping its claim to the Aksai Chin, with both sides making concessions over the middle sector and the Ladakh/Tibetan border. Such a settlement accords with the realities of both geography and administrative control two important criteria in the settlement of border disputes. The N.E.F.A. lies to the south of the Himalayan watershed and is controlled by India. The Aksai Chin, for the most part, lies to the north of the main range, and the Chinese claim to have controlled the area since 1950. In 1956-7, they built a strategic road across the Aksai Chin, linking Sinkiang with Tibet. That the Indians learnt about the road only from a map published by the Chinese in 1958 is substantial evidence that India was not in control of the area.

The historical basis of the border is more confused. The Indian claim to the N.E.F.A. rests almost entirely on acceptance of the McMahon Line, a line agreed to by the Tibetans and British in 1914 as the border in this area. In the Aksai Chin area no agreement has ever been reached on the alignment of the border. Nevertheless, if both sides were to take a generous view of the historical data, a basis for a N.E.F.A./Aksai Chin exchange could be found.

During the post-1954 honeymoon period of Sino/Indian relations, both sides did in fact seem prepared to take a generous view of the situation and to move towards a compromise settlement.

In 1956, Chou En-lai admitted privately to Nehru that, although lie thought the McMahon line "was not fair", nevertheless China would accept the line as the border with India after they had "consulted with the Tibetan authorities". Chinese recognition of the McMahon Line was also implied when its eastern extension was accepted as a basis for border negotiations with Burma, and by Chinese de facto acceptance of the line as the dividing line between Chinese and Indian forces in the area.

Nehru, for his part, appeared willing to play down the Indian claims to the Aksai Chin. He tried to delay disclosure if the news that the Chinese had built a road in the area. After the news had been revealed, he sought to play down the economic significance of the area, describing it as a "barren tundra". He even went so far as to cast doubt on the validity of the Indian claim to the area. In statements to the Indian Parliament during early 1959, Nehru pointed out that "during British rule, this area was neither inhabited: nor were there any outposts", adding that "this place, Aksai Chin area, is distinguish completely from other areas. It is a matter for argument which part belongs to us and which part belongs to somebody else. It is not clear".

Nehru's efforts to take the heat out of the Aksai Chin question were not entirely successful. (One of his critics even suggested building an atomic reactor in the area to promote its economic development.) News of the Chinese road in the area appeared to trigger off long-suppressed Indian sensitivity over the border issue, and, in August 1958, the Indian Government made a formal claim to the disputed territory in all three sectors. In a letter to Nehru of January 1959, Chou En-lai claimed that the Aksai Chin was Chinese territory and added that the McMahon Line was a "product of British aggression", illegal, and had "never been recognised by the Chinese Central Government". He proposed that the existing status quo he maintained, however, pending a negotiated settlement of the dispute, and added that China would take a "realistic attitude" over the McMahon Line.*

The Tibetan uprising of March 1959 upset the delicate balance of Sino/Indian relations. Reports of Chinese military action to suppress the uprising, together with the sight of thousands of

Tibetan refugees crossing into Indian territory, quickly aroused feelings of alarm and anger in India, particularly among those who believed their country had an historic interest in Tibet. Nehru's Right-Wing critics charged that India should never have allowed the Chinese into Tibet in the first place. Nehru, influenced possibly both by Indian public opinion and his own feelings on the question, came out in open condemnation of Chinese behaviour in Tibet.

The Chinese reacted even more strongly than they had in 1950. Nehru, in addition to condemning the Chinese, had spoken of his sympathy with "the aspirations of the Tibetans for autonomy". He had given asylum to the Dalai Lama, who was also allowed facilities to make his 1959 appeal for U. N. action over Tibet. And finally, the Chinese had reason to believe that the Tibetan guerrillas were receiving arms from across the Indian border.

In May 1959 the Chinese published a long article urging, almost begging, Nehru not to be swayed by his reactionary Right-Wing critics and to return to the path of Sino/Indian friendship. With a frankness and detail probably unmatched by any other Chinese statement on foreign policy, the article set out the Chinese case over Tibet, and accused the Indians of unjustified interference. Indian trade with Tibet was greatly restricted. Clashes involving casualties occurred at several points along the disputed border as the Chinese Army extended its control over border areas in an effort to restrict the move- court of Tibetans across the frontier.

These border clashes, following in the wake of the Tibetan uprising, appeared to put an end to Nehru's willingness to compromise over the border dispute. Having earlier in 1959 cast doubt on the Indian claim to the Aksai Chin, in September he stated before the Indian Parliament that the Chinese claims were "absurd" and would mean "handing over the Himalayas to them as a gift". A Chinese call in November 1959 for negotiations and a twenty-kilometre military withdrawal from the McMahon Line in the east and the "line of actual control" in the west to prevent a recurrence of border clashes was met with an Indian demand for a prior Chinese withdrawal from the Aksai Chin. A Chinese reply pointing out that this should also be paralleled by an Indian withdrawal from the NE.F.A. was ignored. In the end the Chinese appeared to settle for a freezing of the existing status quo - without negotiations or a twenty-kilometre withdrawal.

However, if the Chinese were happy to keep things as they were (keeping also their road across the Aksai Chin), Nehru and his Government were not. Throughout 1960-61 Indian opinion progressively hardened, and demands for the Government to do something about Tibet and the disputed border increased. The army was given full control over the frontier districts and it proceeded to build up its strength in these areas.

During the summer (northern) of 1962, Indian military patrols repeatedly crossed the Chinese-claimed line of actual control in the western sector of the frontier. Posts were established well behind the Chinese forward positions in territory claimed and occupied by the Chinese. Frequent and insistent Chinese protests were met with the bald statement that the Indians were merely operating in Indian territory. By August 14, Nehru was able to announce that India had three times as many posts in the western sector as the Chinese. He asked for a free hand to continue the build-up of Indian strength in the area.

The Chinese had repeatedly warned that a continuation of such activity would end in hostilities. On July 9, they had warned the Indians "to rein in on the brink of the precipice". On August 4, they called for immediate negotiations on the border. The Indians replied that negotiations could not be held until the Chinese had ceased their occupation of "every square inch of sacred Indian territory", and that the Chinese must first "vacate their aggression" in the Aksai Chin. The Chinese replied on September 13 proposing talks to begin on October 15 "without preconditions", that is, without a Chinese withdrawal from the Aksai Chin. The Indians refused the offer.

While Indian military pressure was building up along the Chinese-claimed border in the western sector, a curious situation was developing along the McMahon Line in the eastern sector. The Indians claim that at its western end the McMahon Line was not accurately drawn: that it was meant to have followed the crest of a line of hills known as the Thag La ridge. The Chinese claim, and have produced the original McMahon Line from the Tibetan archives to prove their point, that the line as originally drawn lies approximately twelve miles south of this ridge along the southern side of a small river valley. (Western maps show the McMahon Line in conformity with the Chinese claim.) The area between the Indian and Chinese versions of the McMahon Line is described by the Indians as the Dho La strip.

This was not the only unilateral revision of the McMahon Line carried out by the Indians. In his letter to Chou En-lai of September 29, 1959, Nehru admitted that in the Migyitun area (to the east of the Dho La strip) the border shown on Indian maps "differs slightly from the boundary shown in the Treaty map". He claimed that when the McMahon line was drawn, "the exact topographical features in this area were not known". The Indians have also now come to admit that "blind adherence" to the original McMahon Line would leave the Dho La strip on the Chinese side at the border.

It is not clear who first occupied the Dho La strip. The Chinese claim that the area had always been under their control and that Indian troops moved in during 1962. The Indians claim they had long occupied the area and that the Chinese began a to establish posts in the area after September 8, 1962. What is clear is that on October 12, 1962, Nehru announced in the Indian Parliament that he had given the order to drive the Chinese out of the Dho La strip.

Eight days later, on October 20, the Chinese attacked in force across the Thagla La ridge and into the disputed strip, while advancing their troops into the Chinese-claimed territory in the western sector where the Indians had earlier established posts. Four days later, the Chinese called for a ceasefire to be followed by a withdrawal of both sides from the line that separated them at that moment (the so-called October 24 line of actual control). Failing to get a satisfactory response from the Indians, they advanced troops south of the Dho La strip into the N.E.F.A., defeating Indian military forces in the area. Two weeks later, they withdrew to the positions occupied on October 24. The main point of contention between the Chinese and Indians ever since has been whether the Chinese should maintain their October 24 positions or withdraw further to the positions they occupied before fighting broke out.

The Chinese attack of October 1962 has led to an almost complete breakdown in relations between China and India. The level of each country's diplomatic representation in the other has been greatly reduced. Many thousands of Chinese nationals have been expelled from India. The few Indian nationals living in China have, in one way or another, been forced to leave. Border incidents have continued. Both sides have launched extreme propaganda campaigns against each other, the Chinese denouncing Nehru as a representative of the "big bourgeoisie" and a tool for U. S. aggressive designs against Tibet, while the Indians denounce the Chinese for having aggressive, imperialist designs against Indian territory. Both sides have gone to great lengths to discredit each other inter- nationally. Both sides have increased their military preparedness along the Himalayan frontier, particularly India, which has doubled its military budget to a level it cannot afford.

The question thus arises: Who is primarily to blame for the hostility in Sino/Indian relations? From the account already given, the primary cause of the hostility was the post-1959 dispute over the Sino/Indian border leading to the Chinese attack of October 20. But why the sudden emergence of such a dispute between two countries previously enjoying good relations?

Reverting to the terminology of our previous discussion on hostility between states, both sides see the breakdown in relations as being caused by the active hostility of the other side. This hostility, they claim, is both ideologically and national- interest based. The Chinese are accused of having acted in a hostile manner out of a desire to acquire territory and out of strong ideological dislike for the Indian Government. The Chinese claim the Indians have designs against Chinese territory and that their Government is under the influence of anti-Chinese and pro-U. S. reactionary elements.

Both sides realise that they have somehow or other to explain why the other side suddenly, in 1959, decided that its interests were no longer served by the maintenance of normal relations. The Indian explanation is that Chinese pre-1959 policy was designed to lull India into a false sense of security and so facilitate Chinese ambitions. The Chinese explanation was that reactionary elements began to gain the upper hand in the Indian Government in 1959, and point to the post-1959 increase in U. S. aid to India as evidence.

In fact there is good reason to believe that the hostility shown by each side towards the other was reactive rather than active: that each side was reacting to the believed hostility of the other. To take the Chinese side of things first.

In terms of the account already given, it seems likely that the Chinese attack of October 20, 1962, was primarily a reaction to Indian military pressure along the disputed frontier during preceding months. It could be argued, however. that the behaviour of the Chinese before October 20, and in particular their propaganda attacks against the Indians from 1960 onwards, cannot be explained simply as a reaction to previous events: that overall Chinese behaviour must therefore include some aggressive component.

The Chinese had in fact made their first hostile move against the Indians back in 1959 when they restricted Indian trading and other rights in Tibet. The Chinese had also, according to the Indians, extended somewhat the area they claimed in the western sector. And they had, according to the Indians, been responsible for the 1959 border clashes already mentioned. The Indian charge is based on alleged differences between the frontier claimed by the Chinese to 1956 and that shown on a map of the claimed Sino/Indian frontier handed to the Indians by the Chinese in 1960. The Chinese deny any difference between the two lines.

Unless these apparently hostile acts of the Chinese can be explained in reactive terms., in terms of their reacting to previous Indian actions, then it would seem that the Chinese had taken the initiative in hostility towards India and were largely responsible for the eventual breakdown in relations.

The hardening of the Chinese attitude towards India in 1959 was clearly related to Tibetan developments in that year. In judging the behaviour of the Chinese, we need, in effect, to ask whether their sensitivity over Tibet was sufficient to explain this hardening of attitude.

To accept that the Communist Chinese are, in fact extremely sensitive toward Tibet does not necessarily imply a simple acceptance of Chinese propaganda. What we know of Chinese thinking and behaviour, strongly suggests that this sensitivity does exist. If all non-communist Chinese believe that China has the right to consider Tibet as an integral part of her territory, we should accept that Communist Chinese are equally convinced. If many non-communist Chinese believe (as they do) that Britain had designs against Tibet, we should accept that Communist Chinese, educated to believe in the evils of US Western imperialism, will be at least equally fearful. We do not need accept that these views are correct; we may even consider they are absurd. But if we are going to get anywhere in trying to understand China's behaviour, we should start from the assumption that these views may be sincerely hold in Peking.

Nor may it be so absurd for the Communist Chinese to think along these lines. The Chinese legal claim to Tibet, it has been argued, appears difficult to refute. As for fears of foreign designs, if the British had earlier convinced themselves that the activities of one Russian agent in Lhasa could lead the politically unstable Tibetans to ally themselves with Tsarist Russia, the Chinese could be excused for thinking that the presence of a British Mission in Lhasa dealing directly with the independent-minded Tibetans and arranging on occasion for the supply of arms from India was evidence of British ambitions eventually to detach Tibet from China, and that India may have inherited these ambitions. Similarly, it would not be entirely surprising if the Chinese viewed the supply of foreign arms to Tibetan guerrillas from northern India in 1959 as confirmation that such ambitions existed. Finally, the Chinese were hound to be impressed by the demands of the Indian Right Wing for action against the Chinese in Tibet.

For example: some weight could be attached to the fact that the then Chief of the Indian Army Staff wrote a not unenthusiastic foreword for a book published in 1961 entitled The Chinese Aggression. The author of the hook, a Dr. Satyanarayan Sinha, predicted that the "clash of the Indochinese weapons for the possession of the Himalayas will lead to making Tibet an independent country again", and suggested ways in which this could be done.

These, then, are the reasons for believing the Chinese may he sensitive about Tibet. Chinese behaviour provides further confirmation. British officials captured in Tibet in 1950 were subjected to long imprisonment and continual interrogation - treatment far more severe than that meted out to British nationals who fell into communist hands elsewhere in China. And there was Nehru's sad admission to the Indian Parliament in 1959 after talks with Chou En-lai, of the Chinese having "some sort of kink in their minds... of foreign countries, United Kingdom or America, somehow making incursions into Tibet".

In sum, therefore, it does not seem unreasonable to conclude that the Communist Chinese sincerely believed they had a right to Tibet and that their position in the area was threatened from the direction of India. In which case they would have interpreted Indian behaviour in 1959 as an indication of hostility to which they felt compelled, or entitled, to react.

However, if Chinese behaviour in 1959 can be explained in reactive terms, can the same be said about the Chinese attack of October 1962? Even if the Indian claim to the Dho La strip was doubtful, does not the violence and intensity of the 1962 attack suggest that China was doing more than retaliate for any wrongs she may have believed the Indians to base committed?

By 1962, the Chinese were confronted not only by Indian agitation over Tibet, but also by two further aspects of Indian behaviour which would even more easily have been misunderstood. They were: (i) the Indian military build-up along the Sino/Indian border in 1961-2 and (ii) rigid Indian insistence that, as a precondition to border negotiations, the Chinese must first evacuate the whole of the Aksai Chin.

At the time, the Indians justified their position on negotiations and their military build up in terms of the correctness of their border claims. Indeed, the official Indian position was that the line claimed by India as a border had already been defined historically, and that the only purpose of negotiations was to demarcate on the ground the exact alignment of this border. From this it followed that they were justified (a) in regarding rival Chinese claims, and the occupation of the Aksai Chin, as evidence of Chinese hostility, and (b) in insisting that occupied territory had to be vacated before there could be negotiations. In the meantime the Indians had no alternative but to use military means to counter the Chinese "aggression".

If India was in fact the injured party in the territorial dispute, the Indian attitude over the disputed border would have been explicable at least to an impartial observer, and possibly even to the less impartial Chinese. There would be less justification for the Chinese reacting in the way they did. But was this the case? To answer this question we need to take a closer look at the historical background to the Sino /Indian frontier, and shall begin with the eastern sector, or N.E.F.A.

Until the 1920's, the region now known as the N.E.F.A. was largely unexplored. It was, and still is, inhabited by tribes of Tibeto-Burmese origin, some of which enjoyed trade and tributary relations with Tibet. Certain areas in the north of the region, the Tawang district for example, were inhabited by Tibetans and were under administrative control from Tibet.

The McMahon Line was negotiated with the Tibetans in 1914 at the time of the Simla Conference. It was drawn as far to the north as possible, since the British at the time sought to forestall a feared Chinese expansion into the foothills bordering the Assam plains. The McMahon Line as part of a bargain whereby the British would press the Chinese to concede territory elsewhere to Tibet.

Even so, the Tibetans were not entirely happy about losing territory south of the McMahon Line, the Tawang district in particular. Their acceptance of the line was conditional on possible future adjustments in their favour. No such adjustments, were ever made. The British also failed to extract the promised concessions from the Chinese, since the latter refused to accept the Convention produced at the Simla Conference. Thus, even as a Tibetan/British frontier, the McMahon Line does not have full validity, particularly as the Tibetans subsequently, in 1936, made a formal request to the British for revision of the line in their favour a request which the British ignored. As late as 1946, the

Tibetans were still collecting taxes in the Tawang area. And, in 1947, the Tibetans approached the newly established Indian Government, seeking the "return" of "Tibetan territories" from Assam to Ladakh.

The Indian reply to this approach may be of interest in the light of complaints to be voiced later by the Indians over the manner in which the Chinese spoke of their border claims being inherited from previous Chinese Governments "The Government of India should be glad to have an assurance that it is the intention of the Tibetan Government to continue relations an the existing basis until new Agreements are any reached... This is the procedure adopted by all other countries with which India has inherited Treaty relations from His Majesty's Government".

The validity of the McMahon Line as a Chinese/Indian frontier is considerably more doubtful. True, in rejecting the draft Simla Contention, the Chinese did not specifically object to the McMahon Line as drawn on the map of Tibet attached to the Convention. But, as the Chinese point out, the then Chinese Government had no way of knowing what this line was supposed to represent, since the terms of the McMahon Line agreement were for some reason kept secret by the British and Tibetans until 1929. It could, in theory, have been a border between Tibet and a Chinese-owned N.E.F.A. Moreover, Chiang Kaishek's Government was later to make it clear to the British (and the Indians after 1947) that it did not accept the McMahon Line. The Chinese have also pointed out that, since neither the British nor the Chinese regarded Tibet as a sovereign entity, the Tibetans were obliged to obtain Chinese approval for any frontier negotiated with a foreign power. * Failure to obtain this approval, both at the Simla Conference and later, meant that the McMahon Line never at any stage enjoyed international legality. And finally, as the Chinese never tire of pointing out, many Western and Indian maps, including one reproduced in a book by Nehru himself, Discovery of India, have, even in recent years., shown the Sino/Indian border as running along the edge of the Assam plain in conformity with the traditional Chinese claim.

The 1906 Convention between Britain and China (see page 95) had required China to accept responsibility for Tibet's foreign relations. "The 1907 Anglo/Russian Convention required Britain 'not to enter into negotiations with Tibet except through the intermediary of the Chinese Government". Negotiations with the Tibetans over the McMahon Line were thus a breach of both conventions - a possible reason why the terms of the McMahon Line agreement were kept secret.

For the Communist Chinese to appear to be willing to drop their N.E.F.A. claim is no small concession in view of the very considerable doubts as to the validity of the McMahon Line. Indeed, the Nationalist Government in Taiwan feels so strongly shout the justice of the Chinese clams that its official newspapers have accused Peking of being willing to abandon "sacred" Chinese territory. They have predicted that the present Communist Chinese leaders will be condemned by future generations of Chinese for their betrayal of China's interests.

Nevertheless, the Indian position was that the Chinese should not only drop their claim to the N.E.F.A. but to the Aksai Chin also. How strong is the Indian claim in the western sector of the disputed frontier?

The province of Ladakh, which lies on the Indian side of the disputed western sector, was originally a semi-independent state with a complex tributary relationship with Tibet. It was far from being clearly defined Indian territory. These links with Tibet were severed as a result of the 1841 invasion of Tibet from Kashmir, and Ladakh was incorporated into India. In the agreement which followed the invasion, the Ladakh/Tibet border was defined simply as following "the old established frontier", and it was only subsequently that British cartographers decided where this frontier should lie. A small area lying between the Chinese-claimed and Indian claimed frontiers is in dispute.

By far the larger area in dispute, the Aksai Chin, lies for the most part north of the Ladakh/Tibet frontier, and its ownership depends on a definition of the Ladakh/Sinkiang border. At the end of the nineteenth century, the British decided an effort should be made to define this border, and in 1899 a note was delivered to the Chinese suggesting a possible alignment. This alignment is shown on the map above, and it will be seen that it leaves with

China much of the territory at present in dispute. The Chinese never replied to the note. Shortly afterwards, the British attitude changed. Alarmed by growing Chinese weakness in Central Asia, and fearing Russian expansion into the area (fears similar to those being entertained in connection with Tibet), the British felt they should establish the border as far north as possible to forestall any southward advance by the Russians. British maps began to show the border as lying far to the north along the Kun Lun mountains. Chinese agreement was never sought for this claimed border (despite the fact that the British recognised Chinese sovereignty in Sinkiang) ; presumably it was only being put forward as an emergency measure in case the Russians attempted to seize Sinkiang. By the 1920's the Russian threat had disappeared, and it was deemed safe to drop this particular claim.

In subsequent years, British and Indian maps showed a variety of claim lines some coinciding with the present Chinese claim line, some the claim line along the Kun Lun mountains, and some an in-between claim line which ran south of the Kun Lun mountains but which included the Aksai Chin as Indian territory. Maps showing this last claim line were in general use at the time of the 1947 transfer of power, and appear to constitute the basis of the present Indian claim to the Aksai Chin. However, the only border to have ever been officially proposed to the Chinese by the British in this area was that of 1899, and, as already mentioned, this border left most of the Aksai Chin with China.

Whatever the merits of rival Chinese and Indian claims to the Aksai Chin area, it does seem clear that the Indians can hardly speak of the frontier they claim in this area as being already defined by history and therefore subject only to demarcation. In this connection a rather curious aspect of the Indian position should be mentioned - an aspect which has been overlooked by most students of the Sino/Indian dispute. Numerous Indian authorities, including Nehru himself, have claimed historical validity for their version of the Indian! Sinkiang frontier on the ground that the line proposed by the British in 1899 "ran along the Kun Lun range to a point east of 80° longitude, where it met the eastern boundary of Ladakh". In fact, the 1899 line ran well to the south of the Kun Lun mountains, and the text of the proposal speaks only of the tine meeting "the spur running south from the Kun Lun range, which [the spur] has hitherto been shown on our maps as the eastern boundary of Ladakh. This is a little east of 80° east longitude".* A misquotation of these dimensions is rather serious, particularly when it is used to justify an official claim to some 30,000 square kilometres of territory, and when, on the basis of this claim, negotiations are refused in favour of a military solution of a complex border dispute.

The only observer who appears to have noted this misquotation is Alastair Lamb. In his book, *The China-India Border,* he gives the full text of the British note of 1899 and lists some of the Indian authorities who have misquoted the 1899 proposal. Distribution of his book within India has been banned.

It would seem, therefore, that an impartial observer who takes into account not only the historical background of the border dispute, but also the equally relevant criteria of geography and administrative control, would agree that the Chinese are not being unreasonable when they call for border negotiations on the basis of the present status quo. If, as seems to be the case, the Chinese are prepared to do a N.E.F.A./Aksai Chin exchange leaving India in control of far the largest and most valuable of the territories in dispute, he may even feel that the Chinese are being quite generous. And if our impartial observer were to reach such a conclusion, it seems highly likely that the Chinese would be convinced of the reasonableness of their position and the unreasonableness of the Indian demand for a unilateral Chinese withdrawal from the Aksai Chin.

If the Chinese were in fact convinced that they were in the right over the border dispute, they would in all probability have interpreted the Indian military build-up along the disputed border in 1961-2 as evidence of active hostility. Striking confirmation that this was the case is contained in the "Tibetan Documents" - official Chinese documents which were captured by Tibetan rebels in 1961 and which subsequently found their way to the U.S., where they have been translated and published. These documents were intended as background briefing to senior Chinese military commanders stationed along the Sino/ Indian border. As such, their contents cannot be dismissed simply as propaganda. The documents warned of U.S./Indian collusion to build up pressure along the Tibetan frontier as a prelude to a joint attack against Tibet. Military commanders were instructed to observe strictly the twenty-kilometre troop withdrawal from the line of actual control and to avoid clashes with advancing Indian patrols since this would provide the "imperialists" with the pretext they needed to justify their planned attack.*

ACHIEVEMENTS IN THE BORDER NEGOTIATIONS

Since the 1980s, the China-India border talks have experienced three stages, with each stage covering roughly one decade. The first stage covered the 1980s culminated in Indian Prime Minister Rajiv Gandhi's visit to China in December 1988. The second stage covered the 1990s ended with India's nuclear tests in 1998; and the third stage covered the past 10 years marked with Indian President Patil's China trip during the celebration of the 60th anniversary of the establishment of China-India diplomatic relations in May 2010.

The Eight-Round Border Talks in the 1980s

The eight-round border talks took place in the period from hostility to detente in the China-India-relations. The talks obviously eased the tensions in their bilateral relations and resulted in agreement on the disagreements. These talks relieved both governments of pressing too hard on matters of substance while procedural disagreement seemed to be employed as excuse for no-progress. This suggests that neither government found it urgent to resolve the border dispute in the 1980s. Both sides hoped to reduce tensions and stabilize and improve bilateral relations, but they realized it premature to proceed to resolve their border disputes.

The 1988 China-India summit was the first meeting of he top leaders of the two countries in the 28 years since premier Zhou Enlai's visit to India in 1960.

Rajiv gandi's Beijing trip in December 1988 ushered in a new era of China-India relationship. With the detente prevailed in the world during the last years of the Cold War, India's diplomacy has lost the fulcrum of Indo-Soviet strategic partnership while China's diplomacy has lost the pillar of Sino-US cooperation. China and India suddenly found that they needed to re-orient their foreign policies within the context of the changed world power structure. The five principles of peaceful co-existence again became the common basis of their foreign policy reorientation.

In his inaugural address on December 31, 1984, Rajiv Gandhi stressed the continuation of a non-alignment policy and expressed his desire to improve relations with neighbouring countries.

Huang Hua's India's trip was marked by the agreement to open negotiations on the border dispute and the development of China-India relations. There followed eight rounds of China-India talks as an official channel of the China-India dialogue on the border dispute.

China's strategy on the eight-round border talks comprised two main aspects. One was to insist on a package deal, and the other was to develop their bilateral relations in other fields with the border dispute shelved. During his interview with Krishna Kumar, the editor of *Vikrant,* on June 21, 1980, Deng Xiaoping renewed the "package" approach on the border issue. He stated that China would be willing to accept the watershed principle in the eastern sector in exchange for India's renunciation of claims to Aksai Chin. In other words, both sides should agree to accept the present line of actual control as their boundary. During his meeting with Indian Prime Minister Atal Vajpayee in February 1979, Deng stated that " We shall seek common ground while reserving our differences. We can solve the boundary question through peaceful consultation. This question should not prevent us from improving our relations in other field.

India insisted on sector-by-sector negotiations and refused China's package deal and both sides failed to narrow their differences during the eight rounds of talks. However, all the principles and concerns put on the table by both sides constituted sme mutually acceptable principles for substantive discussions on the border question. Both sides cautiously inched forward without getting bogged down in differing interpretations.

At the eighth round held in New Delhi, on November 14-17, 1986, India gave up its position of "boundary settlement or nothing." China had accepted the approach of the sector-by-sector review within the framework of comprehensive settlement in 1984.

Both agreed that pending a settlement of the border issue, the two governments should develop friendly relations and strengthen cooperation in other fields. Both sides agreed that peace and tranquility should be maintained all along the border. Both sides are prepared for Rajiv Gandhi's Visit to China. Apparently, the stage as set for raising the border dialogue to the political level.

The eight rounds of the border talks in the 1980s showed that India's policy on the border talks changed first from non-negotiation to negotiation, and then from "boundary settlement or nothing" to overall development in all fields. China-India dialogue of the 1980s substituted China-India Detente for their enmity.

Rajiv's visited symbolized the general trend of transition from hostility and confrontation to detente and dialogue. The 1988 summit also marked a departure from the previous approach, political settlement approach substituted for the legalistic approach. Both sides reduced their stress on historical documents and focused instead on their respective security interests by attaching inpotance to mutual bargaining and mutual understanding.

Line of Actual Control Clarification and CBMs Implementation

The eight rounds of border talks demonstrated that their conflicting border versions, based on historical-legalistic arguments, could not find common ground because no mutually acceptable border treaties or agreements existed. The eight rounds of border talks raised the hope for a political solution to the border dispute.

In 1991, Premier Li peng visited India and signed the Sino-Indian Joint Communique on December 16, 1991. In the joint communiqué, they reaffirmed their independent foreign policy and the five principles of peaceful co-existence. The two sides appealed for the joint efforts for the establishment of a new international political and economic order. India reiterated its position that Tibet is an autonomous region of China and it does not allow Tibetans to engage in anti-china political activities in India.

After the two summit meetings in 1988 and 1991, China-India interactions shifted from the border dispute to the identification of a mutually acceptable lie of actual control along the China-India border. In 1993, Indian Prime Minister Rao visited China and signed an agreement on maintaining peace and tranquility along the line of actual control and reduced military forces in the border areas. This peace pact, under which both sides agreed to respect and observe the LAC, is a big step forward in exploring a lasting border solution, eliminating concerns about events such as the Sumdurong Chu incident which nearly sparked another border war in 1987. Under the LAC agreement in 1993, the two sides agreed that the boundary question shall be resolved through peaceful and friendly consultations. Neither side shall use or threaten to use force against the other by any means. Pending an ultimate solution to the boundary question, the two sides shall strictly respect and observe the LAC.

Each side will keep its military forces in the areas along the LAC to a minimum level compatible with the friendly and good-neighborly relations between the two countries. Both sides shall work out effective confidence-building measures (CBMs) in the areas along the LAC.

However, the two sides agreed that references to the LAC in this agreement do not prejudice their respective positions on the boundary question.

Under this agreement, both sides agreed that each side of the China-India Joint Working Group on the boundary question shall appoint diplomatic and military experts, advising the Joint Working Group on resolution of differences on the alignment of the LAC and address issues relating to military redeployment in the border areas along the LAC.

In 1996, the Chinese president Jiang Zemin visited India and both sides decided to develop a cooperative and constructive partnership, further raising political level of bilateral cooperation between the two countries. However, the Indian nuclear tests in 1998 and its leaders indicated India's nuclear tests for counter-China's nuclear threat dashed the healthy momentum of China-India relations in the late 1990s.

Apparently, China-India interactions in the 1990s focused on political and security fields. The line of actual control, the CBMs in the areas along the China-India border, and emphasis on the establishment of an international political and economic order and even India's nuclear tests are all pointed to political and security dimension of the China-India relations.

Shift Back to the Settlement of the Border Dispute in the New Century

Ushering in the new 21st century, China and India, the two Asian giants, are rising at the same time. Their bilateral relationship has its regional and global significance. As the two largest emerging powers in Asia and the world, their roles have been played far beyond the bilateral context. Certainly, their bilateral dispute, particularly the border dispute, has constrained each other's capability to play their responsible role in the regional and global affairs.

If they focused on stabilizing their relations and securing their border areas in the 1990s, they have shifted their attention to the settlement of their border dispute by developing their political and economic relations while taking concrete and substantive measures to resolve the border dispute. They understand that their bilateral problems have complicated their policy coordination and cooperation in the regional and global issues. Their bilateral differences have tended to be manipulated by other powers to serve their geostrategic interest.

For the past decade, in terms of the border dispute, they have taken three substantive steps to intensify their efforts to resolve it.

The first step is that India has accepted Tibet is an autonomous region of China, implying that India has given up the intention to use Tibet as a buffer zone between China and India and recognizes China's sovereignty over Tibet. However, although

India does not allow the Tibetans in India to engage in Anti-China political activities, it still hosts the Dalai Lama's government-in-exile. China has recognized Sikkim's status as a state of India's federation by signing the agreement on the cross-border trade with India.

The second step is that China and India signed an agreement on political parameters and guiding principles on the settlement of the China-India border dispute. This document is regarded as a big breakthrough in the joint efforts for resolving the border dispute.

The third step is that the two governments have appointed their special representatives to promote the negotiations on a framework of the border settlement. The two governments have paid importance to the annual meetings of the two special representatives. The Chinese special representative is State Councilor Dai Bingguo and The Indian special representative is India's National Security adviser M. K. Narayanan.

After the two special representatives were appointed, they started to work together for a framework settlement of the border dispute according to the agreed political parameters and guiding principles.

Under the current circumstances, although the two governments continue to work on the settlement of the border dispute, peace, stability, and tranquility in the border areas have remained. No armed conflicts or even skirmishes happened although some media has played up such noises of China's invasions into India's territory dozens or hundreds of times.

PROSPECTS OF RESOLVING CHINA-INDIA BORDER DISPUTE

Today, some security experts such as Mr. Bharat Verma, the editor of *Indian Defence Review,* in this world are still talking about China's military attacks on India before 2012, or even within 6 months. However, such noises cannot halt the historic wheels of Chindia partnership from rolling forward. As the two new emerging powers, their leaders know clearly that each is not a threat to the other. China has been called the world workshop while India the world office. In the course of their rise, the challenges they will face are the same or similar. They need more policy coordination and more functional cooperation in the world dominated by the developed nations in the global platforms such as G20, BRIC, BASIC, and China-Russia- India Trilateral Dialogue. China and India joined hands last year during the United Nations Climate Change Conference in Copenhagen, effectively presenting the stance of emerging economies and developing countries on climate change.

For the past 10 years, the two governments have made joint efforts to cement and strengthen their bilateral relations. In 2003, Indian Prime Minister Atal Vajpayee visited China and signed Declaration on Principles for Relations and Comprehensive Cooperation between China and India. Both sides reaffirmed that they would promote a long-term constructive and cooperative partnership.

They emphasized that their common interests outweigh their differences. The two countries are not a threat to each other. Neither side shall use or threaten to use force against the other.

They are committed to qualitatively enhance the bilateral relationship at all levels and in all areas while addressing differences through peaceful means in a fair, reasonable and mutually acceptable manner. They emphasized that the differences should not be allowed to affect the overall development of bilateral relations.

On the border question, they reiterate their determination to seek a fair, reasonable, and mutually acceptable solution through consultations on an equal footing. They agreed that pending an ultimate solution, they should work together to maintain peace and tranquility in the border areas, continue implementation of h agreements signed for this purpose, including the clarification of the line of actual control. The two governments decided to appoint special representatives to promote the process of the border negotiations.

As one of the sensitive issues in the China-India relations, India recognizes that the Tibet Autonomous Region is part of the territory of the People's Republic of China and India does not allow Tibetans to engage in anti-China political activities in India. In recent years, the trade relationship between the two countries has been seen in both countries as a crucial driver of overall bilateral relations, amid persisting political strains over the long-running border dispute. China became India's largest trading partner in 2008, with bilateral trade reaching $52 billion. Trade fell to $43 billion on account of the financial crisis, but has rebounded in the first two months of this year with Indian exports, mainly driven by iron ore, rising 75 per cent. It is predictable that rapid development of trade relations will certainly affect bilateral political relations in a positive manner.

Fast growing trade relations have come under increasing strain with India's trade deficit continuing to widen. India filed a record number of anti-dumping investigations against China at the World Trade Organization in 2009. India's recent restrictions on the import of Chinese telecom equipment, in light of security concerns, have added to the list of strains. The telecom issue, however, was not raised by China during the President's ongoing visit. With the bilateral trade rapidly growing, these differences or disputes are normal. We believe that all these problems can be resolved by bilateral consultations. Describing trade and economic cooperation as a pillar of bilateral ties, Indian president Patil said India and China should work together to realize trade target of US$ 60 billion in 2010 that had been set.

In 2006 Presiden Hu Jintao visited India and the two sides agreed on a 10-pronged strategy to expand and intensify bilaterlal strategic and cooperative partnership.

In 2008, during the Indian Prime Minister Manmohan Singh visit to China, the two countries concluded a " Shared Vision for the 21st century", which forms the basis for bilateral cooperation on global issues.

China and India have agreed to enhance political, economic ties and bolster people-to-people contact during a meeting between Indian President Pratibha Patil and Chinese Premier Wen Jiabao here on May 27, 2010. President Hu Jintao held talks with her. President Patil said India-China relations were of global and strategic significance, and all political parties in India were supportive of further advancing such relations. President Hu said that China and India should work more closely to address global issues such as economic downturn, climate change, energy security and food security. The two countries should maintain close communication and coordination within multilateral mechanisms such as China-Russia-India, BRIC, BASIC, and G20, in a bid to increase the voice of developing countries.

China and India do not pose as threat to each other and their common interests far outweigh their differences. The two countries should understand and respect each other's core national interests and major concerns, properly handle their differences, and seek common development and a win-win situation. A good China-India relationship makes both winners while a confrontational one makes both losers.

CHINA-INDIA BORDER TALKS PIVOT ON TIBET

Throughout the protracted Sino-Indian border dispute, Tibet and its status has always been a predominant influence, whether implicitly or explicitly on the negotiating table. This has both historical and contemporary ramifications.

India, much to China's chagrin, utilized the Tibet issue as a key point of departure in order to strike a grand bargain with Beijing after China occupied Tibet in 1949. Jawaharlal Nehru was of the firm conviction that China and India could encapsulate a grand cooperation in Tibet based on which India would recognize Tibet as part of China while China would recognize Tibetan autonomy.

To Nehru, Tibetan autonomy meant safeguarding Tibet's cultural and social uniqueness. It also meant that China would not militarize Tibet with a massive People's Liberation Army (PLA) presence which could pose a security threat to India.

Propelled by this belief, Nehru recognized Tibet as part of China in 1954. Mao Zedong, however, interpreted Nehru's insistence on Tibetan autonomy as a diabolical plan to turn Tibet into an Indian "protectorate or colony". In the several meetings that he conducted with his Politburo colleagues in the run-up to the 1962 war with India, he argued that the "Indian expansionist" had devious plans to occupy Tibet. In an essay titled "The Revolution in Tibet and Nehru's Philosophy", published in The People's Daily on May 6, 1959, at the behest of Mao, Nehru was faulted for his sympathy for the Tibetan people and accused of upholding the Tibetan upper-class structure to the detriment of what the essay termed as "Tibetan serfs".

Nehru, the essay argued, wanted to turn Tibet into an "Indian colony". By extension, India's "forward policy" activated since November 1961 to establish forward posts in unoccupied territory that China and India each viewed as its own was also interpreted by Mao as an Indian design to create the logistical conditions to occupy Tibet in the long run.

These differences and a "no-negotiation" posture by India on the border from 1961 onwards in the face of what Nehru interpreted as Chinese aggression on Aksai Chin led to the China-India border war in October 1962 in which India suffered defeat.

While both countries have come a long way since then, having re-activated diplomatic relations in 1976 and border negotiations since 1981, the border talks were stalled at this stage due to increased Chinese territorial posture in 1985 especially with regard to Tawang. In 1988, a Joint Working Group (JWG) was institutionalized during the visit of Rajiv Gandhi to China.

At present, there is talk of "progress" on the border issues and statements from high-level officials representing both parties on not letting the border dispute affect the bilateral working relationship. Yet, both China and India remain deeply entrenched in their rigid negotiating positions.

The border dispute, especially in the eastern side, is becoming financially costly to both parties, particularly as resources are diverted to build up militarily at the border to deter the other while additional political resources are utilized to continue the negotiations in official diplomatic fora.

India has planned to invest US$100 billion in military modernization in the next decade, with $15 billion already under negotiations for 126 French Rafale Multi Medium Role Combat Aircraft to be deployed in the eastern sector. China has also visibly demonstrated its military presence in Tibet with nearly 300,000

PLA troops and fighter aircraft like the J-10 deployed at the Gonggar airport in Lhasa. Military exercises by both China and India along the eastern frontier have also increased since 2012.

The territorial dispute has lingered for decades, crippling the bilateral relationship and thus preventing the two countries from working as closely together as could have been possible had the border dispute been resolved. The bottom line: as China and India rise as global powers, now is the time to pursue real conflict resolution on the border dispute.

The border dispute will only continue to divert resources and time from both countries which could better contribute to enhance China and India on their way to becoming stronger global actors on the world stage.

Why is the border dispute so intractable and why has it continually resisted resolution in the past 60 years? The answer is threefold - the inflexibility of negotiation positions, the choice of conflict resolution mechanisms utilized, and the mistrust that perpetuates and further prevents progress from being made toward a lasting resolution.

With regard to flexibility, at present, both parties seemingly remain firmly committed to their territorial claims and these claims are at times strategically utilized as leverage in the negotiations. China maintains its claim to Arunachal Pradesh, which India has administered since the British left India in 1947, while India seeks control of Aksai Chin, which is under Chinese control.

Despite China's claims, India firmly maintains that Arunachal Pradesh is and will remain Indian territory, while implicitly utilizing the Tibet issue and India's spiritual connection to the Dalai Lama, a great insecurity for China, as leverage.

The Tibet issue is distinctly intertwined with the greater Sino-Indian border dispute along the borders of Arunachal Pradesh because China maintains that Tibet is an integral part of Chinese sovereign territory and considers Arunachal Pradesh to be "Southern Tibet".

Recently, a Chinese scholar from Huazhong University, Du Dacai, argued that "solving the problem of our territory of South Tibet [as China refers to Arunachal Pradesh]" should be China's fourth priority territorial unification issue after Taiwan, the Diaoyu (or Senkaku) Islands and the South China sea issue "to realize the Chinese dream and China's unification."

This conceptualization of "Southern Tibet," whether legitimate in the minds of the Chinese or a negotiation tactic to try to gain control of Arunachal Pradesh from India, links the Tibet issue to the border dispute because if China and India's borders are to be delineated, Tibet's borders with India must also be determined.

The fact that Tibet's status within China itself is not accepted by many Tibetans and that the Tibetan government-in-exile and Dalai Lama reside in India, threatens China. This also contributes to the intensity of mistrust among both parties and complicates the already complex process of negotiating the disputed borders.

In order to resolve the dispute through negotiations, both China and India should seek to take another evaluation of their core interests and determine possible areas of flexibility on certain issues.

The Tibet issue is also incredibly important to both China and India because the Tibetans' struggle for independence affects both countries greatly from a national security standpoint. China views the Tibetans' struggle for independence as a great source of instability because it directly threatens China's domestic social stability and territorial integrity.

India's spiritual connection to the Dalai Lama and tenuous relationship with the Tibetan government in exile further exacerbates this insecurity. The Indian government has made public statements expressing India's "official" policy of not supporting the Tibetans or the Dalai Lama, such as Prime Minister Manmohan Singh's comments that "India will not allow Tibetans to conduct anti-China activities in the country [India]", but India may hesitate to make further statements regarding the status of Tibet while China is pressuring India to do so. Despite these official statements, the Dalai Lama holds spiritual significance in India, thus making China more dubious about India's intentions.

In this respect, India isn't exactly helping to resolve that tension by refusing to make bolder statements on China's claim to Tibet, and from the Indian perspective, why should it? From a purely bargaining perspective, India retains more leverage to potentially use against China to gain concessions in the border negotiations. The real issue here is that ultimately, this play for leverage further breaks down trust and makes the process of negotiating more difficult.

Another key issue at play, is that of Tawang, which is in Arunachal Pradesh, closely linked to the Tibet issue and considered to be a holy place for Tibetans. This further complicates the Tibet issue and thus the overall border negotiations because if Tibet is a part of China and Tibetans consider Tawang to be culturally linked to Tibet, then China has an incentive for why it should obtain Arunachal Pradesh from India in the negotiations.

If Tibetans seek independence from China, this claim becomes less legitimate, but as the Tibetan government-in-exile and Dalai Lama currently reside in India, it again causes insecurity for China. India has likely recognized this concern and in response to China's aggressive posturing towards Arunachal Pradesh, India has increased the civilian and military presence in that area, similar to what China has done in increasing the Han Chinese and PLA presence in Tibet.

Another key concern on the Tawang issue is whether the next Dalai Lama will come from Tawang, and if so, will that further complicate the Tibet issue and tensions between China and India if China does not approve of the new Dalai Lama? The Dalai Lama will always have spiritual connections with India, even if the current Dalai Lama has renounced former political ties, and given that it is a religious issue, it is not plausible that India would break these spiritual and cultural ties it has historically respected.

As long as the Tibet issue remains unresolved and the questioning of Chinese legitimacy over Tibet continues, China remains fearful of India's intentions for Tibet, and as long as India does not make those intentions more clear, it will be increasingly more difficult to resolve the ongoing border dispute.

Although China and India have made progress in developing economic and diplomatic relationships with an attempt to disregard the Tibet issue, the border issue is time and time again raised. The current pace of negotiations has not resulted in progress on the resolution of the border dispute. China and India have less to lose and more to gain by rethinking how to resolve this dispute. First off, the mechanisms for resolution should be expanded. On their own, the Special Representative talks set up since 2003 may not be enough to come to a mutually beneficial negotiated solution.

There are other possibilities for creating a common border mechanism outside of the Special Representative talks to supplement conflict resolution efforts, such as talks on the Track I5 levels. Within the field of conflict resolution, one such conflict resolution method is known as the "Problem-Solving Workshop" (PSW).

The PSW emerged from the field of social psychology and was pioneered by several scholars and practitioners including Herbert Kelman, John Burton, Benjamin Broome, Ronald Fisher, and Leonard Doob. This method of conflict resolution was designed to bring together influential people who have connections to high-level decision makers but the flexibility to more freely discuss the key issues, various parties' perspectives, and explore creative options for conflict resolution, all the while building trust among the participants.

In the beginning, this could be conducted as unofficial sessions internally within India and China respectively to explore key issues and perspectives before meeting with their counterparts. Once the participants become comfortable with the process, Indian and Chinese influentials could be brought together to engage in a PSW on the border issue.

In addition to PSW among influentials, a forum should be created between the think tanks and academic communities (Track II) in China and India to bring together the brightest minds working on these issues. While there are many within both China and India who work on these issues and related ones, there is little sharing or joint work among these individuals and groups together.

A joint forum, roundtable discussion or partnership among think tanks working on these issues would act as a way in which to collective brainstorm with a problem-solving approach to determine options for resolution of the border dispute. At this point in time, it is clear that official negotiations alone may not resolve the border dispute. Additional mechanisms of conflict resolution like the Track II should be sought after, and if deemed appropriate by each party internally, Problem Solving Workshops and partnerships among those working on these issues may provide additional methods in which to unofficially explore options that could be proposed to the negotiators with an aim at resolving the border dispute.

SINO-INDIAN BORDER DISPUTE: IS A RESOLUTION ESSENTIAL?

Beijing has re-ignited the decades old Sino-Indian border dispute by recently publishing a map depicting India's Arunachal Pradesh state and parts of Jammu and Kashmir as Chinese territory. The Sino-Indian border dispute is a legacy of British rule in India and so far has defied resolution. In 1962, war broke out between India and China over territorial boundaries. At its conclusion, however, the two sides still failed to agree on where the Line of Actual Control (LAC) lay.

This situation has resulted in "incursions" into each other's territory, most notably in April-May 2013, when India claimed that the Chinese military had crossed into the Indian territory of Ladakh. The incident triggered the most serious escalation in tensions between the two states in a quarter of a century; it ended after three weeks with an agreement negotiated by military commanders. China and India have managed to create a durable framework to manage the dispute since negotiations began in 1981, but progress has slowed in recent years.

Comment

Despite recent episodes of heightened tensions, trade between China and India has increased exponentially. According to the Indian Department of Commerce, China was India's largest trading partner in 2012, with trade exceeding US$73 billion. India's growing economy and its rising middle class present a vast opportunity for China's economy, particularly at a time when its markets in the West are declining. While the two countries have a long way to go in establishing mutual trust, they are showing increased collaboration in areas such as anti-piracy patrolling off the Gulf of Aden, military-to-military dialogue, international negotiations on critical issues, such as climate change, and within multilateral organisations, such as BRICS (Brazil, Russia, India, China and South Africa) and BASIC (Brazil, South Africa, India and China).

Strategic competition between the two states, however, is beginning to manifest itself, both regionally and globally. As they continue to grow, it is becoming increasingly apparent that they are beginning to encroach upon each other's spheres of influence. China is increasing bilateral trade relations with countries such as Sri Lanka, Pakistan and Bangladesh, while also extending its naval presence in the Indian Ocean. India, on the other hand, is courting further investment from Japan, China's rival.

Recently-elected Indian Prime Minister, Narendra Modi, fought his election campaign on the platform of economic growth. He understands that India will need strong relations with China to achieve the high levels of economic growth that he has promised to deliver. China, for its part, has invested considerable military and political resources in its ongoing territorial disputes in the East and South China Seas; it will be reluctant to ignite further problems on its western flank as well. So far, China has reached out to Modi's new administration; any real progress, however, is unlikely, as New Delhi and Beijing differ in their opinions on how the dispute should be resolved. Beijing believes that it is a difficult issue, rooted in history, and should be put aside, to allow them to focus on strengthening bilateral relations. New Delhi, however, sees the resolution of the boundary dispute as essential if a strong relationship is to be realised. The resultant stalemate makes a resolution of the issue unlikely in the near future.

Incursions by both sides are likely to continue as long as the LAC is not demarcated. The long-standing engagement mechanisms between the two states have so far maintained the uneasy peace along the disputed border. The principal reason that a resolution has eluded both sides for so long, is that it would require at least minor territorial concessions from both China and India. A resurgence of nationalist passions in both countries means that these concessions are unlikely to eventuate in the short-term. While the lack of a final resolution to the boundary dispute may continue to inhibit strong Sino-Indian relations in the longer-term, for now it appears as if the status quo will be maintained. Igniting a dormant issue would not be in the interests of either India or China.

INDIA & CHINA: LOOKING BEYOND BORDER INCURSIONS & LI KEQIANG'S VISIT

As the dust settles after Chinese Premier Li Keqiang's visit to India and accompanying intrusions, it will be prudent to objectively assess the nature of the China-India relationship over the longer term. An episodic evaluation will be misleading, particularly as the timing of these intrusions marks them out as of significance. They are also an escalation of the unfriendly Chinese behaviour demonstrated shortly before the visits of Chinese President Hu Jintao in November 2006 and Chinese Premier Wen Jiabao in December 2010.

Just prior to Hu Jintao's visit to India in 2006, China's Ambassador in New Delhi, Sun Yuxi, publicly declared: "In our position, the whole of the state of Arunachal Pradesh is Chinese territory. And Tawang is only one of the places in it. We are claiming all of that". Later, in the months prior to Chinese Premier Wen Jiabao's visit in December 2010, Beijing denied a visa to India's Northern Army Commander and began issuing stapled visas to residents of J&K thereby implicitly designating the entire state as 'disputed', a stand from which it has not backed off. Barely a month earlier around the visit of Politburo Standing Committee (PBSC) member Zhou Yongkang in November, an article by a senior commentator in the Party mouth-piece 'People's Daily' had warned India against drawing closer to Japan in pursuit of its 'Look East' policy.

CONTEXTUALIZING LI KEQIANG'S INDIA VISIT

The circumstances surrounding Chinese Premier Li Keqiang's visit are relevant as are Beijing's other actions and pronouncements. These need to be viewed in the larger perspective of the new Chinese leadership's strategic foreign policy. Chinese President Xi Jinping's 'China's Dream', in fact, promises to wipe out past humiliations and lays bold emphasis on a strong and wealthy

China. There are adequate indications that Beijing assesses that the time is now opportune for it to push for international acceptance of what it perceives is its pre-eminent position in the region, including the Asia-Pacific. It considers that it has adequate stature and strength for it to partner the US in the resolution of international and regional issues. The recent (June 7-8, 2013) Sino-US Summit publicly stated that a start had been made in building a "new type of major power relationship", a point which was often reiterated by the two senior Chinese interlocutors, Vice Premier Wang Yang and State Councilor Yang Jiechi, at the US-China Strategic and Economic Dialogue (SED) held soon after on July 10-11, in Washington DC.

Tacit US acceptance, at least for the short-to-medium term, seemed apparent in US National Security Advisor Tom Donilon's disclosure that the Summit had taken place at a time when the US faces "an intense range of bilateral, regional and global challenges on which U.S.-China cooperation is critical". Describing discussions as "quite unique and important" he added that the Summit aimed to start building a "new model of relations between great powers".

Relevant in this context are the lessening references to the 'Asian pivot', for which the preferred term is now 'rebalancing'. The emphasis seems also to have shifted from the military to the economic sphere with focus on the Trans Pacific Partnership (TPP), which envisages a whole new set of rules for the international economy and trade. The US and West possibly expect to retard China's economic growth and rise by these new rules, which will also adversely affect a number of other countries too.

Shortly prior to the Summit, China's self-image was clearly outlined in two articles by senior commentators which were published in the Party's official mouthpiece 'People's Daily'. On May 28, 2013 Jiemian Yang, Dean of the Shanghai Institute of International Studies (SIIS) and younger brother of Chinese State Councilor and former Foreign Minister Yang Jiechi, candidly declared that the increase in China's comprehensive national strength had given its new leaders more confidence in dealing with the international community. Stressing that China will adhere to its own theories, systems and path of development, he emphasized that this "self-confidence" has enabled China's leaders to be "very firm" in safeguarding sovereignty and territorial integrity while simultaneously being flexible in dealings with smaller countries. He revealed that they will focus more on the neighbourhood and travel oftener in the region.

Conceding that China needs to "normalize relations with Japan" and that the "many maritime disputes" are major challenges, he concluded that so long as "the United States, other major powers, neighbouring countries and other members of the international community" cooperate and support China, "it will eventually emerge as a very peace-loving, powerful and prosperous nation".

The second article was published on June 4, 2013, and written by Li Wen, a scholar from the 'Centre for Research on the Theory of Socialism with Chinese Characteristics' of the Chinese Academy of Social Sciences (CASS). Stating that Beijing wanted cooperative relations with major powers, it advised major powers to discard 'Cold War' ideas and hegemonic policies. It urged major countries not to depict a country as a "strategic competitor" and seek to "contain it", but to "show more kindness and less hostility, and respect each other's core interests".

The reference to "core interests", which is China's short-hand for territories claimed by it, is pertinent. While these "core interests" currently include Taiwan, Tibet and Xinjiang, some months ago a Chinese Foreign Ministry spokesperson repeatedly referred to the Senkaku islands, called Diaoyu in Chinese, as China's "core interest". In 2011 and 2012 there were numerous references to the South China Sea as China's "core interest", though these have since tapered off.

This increased self-confidence of China's leadership is visible in its more activist and muscular foreign and strategic policy of the past few months, particularly in its strategic periphery. Beijing has continued to consolidate and expand its strategic investments in Pakistan notwithstanding India's objections or the disturbed conditions there. A slew of new agreements were signed during Chinese Premier Li Keqiang's visit to Islamabad in May this year and newly-elected Pakistan Prime Minister Nawaz Sharif broke with past practice and travelled to Beijing on his first visit abroad during this tenure.

While he has not returned with financial assistance, there is renewed talk in Pakistan of a Chinese-built railway line linking the Chinese province of Xinjiang with Pakistan's port city of Gwadar. Similarly, the Chinese Embassy and its diplomats are noticeably more active in Nepal. Their primary objectives are to monitor and curb the activities of the Tibetans residing in Nepal and to prevent Tibetans from escaping into Nepal. In Myanmar too, Beijing has moved to safeguard its strategic investments. It has, for the first time in decades, overtly engaged in the internal affairs of another sovereign nation – albeit at its request – and brokered at least six rounds of 'peace talks' between the Kachin Independence Army and Myanmar's military.

Significantly, senior officials of China's Ministry of Foreign Affairs attended the talks where China flaunted its influence by guaranteeing the security of all participants. This has been buttressed by increased, though quiet, contacts between the Chinese and Myanmar's military and Intelligence establishments.

The Chinese Premier's visit to India and premeditated military intrusion that preceded it had multiple objectives. They brought into sharp definition China's new policy towards its neighbours and countries in the region with which it has unresolved sovereignty and territorial disputes. As evidenced by its policies towards Vietnam, the Philippines and Japan, Beijing is uncompromising on the issues of sovereignty and territorial integrity. China's official news agency, 'Xinhua', has earlier publicized that growing economic and trade ties will not translate into good bilateral relations unless China's "core interests" are acknowledged. For the first time it used the economy as a lever against Japan when it banned the export of rare earths to Japan. It repeated this months later against the Philippines over the Scarborough Reef issue, thus making it amply clear that regardless of international trade laws and practices Beijing will not hesitate to use economic pressure to achieve its objectives.

The texture of all these relationships is assertive and differs from China's pragmatic, conciliatory, non-confrontational stance with the US. They make clear that while China's new leaders could show flexibility in formulating the framework for a bilateral relationship, there will be no willingness, or concession, on matters perceived as impinging on China's sovereignty or territorial integrity. They also reinforce the assessment that on issues concerning sovereignty and territorial integrity, China's People's Liberation Army (PLA) and the security establishment continue to exercise a prominent role as they have for the past some years.

Some reports circulating in April-May 2013 wildly speculated that a group of Chinese Generals not amenable to control by Central Military Commission (CMC) Chairman, Xi Jinping, were responsible for the 'action', or that it was an isolated action by a local commander. The number of such so-called rogue Generals was even mentioned as 45! There is not a shred of evidence to support such speculation.

On the contrary, since at least 2002 the Chinese Communist Party (CCP) has steadily and inexorably tightened its grip on the PLA. Political Commissars, who monitor the political reliability of all personnel, have been granted the power of veto over promotions and three successive year-long campaigns were carried out throughout the PLA to ensure political reliability and loyalty to the CCP. One such campaign is presently underway. Political reliability and loyalty to the CCP has, for at least the past year and a half, been listed as the most important criteria for promotions and was reiterated by Xi Jinping promptly on taking over as CMC Chairman. Additionally, thorough background checks to ascertain the political reliability of officers were conducted last year in the wake of the Bo Xilai affair.

Xi Jinping, who succeeded Hu Jintao as CMC Chairman at the 18th Party Congress in November last year, exercises firm control over the PLA. The new members of the CMC, Commanders of the ground forces, Air Force, Navy and Second Artillery, Military Region Commanders and Generals appointed to key positions have all been selected by Hu Jintao and Xi Jinping. Since his elevation as CMC Chairman, Xi Jinping has paid a lot of attention to the PLA and been continuously visiting military establishments. He also has considerable personal influence in the PLA and knows a number of high-ranking PLA officers, especially the 'princelings'. The current Director of the important General Political Department (GPD), General Zhang Yang, is also a close long-time associate of the PLA Chief, General Fang Fenghui. These factors preclude the possibility of any local commander attempting such an adventure. Furthermore, there have been no such behavioral aberrations by local Chinese troops over the past so many years. Importantly, Xi Jinping presides over the powerful Foreign Affairs Small Leading Group. The action was undoubtedly approved by the top CCP leadership in Beijing.

THE INDIA-CHINA MILITARY STANDOFF (APR-MAY 2013): A POST MORTEM

An important attribute of the stand-off that stretched over twelve days in April-May 2013, was that Beijing remained transparently impervious to the three flag meetings at the level of local army commanders, communications from New Delhi and, to the prolonged and adverse media publicity which was embarrassing to the Indian government and damage it caused to India-China relations. The clear message was that for Beijing's leadership the issues of sovereignty and territorial integrity trump all other considerations. This stance is additional confirmation that the stand-off was not a local incident provoked by the action of a local commander, but one initiated with the full knowledge of China's senior leadership.

At the tactical level the prolonged military intrusion by Chinese forces near Daulet Beg Oldi in the Aksai Chin area was intended to send three clear signals. Very pertinently the equipment carried by the PLA troops involved in this act did not point to any military intent. The objectives were to:

continue the practice of· marking out the increasing extent of Chinese claimed territory along the entire length of the border with India and inhibit India from activities, including civil construction, near the border on its own side; test the rapid reaction capability· of Indian forces to deploy to counter a threat, and to test the time it takes for India's military command and political leadership to respond to a threat; and signal that the border can be· activated militarily at any time of Beijing's choosing. In addition to demonstrating the extent of China's territorial claims and attempting to capture areas of importance along the border, of particular importance to PLA Commanders is ascertaining the readiness and response capability of the Indian forces deployed along the border and that of the Indian military and political commands.

This has become important as preparations by PLA Commanders are for a quick, decisive local war. Current Chinese military literature makes amply clear that China's leadership and the PLA envisage a decisive short-duration conflict using overwhelming firepower that concludes with a Chinese victory within a few days and certainly before it can enlarge and involve other powers. In fact, China is preparing for a local war where the initial first phase opens with a cyber-offensive targeted at military and civilian public utilities. The next stage involves the use of missiles and that is followed by use of the PLA Air Force. Ground troops would be used only in the final mopping up stage if required. This doctrine is a major factor prompting Beijing's recent proposal to Delhi on border management. Realities of capability and terrain would place India at a severe disadvantage in case this is accepted.

Interesting is that during the period of the intrusion, senior Chinese diplomats based in Delhi dissimulated to some foreign diplomats that approval for the action near Daulet Beg Oldi in Aksai Chin by People's Liberation Army (PLA) troops had been granted by China's top leadership in Beijing. The decision regarding timing of the action was left to the local Commander. This green light was given prior to the leadership's final approval for Chinese Premier Li Keqiang's 4-nation tour abroad. Significantly, they added that it was Beijing's assessment that India would not cancel the Chinese Premier's visit to avoid damaging relations with China.

These Chinese officials also predictably dismissed description of the PLA's action as "intrusion" or "incursion" and asserted that the troops were within Chinese territory. They added that Chinese Premier Li Keqiang would reiterate China's position in his meetings and not yield ground. At least one Beijing-based foreign diplomat was told by an official in Beijing that there had been no intrusion and that the Chinese troops were inside their territory. Intrusions by Chinese forces are not a new feature. They have been occurring with increasing frequency since 2008 along the length of the entire 4,057 kilometres border and in each case are intended to test Indian responses and preparedness in addition to keeping India under pressure. China has, in the past few years, actually sought to increase pressure by expanding its territorial claims.

Examples of the above include the expansion a couple of years ago of the policy of issuing 'stapled visas' — followed in the case of residents of Arunachal Pradesh — to residents of Jammu and Kashmir thereby depicting the entire state as 'disputed'; reinforcing their territorial claims by successfully preventing international financial organisations from extending developmental aid to projects in Arunachal Pradesh; officially declaring a considerably reduced length of the border with India; re-opening the settled issue of Sikkim; and forcibly seizing, or nibbling away, the traditional grazing grounds of Indian herders in areas of Ladakh and Barahoti-Kaurik in Himachal Pradesh and denying them their use.

China has also been steadfast in its opposition to the India-US Civil Nuclear Agreement when it coordinated actions with Pakistan and warned the US that it would assist Pakistan in like manner. When Beijing did make good on its threat and agreed to add to Pakistan's nuclear reactors there was no reaction from the US.

The intrusion of this April and the subsequent ones are assessed to have had at least two major objectives. A major military objective concerns border defences. The PLA has completed construction and refurbishing of border defences along the entire length of its border, including construction of adequate accommodation for additional troops that may be inducted, ammunition and storage dumps and secure fibre-optic communications linking each border and command post. This is a major factor prompting Beijing's proposal to Delhi on border management made late last year at the time of then Chinese Defence Minister Liang Guanglie's visit. The proposal, in effect, suggests that neither side should patrol the LAC up to a specified depth on their own side or augment existing border defences or build new ones. Realities of capability and terrain will place India at a severe disadvantage in case this is accepted.

The larger objective was to warn India against expressing support to Japan during the scheduled visit of the Indian Prime Minister to Tokyo. The CCP leadership at the highest levels continues to be very suspicious of US designs and apprehensive that the US is intent on putting together an anti-China coalition aimed at 'containing' China. It sees this US-sponsored coalition as comprising Japan, Australia, India, Vietnam and the Philippines. Pertinent was the observation in the context of the South China Sea dispute as far back as July 2010, in a Hong Kong-based pro-Beijing newspaper, that: "the issue of China's territorial disputes with neighbouring countries will ignite the flames of war sooner or later. If a country must be chosen for sacrifice, India will be the first choice...India's long term occupation of southern Tibet is indeed worrying...If armed force is used to resolve border disputes, China must pick a country to target first, and it will definitely pick a big country, which means choosing between Japan and India...". Other references stated that China's relationship with India and Japan had limits imposed by history. The references unmistakably draw India into the ongoing confrontation in the South China Sea.

China's deliberate and prolonged military intrusion near Daulet Beg Oldi in the Depsang Plains in Aksai Chin did cast a perceptible shadow over Chinese Premier Li Keqiang's first visit (May 19-22, 2013) to India as Premier, despite the overt display of courtesy. It embarrassed the government and starkly outlined China's policy towards India and has had an impact on India's relations with China. Indications were immediately available in the 35-paragraph joint statement issued at the end of Li Keqiang's stay in Delhi on May 20, which revealed little forward movement on substantive issues.

There was negligible progress on economic issues which mainly comprised Li Keqiang's agenda. India raised the issue of the border incursion and incident in Ladakh, making it clear that such incidents could not form the basis for trying to build friendship. Beijing would have also noted India's departure from usual practice and refusal to reiterate that Tibet was an integral part of China in the joint statement. The last occasion such a stand was taken was during Chinese Premier Wen Jiabao's visit in 2010. China also did not have its way in the references to the Asia-Pacific and South China Sea in the joint statement and received, instead, an ambiguous comment on international cooperation and freedom of navigation. Importantly, it ensured a more fruitful and positive visit by the Indian Prime Minister to Japan.

China's deliberate and prolonged military intrusion could well have been prompted by the rapid progress by India in the past few years in building forward border defences and intended to slow it down. Instead, China's action cast a perceptible shadow over Chinese Premier Li Keqiang's visit and brought China's policy towards India into bold relief. This and similar intrusions along with Beijing's other actions that impinge on India's sovereignty, make it imperative that there should be no easing in the construction and augmentation of India's defence build-up. Construction of border defences, including of border roads and ALGs in forward areas, should continue apace as also the acquisition of modern military hardware, equipment and effective strategic deterrent capability.

CONCLUSIONS

Any evaluation of India-China relations over the longer term needs to factor in Beijing's views. In this context worth recall is Mao Zedong's telegram to Stalin around 1950 when he conveyed Zhou Enlai's very unfavourable opinion of Indian Prime Minister Jawaharlal Nehru and observed implicitly that this would guide the tenor of the relationship for a very long time.

In recent conversations with foreign diplomats and analysts their Chinese interlocutors list three main issues as responsible for the strain in India-China bilateral relations. These are: the Dalai Lama's presence and activities in India; the unresolved border dispute; and India's international aspirations. Viewed along with the statements publicized by China's official media that 'limits have been imposed by history on the extent to which China can develop relations with India', it is clear that tensions will exist in India-China relations for the forseeable future.

Two other major issues, in addition to the unresolved border or shrinking export markets sought by both countries and competition for scarce energy, natural and mineral resources, have a real potential to erupt into serious confrontation between India and China. Water is the most important. Much of north China faces severe water shortages and as this gets increasingly accentuated it will probably accelerate Beijing's ambitious plans to divert waters from the south to the north. Diversion of the Brahmaputra River to the north at a currently estimated cost of US$ 66 billion is a major part of these plans. Chinese engineers are going ahead with the construction of a series of dams along the course of the Tsangpo (Brahmaputra) and the project is presently under the direct supervision of Chinese Premier Li Keqiang.

Thus far Beijing has exhibited marked insensitivity to either India's concerns or those of other lower riparian nations as in the case of the Mekong River. The deleterious effects of diversion of the river will be heightened by the quickening retreat of the snow-fed glaciers in Tibet caused by warming and the rise in temperatures because of the new dams and development projects undertaken by China in Tibet. Together this will affect the 40 crore people residing in the Indus, Ganges and Brahmaputra river basins.

The other area of likely competition is food. At a time when global population is rising, both China and India, according to analysts, will move from their current self-sufficiency in food to become food grain deficient nations between 2045-50. Global warming has an adverse impact on food production which registers a decline for each degree Celsius rise in temperature above the norm. During the growing season, farmers can expect a 10 per cent decline in wheat, rice, and corn yields. Four countries namely the US, Canada, Russia and Australia will remain the main sources of food grain supply for the world. China and India will compete for the limited supplies and grain prices will soar. China will also try and enhance food production by using the large tracts of arable land in its water starved north, thus accelerating implementation of the south-north water diversion project.

If India is to persuade China to cooperate, it must accelerate efforts to, at least in asymmetric terms, acquire the ability to impose costs and deter China. The growing restiveness among China's minorities and increasing societal discontent, are vulnerabilities that will potentially constrain Chinese leaders in the not too distant future.

Meanwhile, India should build the capacity to frustrate Chinese ambitions and ensure a calibrated enhancement of resistance to Chinese pressure. For this India will need to recast its strategic foreign policy objectives to enable it to urgently find and attract good sources of large scale capital investments, advanced technology and hi-tech joint manufacturing ventures. India will simultaneously have to upgrade the skills of its workers; favour establishment and growth of a manufacturing industry especially in the hi-precision and advanced technology sectors; and, put in place the back-bone for a secure, modern telecommunication and global navigation systems. China's entry into the Indian economy will require to be controlled and India's indigenous critical industries safeguarded.

BORDER DEFENCE

With unity of command having been compromised, our border defence has been woefully inadequate. Reportedly, some 400 sq.km. of territory has been lost in Ladakh over and above the Aksai Chin. Responsibility of border defence is divided between the Ministry of Defence (MoD) and the Ministry of Home Affairs (MHA), with the Central Armed Police Force (CAPF) deployed in sensitive areas without placing them under the command of the Army. This facilitates smuggling of narcotics, fake currency, goods and even illegal immigration with indicators that some of these activities are institutionalised. Chinese goods are being smuggled into India also through the India-Myanmar border. Not only is the ULFA hierarchy located at Ruli on Chinese soil but China is also pumping in weapons and communication equipment through the Kachen rebels in Myanmar to the PLA in Manipur and onwards to the Maoists in India. Deployment of the Indo-Tibetan Border Police (ITBP) in sensitive areas of Ladakh without placing them under the command of the local Army formation is a folly that has been capitalised by the Chinese who have made deep intrusions without qualms.

Border Infrastructure

Despite the Border Road Organisation (BRO) being directly under the MoD, border infrastructure has been severely neglected. In February 2014, NDTV reported that out of the 26 border roads sanctioned in recent years, only one has been completed. China, on the other hand, has developed excellent infrastructure that permits quick mobilisation and vehicular movement. This includes construction of a ten-kilometre road in Pangong Tso area. In 1970, at Nathu La, the Chinese could ply a five-tonne vehicle vis-à-vis a one-tonne vehicle of ours. Today, over four decades later, the status remains the same. Lack of development of border infrastructure on the Indian side is the main reason why the Chinese could intrude freely and our security forces are unable to react effectively and in time.

Intrusions

Similar is the story with our poor response to Chinese intrusions. Criticism and shame had to be faced in wake of deep intrusions such as the one at Raki Nala in Depsang during April 2013 when even the MEA admitted that the intrusion was five to seven kilometres beyond the line of Chinese claim. It is a wonder how a 1.2 million strong army could permit 20 Chinese soldiers to sit 19 km deep inside Indian territory for 25 days. Ironically, Chinese troops had reportedly intruded into the same area on earlier occasions albeit this time the media got wise.

Such intrusions have been occurring at many places along the LAC despite the 1993 India-China Agreement on Maintenance of Peace and Tranquility Along the Line of Actual Control in the India-China Border Areas, Agreement on Confidence Building Measures in the Military Field Along the Line of Actual Control in the India-China Border Areas, 2005 Protocol on Modalities for the Implementation of Confidence Building Measures in the Military Field Along the Line of Actual Control in India-China Border Areas, and the 2012 Agreement on Establishment of a Working Mechanism for Consultation and Coordination on India-China Border Affairs. Now, even after signing the China-drafted Border Defence Cooperation Agreement (BDCA) in 2013, the

Chinese intruded into Depsang and Chumar on December 19 and 20. Then, in the first week of January 2014, intrusions took place in the Takdip area where incursions had been spotted in December 2013 as well. Now, China has proposed a Code of Conduct to be introduced along the border. Obviously China wants to play at signing agreement after agreement without changing her aggressive stance. Chinese occupation of the Depsang plains in conjunction with her presence in Gilgit-Baltisatn would threaten India's deployments in Siachen and sever the approach to Karakoram Pass. India has also lost substantial territory in the India-China-Myanmar tri-juncture area; China is also staking claims to the Tatu Bowl, loss of which would enable the Chinese to easily roll down the plains. POK is already a strategic objective of China that provides her access to the warm waters of the Indian Ocean, to Afghanistan and the CARs.

Prospects of Conflict

Much has been talked of about the possibilities of future Sino-Indian conflict from the Chinese gameplan to place India in the vice-like grip of a python to gobble up what the former wants, active defence to short swift offensive even using tactical nuclear weapons to force India to surrender territory, acupuncture warfare and the like. China's 'active defence' doctrine is a transformation from Mao's large scale people's land-centric war to high intensity, short duration localised war under informationised conditions. In this context, the chances of conflict remain.

Despite the progressing economic relations, China's focus in the Indian Ocean Region (IOR) remains a cause for concern. China has been making every possible effort to find her way to the Indian Ocean through Myanmar and Pakistan along the land routes. Her strategic interests clash with the US and her allies in the Asia-Pacific; China desperately needs another oceanic front and a strong India is hardly to her liking. Besides, for Chinese Carrier Battle Groups (CBGs) to operate effectively in the IOR, China needs land-based air and missile support. This is one reason why China is deploying missiles in the Gilgit-Baltistan area of Pakistan and developing or planning to develop ports in countries such as Myanmar, Thailand, Bangladesh, Pakistan, Maldives, Sri Lanka and Seychelles in the IOR. Not only has China colluded with Pakistan on a conventional and nuclear front but also in the sub-conventional field by waging a collusive asymmetric war against India including through irregular forces and proxies. With China's aggression on the rise, the collusive China-Pakistan threat has multiplied exponentially with both countries following a policy of ambiguity, denial and deceit, what with repeated Chinese intrusions, claim to entire Arunachal Pradesh as "South Tibet" and now demanding a Code of Conduct for forward troops, indicating the futility of the recently signed Border Defence Cooperation Agreement (BDCA).

On balance, the prospects of Sino-Indian conflict remain. What appears certain is that China's aggressive stance and the initiation of conflict will be aimed at undermining India's status as a regional power. If India fails to respond adequately, she will be projected as a 'Soft State' susceptible to coercion. Simultaneously, the Chinese aim would be to keep India embroiled in fighting internal/regional conflicts. In doing so, China maybe expected to virtually abrogate any agreements such as Border Peace and Tranquility Agreement and Confidence Building Measures and BDCA leading to incremental build up and conflict.

Should the US get more involved in the Middle East or in new and likely hotspots such as Ukraine and the CAR, Chinese adventurism in India can be expected to escalate. The US may have announced the Asia Pivot in recent months but China already has in place a globally deployable military force with nuclear/non-nuclear allies/proxies in North Korea, Pakistan, Iran, Libya, Sudan and Syria as a countermeasure even if one discounts China not resorting to the employment of large scale nuclear force.

6

Disputed Territory between China and India

ARUNACHAL PRADESH

Both countries retain their strong claims to the disputed territory, however, fueled by national pride and national security interests. China's "Go West" development policy and July 2006 opening of the Qinghai-Tibet railway have received mixed responses from Indian policymakers; those who favour expanded trade and people-to-people contacts have regarded the developments as positive, but some within the national security establishment have raised concerns that they will allow Beijing to extend its military power projection into Tibet and beyond into South and Central Asia.

Three rivers running through India—the Indus/Sengge Chu, Sutlej/Langqen Tsangbo, and Brahmaputra/Sang Po—originate in Tibet, a fact that has spurred Indian fears that China could use upstream dams and barrages to control the flow of water into India.

India, for instance, has blamed a series of flash floods along the Sutlej River in its state of Himachal Pradesh to China's reluctance to supply hydrological data to India in a timely manner or allow Indian scientists to conduct surveys of melting glaciers on Chinese soil. The absence of any water-sharing treaty between both states as a result of the disputed status of their borders contributes to these water tensions.

Regional Affairs

Regionally, Sino-Indian cooperation has been the exception rather than the rule. Beijing watches closely New Delhi's increasing engagement of East Asia, including relations with nations that have historically had particularly difficult interactions with Beijing, such as Japan, Vietnam, and Indonesia. At the same time, Indian strategists have expressed quiet concern over China's growing influence in the subcontinent, not only its maintenance of a robust political and military relationship with India's rival Pakistan, but also its extensive political, economic, and security relationship with Burma, growing relations with Bangladesh and Nepal, and increasing naval presence in the Indian Ocean. China's admission as an observer to the South Asian Association for Regional Cooperation (SAARC) in November 2005, with New Delhi's reluctant acquiescence, has been cited as further evidence of China's emergence as a player in India's backyard and the desire of India's smaller neighbours to draw China into the region as leverage.

India has viewed growing Chinese influence in Burma, which is strategically located along the eastern end of the Indian Ocean, with great suspicion. In the mid-1990s, India had been one of the most vocal and ardent supporters of Burma's democracy movement, led by Aung San Suu Kyi. However, the combination of India's aim to forge closer links with Southeast Asia as part of its "Look East" policy, its need for Burma's support in countering insurgent groups in India's northeast, its desire for access to Burma's natural resources, including energy (often in competition with China), and its alarm over China's growing military ties to the Burmese junta led India to adopt a more conciliatory engagement policy with the Burmese leadership by the late 1990s to counterbalance Chinese influence. Most notably, the presence of Chinese radar technicians in Burma's Coco Islands, which border India's Andaman and Nicobar

Islands, has fueled concern in New Delhi (and Washington) that Beijing is monitoring naval activities in the region.

Furthermore, China's efforts to develop alternative overland routes to transport oil and gas imports through port facilities at Gwadar in Pakistan's Baluchistan province, which is at the entrance of the Strait of Hormuz, as well as through Bangladesh and Burma, have been viewed by India as part of a Chinese "string of pearls" strategy of economic and military encroachment into South and Central Asia. Indeed, China's senior-most leaders have openly declared Beijing's attention to placing priority focus on naval modernization, including greater power-projection capability. Indian policymakers fear that China's moves could undermine India's regional preeminence.

At the same time, India's joint naval exercises in the South China Sea—with Vietnam in 2000 and Singapore in 2005, joint patrols with Indonesia in the Andaman Sea beginning in 2002, and exercises off the Japanese coast with the U.S. and Japanese navies in April 2007, have sparked concerns in Beijing. The Indian Navy, the world's fifth-largest, has also set up a Far Eastern Naval Command (FENC) off Port Blair on the Andaman Islands to increase its presence in the Strait of Malacca and potentially monitor Chinese naval activities in the region. Such mutual suspicions could result in China-Indian naval rivalry in and around the Indian Ocean over time. For their part, East Asian nations have increasingly looked to India as a potential partner in economic and regional security affairs, with some, such as Japan, apparently considering India as a potential element in a hedging strategy against China. South Asian countries have likewise begun to play the "China card" in order to counterbalance India's influence in their affairs or gain policy concessions from India and the West.

For instance, as relations have soured between New Delhi and Dhaka in recent years, China has become Bangladesh's largest supplier of military hardware and has replaced India as Bangladesh's overall largest trading partner. In Nepal, China defied international suspension of military aid and other support to King Gyanendra's regime after the monarch suspended democracy from February 2005 to April 2006, calling the situation Nepal's "internal affair." King Gyanendra reciprocated by shutting down the office of the Dalai Lama's representative in Nepal as well as the Tibetan Refugee Welfare Office.

In the end, China and India each recognize the inexorable reality of the other's increasing involvement in its neighborhood.

In response, the two nations are quietly balancing the prospects for cooperation and competition in their relationship without letting any residual suspicions, tensions, or mistrust derail their mutual desire to test the possibilities of political rapprochement, economic engagement, and confidence-building in the years ahead.

People-to-People Contacts

People-to-people contacts between China and India have increased in recent years, albeit from a low base. Regular direct flights were established in 2002, when China's tourism authorities designated India as an "authorized destination." More than 5,000 Indian students are currently studying in Chinese universities. In India, enthusiasm for Chinese popular culture is growing, and Indians tend to respect, if not envy, China's economic and political rise, which they would like to have their own country mirror. India dubbed 2006 the "Year of Friendship with China," and China declared 2007 the "Year of China-India Friendship through Tourism."

Nonetheless, while official interaction is on the rise and public opinion polls suggest that a majority of citizens and businessmen in both states hold favorable views of each other overall, popular interaction remains relatively minimal, restricted by the language barrier, cultural differences, and other factors. Chinese and Indian observers alike will note that the Chinese have more natural affinity with countries in East and Southeast Asia, while Indians are more comfortable in dealing with English-speaking countries and other South Asian states.

Mutual mistrust persists, particularly within India's older generation, whose memories of the Sino-Indian border conflict lead it to view China with suspicion. India's media and educational system have also nurtured the notion that China "stabbed India in the back" in 1962 and is sitting on Indian land. India's visa policy, in fact, is very restrictive and suspicious of the entry of citizens from China (among other nations, including the United States), further constraining popular contact.

For their part, the Chinese have expressed difficulty in understanding India's cultural and interpersonal style and have tended to be snobbish in their view of India and its state of development relative to China. While Indians may be focusing increasingly on China, relatively little Chinese popular attention is directed toward India. Few Chinese students study in India, for instance. Even at the official level, a similar lack of symmetry in the level of attention paid by China and India toward each other appears to prevail.

THE INDIAN NAVY'S CHANGING FORCE POSTURE

Despite traditionally being perceived as adhering to pacifist principles, India has undergone a dramatic shift in its stance on self-defence. Correspondingly, its military doctrine has also undergone significant change. India has fought four wars since independence in 1947 and as its economic and political power grew, its military situated these experiences into its doctrine. For instance, in 2004 the Indian Army began to roll out its "Cold Start" doctrine. This grew from political and military frustration with India's inability to deter or respond to incursions such as those which led to the 1999 Kargil incident and terror attacks like that which occurred in December 2001 on the Indian Parliament. Indian leaders wanted the military to rapidly mass its troops on the Pakistani border, threatening overwhelming conventional attack on that country if it did not cease its support for attacks on India by groups based there. The military, however, was incapable of such rapid deployment. Cold Start emphasised forward deployment, decisive offensive strikes launched from a standing start with a minimal mobilisation period, and pre-emptive strikes on enemy forces. It had three main objectives: 1) to avoid triggering an enemy's nuclear response; 2) to move so fast that Indian political leaders could not halt or terminate it; and 3) to secure India's objectives before the international community could intervene.

Concomitant with this change in the Army, the Indian Navy's *Maritime Doctrine* released in 2004 also shows a major change in its outlook. Echoing the statement of Indian strategist, K. M. Panikkar, the document implies that the Indian Ocean is, in a singular way, Indian. Thus, Admiral Mehta, the Navy Chief of Staff remarked, "The Indian Ocean is named after us. ... If required in this IOR, we will undertake humanitarian missions, stop piracy and gun running, and all those kinds of things in asymmetric warfare." Left unstated was the role of aircraft carriers and nuclear submarines in achieving these goals.

The Maritime Doctrine is designed to maintain Indian autonomy and security against any regional threat. China is defined as a competitor, but as Sakhuja writes, the Navy is required to "provide maritime security in all directions – the classical doctrine of 'tous azimuths'", a clear reference to the US, which, unlike China, is accepted as a comparatively benign presence in the region. However, the Indian Navy does not see itself as primarily a defensive force. Specific undertakings of the Indian Navy include exercising sea control in designated areas of the Arabian Sea and the Bay of Bengal and at the entry/exit points of the IOR; in case of war to carry the conflict to the enemy's territory, to strangulate his trade/oil arteries, to destroy his war waging potential and naval assets and to ensure a decisive victory; to provide power projection force; and to work in conjunction with the two other services to preserve, protect and promote India's national interests.

The 2004 Maritime Doctrine notes China's naval-building and pays close attention to its submarine acquisition. It also considers the PLANs power projection abilities using aircraft carriers. The 2007 Maritime Military Strategy emphasises three new issues: power projection including the development of expeditionary forces, securing Indian interests in a wide arc including the Indian Ocean, the Middle East / Persian Gulf and East Asia, and strike capabilities in littoral warfare to support land forces in war. It also lays emphasis on developing a sea-based nuclear deterrent.

The Indian Navy is primarily focused on a possible confrontation with Pakistan. This was made evident during the Kargil Crisis in 1999 when it was used to blockade the Pakistani Navy, preventing vital supplies from reaching Karachi. Margolis believes it could be used in any future confrontation to overwhelm Pakistan's aging navy. He further notes, "Pakistan could not fight for longer than a week in the face of an Indian naval blockade – unless the U.S. Navy challenged it." This assertion appears to have its roots embedded in history; many Indians believe that a US carrier group in the Arabian Sea to support Pakistan during the

1971 Indo-Pakistani War forced New Delhi to halt its plan to crush West Pakistan. This has led for calls ever since for a naval build-up to counter any future US intervention.

Pakistan aside, Indian strategists are today very aware of China's increasing activity in the IOR. China's development of a blue-water navy has caused a great deal of concern in New Delhi. Margolis again observes,

In coming decades, geopolitical tensions between the two uneasy neighbours and rivals easily could intensify as they vie for hegemony over South and Central Asia, Indonesia and even the South China Sea, political influence, oil, resources and markets.

In India's perception the IOR holds the same interests for itself as Central America and the Caribbean do for the USA. As such, China's activity in the region causes India concern. This concern partly stems from the Communist takeover of China in 1949, when the Indian politician, Vallabhbhai Patel, enunciated his concerns with China in the IOR. This concern grew after India's defeat by China in the Sino-Indian War of 1962. Since relations were normalised in 1988, this view has been modified to an extent but fundamentally remains the same. As Indian strategists see it, any Chinese activity in the IOR diminishes India's security. These concerns have been compounded over the last twenty years with five categories of Chinese activity in the IOR. These are (1) covert and overt assistance to Pakistan's nuclear and missile development, assistance to its military development and enhancement of its military-industrial capability, (2) initiation of defence relations and intelligence-sharing with Nepal, (3) military and deep economic co-operation with Myanmar including development of its transport and maritime infrastructure, (4) growing PLAN activity in the IOR including ship visits and the creation of electronic monitoring facilities, and (5) the cultivation of ties with Bangladesh and the normalisation of ties with Bhutan.

It is likely with this in mind that the Indian strategist, C. Raja Mohan, conceives of an Indian maritime strategy premised on three concentric geographic circles. The innermost circle contains India and its immediate neighbourhood, a view consistent with that of the Indian Navy's doctrinal statement, *Freedom to Use the*

Seas: India's Maritime Military Strategy. The neighbourhood also contains Bangladesh, the Maldives, Myanmar (Burma), Pakistan and Sri Lanka. Mohan alleges that India's goals in this region are to ensure its primacy and to retain the capacity to veto actions seen as infringing on India's interests. Needless to add, this is not stated in the Navy's public document. Primacy implies India's capacity to impose its will and influence the states of the region, including militarily. While the naval document is less aggressively stated than Mohan's article, the section titled "Strategy for Employment in Conflict" envisions the conduct of sea-control and sea-denial operations in wartime in India's vicinity, including at the entry/ exit points of the IOR. This appears to be aimed at China, it being a prerequisite to denying China's ships access to and from the Straits of Malacca. Such an action would shut off China's and other "hostile extra-regional powers with inimical intentions" access to India's immediate maritime neighbourhood.

Mohan's middle circle encompasses the rest of continental Asia, including China. Again the naval document does not treat this area in as starkly plain terms as Mohan does. It instead emphasises its role in naval diplomacy and maritime cooperation so as to prevent "incursions by powers inimical to India's national interests by actively engaging countries in the IO littoral and rendering speedy and quality assistance in fields of interest to them." This clearly alludes to China's increasing activity in East Africa, Persian Gulf, and the rest of the IO littoral. It was likely this thinking which saw the Indian Navy dispatch four warships on a two-month journey along the coast of East Africa to engage in "naval diplomacy" and offer a counter to China's influence and activity there.

Mohan's third circle, consisting of the rest of the world, envisions India as a world-power in maintaining international peace and security. Prime Minister Singh endorses this view in his introduction to the doctrinal statement, stating "current power projections indicate that India will be among the foremost centres of power". He also notes that military capacity will be a critical component of India's increased power. Given India's interests in acquiring aircraft carriers and its doctrinal statements regarding sea-control and sea-denial, it appears that India, like China, seeks regional hegemony. It could be argued, however, that the acquisition of aircraft carriers is purely deterrent in nature and cannot be construed as being offensive in this case. To place the matter beyond reasonable doubt, therefore, it will be instructive to examine India's activities in this regard to determine if its intentions are defensive or offensive in nature.

India has emphasised its requirement for a dominant position in the north-eastern IOR and more so towards the western approach to the Malacca Strait since the 1990s. This, according to Brewster, is part of a broader strategy of projecting power into the main entry and exit choke points of the Indian Ocean. These points include the Mozambique Channel, the Strait of Hormuz and Bab el-Mandeb around the Arabian Peninsula and the Malacca, Sunda and Lombok Straits in the east. These choke points, recognised as being vital to the control of the Indian Ocean, apparently guide India's regional maritime strategy. This may also be gauged from the Indian Navy's doctrinal document, *Freedom to Use the Seas*:

> By virtue of geography, we are ... in a position to greatly influence the movement/security of shipping along the [sea lines of communication] in the [IOR] provided we have the maritime power to do so. Control of the choke points could be useful as a bargaining chip in the international power game, where the currency of military power remains a stark reality.

Over the last two decades, India has constructed a new base for the Eastern Fleet south of Vishakhapatnam and sophisticated naval and air force facilities in the Andaman and Nicobar Islands. These islands constitute a seven-hundred mile chain at the western approaches to the Malacca Strait, and provide the perfect basis for projecting power into the Malacca Strait. The Eastern Fleet apart, the aircraft stationed at this base have an operational radius sufficient to project power into the Malacca Strait and into extensive areas of the South China Sea. Additionally, Indian Special Forces conduct regular training operations from the Andaman Islands base. The islands have received much attention in Beijing, with one Chinese analyst describing them as a "metal chain" which could lock the western end of the Malacca Strait. The militarisation of India's east coast and the approaches to the Strait of Malacca are a clearer indication of India's intention to be the predominant power in the Bay of Bengal and the Andaman Sea.

India's Maritime Engagements

The potential power of the Indian Navy is not the only aspect of sea power which is growing increasingly visible. It has also undertaken several functions to prove itself a useful partner to South-east Asian states in dealing with instances of disaster relief, piracy, smuggling, refugee issues and terrorism. Since 1995 it has also conducted the biennial MILAN (Togetherness) naval meetings at Port Blair in the Andaman Islands. In 2012 the five-day meet had fourteen participating countries including Australia, Bangladesh, Brunei, Indonesia, Malaysia, the Maldives, Mauritius, Myanmar, Sri Lanka, Thailand, Singapore and the Seychelles. This meeting is not a naval exercise, *per se*, but an opportunity to increase military-to-military relationships with the navies of regional states. Neither China nor the USA is invited, presumably to assert India's regional primacy. Since 2008 the Indian Navy has also sponsored the biennial Indian Ocean Naval Symposium (IONS) at which the heads of the navies of littoral states may express issues of concern. The Indian Navy has emphasised its strengths in maritime policing and counter-terrorism since 2001. It has interdicted supply routes in the Andaman Sea by Indonesian and Thai separatists, drug smugglers and refugees. It made a strong contribution to disaster relief in the wake of the December 2004 tsunami. Furthermore, joint India-Indonesia naval patrols off Sumatra and similar patrols (and training) between the Indian and Thai navies (as "funnel states" to the Malacca Strait) arguably demonstrate a general acceptance of India's role in Southeast Asia.

In 2002, India began to provide naval escorts to high-value commercial shipping through the Malacca Strait, after being requested to do so by the USA, as part of Operation *Enduring Freedom*. Singapore, which hosted Indian naval ships, supported this request. India consulted with Malaysia, Indonesia, the Philippines and Australia. Indonesia, however, rebuffed India's request for a more permanent role in the Strait, stating that the strait's safety lay with Indonesia, Malaysia and Singapore. This led

Chief of Naval Staff, Admiral Arun Prakash, to deny India had any intention of patrolling the Strait. Malaysia has since accepted an Indian presence in the Strait and was ready to accept a strategic relationship with India, provided India's security ties with Thailand are scaled down. Malaysia, however, agreed to an Indian aircraft presence in the "Eye in the Sky" project to provide air surveillance over the Strait. In return India has offered to provide training and support for Malaysia's MiG-29 aircraft and Scorpène submarines. This has led some analysts to believe Malaysia is now more amenable to an Indian presence in the Malacca Strait.

It would be naïve, however, to believe India's interests remain confined to the Indian Ocean. It also has strategic ambitions in the West Pacific region including the South China Sea. Daly, for instance, claims India is a factor in the balance of power as far as the Taiwan Strait. Likewise, Mohan believes that India will become an East Asian power because of its military and economic growth. More importantly, the Indian Navy, agreeing with Mohan's three circles, itself identifies the South China Sea as an area of interest after the Indian Ocean. This, though, is not new. In 1945 K.M. Panikkar recognised Vietnam's importance in controlling China's entry into the Indian Ocean and the South China Sea, probably underscoring India's attempts to secure a deep security relationship with Vietnam.

Since 2000, India has extended its reach into the South China Sea through regular naval visits, unilateral exercises, and bilateral exercises with regional states. In 2000, Indian warships visited ports in Vietnam, China, the Philippines, South Korea and Japan. In 2004 the Indian Navy deployed ships to the South China Sea on "presence cum surveillance" missions on three occasions, and in 2005 the aircraft carrier, *INS Vikraant*, and a task force visited Singapore, Malaysia and Indonesia. Perhaps as a sign of China's concern, in September 2011 an Indian Navy ship, sailing from Nha Trang port in Vietnam to Haiphong, was challenged by an unidentified radio call in which the announcer identified himself as the "Chinese Navy". Early this century India sought long-term access to Vietnam's Cam Ranh Bay air force and naval bases. The then Indian Defence Minister, George Fernandes, suggested Indian ships could patrol local sea lanes and contain local conflicts. More recently, it was reported that India would train around five hundred Vietnamese submariners as part of the expansion of their military ties.

In October 2013 the Indian External Affairs Minister, Salman Khurshid, visited the Philippines to upgrade Indo-Filipino ties to a comprehensive partnership prior to Indian President Pranab Mukherjee's visit in 2014. Khurshid and his Filipino counterpart, Albert del Rosario, agreed to expand defence cooperation between the two countries; reportedly Manila may purchase two frigates from India. Saliently, their joint statement calls the South China Sea the West Philippines Sea, by which name Manila refers to the disputed sea, contradicting India's policy until now of calling the area the South China Sea so as to avoid upsetting Beijing.

India has had a fairly stable relationship with Japan, despite Japanese debate on whether India is Asian. During the Cold War, Japan saw India's non-alignment as untenable and its economic policies unattractive to investment. This has changed. Prime Minister Shinzo Abe's statement in 2007 that the India-Japan relationship "will be the most important bilateral relationship [for Japan] in the world" gives some indication of the extent of the change in perception. Despite a brief interregnum after India's 1998 nuclear tests, Japan enhanced its ties with India because Japanese officials realised they could be left isolated due to India's growing regional relationships. A strategic relationship was proclaimed in 2005 and was extended to include the formalisation of defence ties, especially maritime co-operation, in 2006. Foreign Minister Taro Aso proposed closer ties with India, Australia and the North Atlantic Treaty Organisation (NATO) states on the basis of shared values.

This translated into the proposal by Prime Minister Shinzo Abe for a "Quadrilateral" initiative in which Australia, India, Japan and the USA would hold a security dialogue. April 2007 saw the first trilateral naval exercise between India, Japan and the USA in the Western Pacific, and in August of that year, the annual India-USA Malabar exercise was transformed into large-scale exercises involving Australian, Indian, Japanese, Singaporean and US ships.

Speaking in the Indian parliament in the same year, Prime Minister Abe referred to an India-Japan relationship which could "evolve into an immense network spanning the entirety of the Pacific Ocean, incorporating the US and Australia". In 2008 the Indian and Japanese Prime Ministers formalised an India-Japan Joint Security Declaration, "an essential pillar for the future architecture of the region".

Both Prime Ministers emphasised that these treaties did not seek to isolate or contain China. Nevertheless, in the aftermath of the April – May 2013 border stand-off between China and India, and barely a week after Chinese Premier Li Keqiang visited New Delhi on his first international trip as Premier to calm the situation, Prime Minister Singh visited Japan. During this visit the stand-off was discussed by the USA, India, and Japan at their fourth trilateral dialogue, emphasising "greater security cooperation at a time all three countries are facing what they perceive to be an increasingly belligerent China". Though not a formal ally, India has reportedly "signed up for the dialogue that goes beyond security cooperation."

The relationship has grown since late 2013. Prime Minister Abe was Chief Guest at India's Republic Day parade on 26 January 2014. Japan has, furthermore, been asked to invest in areas that are strictly off-limits to China, notably in the north-eastern states. This is all the more telling since China, which claims the Indian state of Arunachal Pradesh as South Tibet, worked to deny an Asia Development Bank loan in 2007 to Arunachal Pradesh, claiming it was 'disputed territory'. Furthermore, Japanese organisations have been invited to construct a new port in Chennai. The two countries will hold their third 2 + 2 Dialogue and fourth Defence Policy Dialogue later this year (2014). Also, in the immediate wake of the Imperial visit to India by the Emperor and Empress of Japan, Japanese Defence Minister Itsonuri Onodera spent four days in India, which culminated in a joint statement with his Indian counterpart, A. K. Antony, that Japan and India will "further consolidate and strengthen their strategic and global partnership in the defence arena through measures ranging from regular joint combat exercises and military exchanges to cooperation in anti-piracy, maritime security and counter-terrorism."

As with Japan, India seeks to develop closer strategic ties with South Korea and Taiwan. Though not as sophisticated and formalised as Indo-Japanese ties, these are being gradually developed. South Korea sees India as a potential market for its defence and civil nuclear technology and, importantly, as an important security provider in the Indian Ocean. India has sought to deepen its defence ties with South Korea by purchasing eight mine-sweeper ships from Seoul. Similarly, India and Taiwan have increased their non-official and non-public security contacts in recent years. The non-official description of these contacts enables India to maintain its claim of non-alignment and non-interference in the affairs of other states. It also enables India to maintain its façade of adhering to a one-China policy.

It comes as little surprise, then, that some Chinese observers see these actions as a subtle Indian attempt to encircle China by itself and together with the United States and Japan.

To conclude, this study notes that while India does not display Mahanian principles as overtly as China does, these are observable upon closer examination. For instance, while India's modernisation of its navy may be seen as a step towards ensuring its own maritime security, the use of the navy to project force into and beyond the Strait of Malacca is not defensive. This is the action of a state which seeks a degree of power beyond that which is purely defensive in nature. Similarly, while India's ship-building capacity may not match China's, its actions – political and maritime – in the Western Pacific demonstrate a trend towards countering China's actions in the Indian Ocean. The principles behind these actions may be discerned by an examination of the Indian Navy's doctrinal statements published over the years. Furthermore, formalised agreements between India, Japan and the USA, naval exercises between these three states, and further nascent relationships between India and South Korea and India and Taiwan, point to at least indirect or consequential Indian efforts to encircle China, just as it believes China is attempting to do to it. These actions are not defensive in any way. These are Mahanian principles cloaked in politics and security ties. They are, furthermore, the actions of a state which, recognising its maritime shortcomings, seeks to alleviate those through shared security relationships against a perceived common (potential) enemy.

By seeking to project its power through the Strait of Malacca and into the Western Pacific, India demonstrates its adherence to Mahan's principles of sea power and Mearsheimer's tenets of offensive realism. Its actions are aggressive in nature, which lead this examination to conclude that it seeks to counter China's emphasis on regional hegemony by firstly securing its own region, the Indian Ocean, and then projecting its power while taking into account its presently limited ability to do so, into the Western Pacific region. To this extent, at least, India also seeks a degree of regional hegemony and, again like China, seeks to use its modernised and upgraded navy to achieve this end.

BEIJING'S RESPONSE TO INDIA-PAKISTAN TENSIONS AFTER 9/11

Since the late 1990s, China had become increasingly concerned over the gradual shift in the regional balance of power in South Asia, driven by the steady rise of India coupled with the growing US-India entente and the talk of "India as a counterweight to China" in Washington's policy circles, and by Pakistan's gradual descent into the ranks of failed states. Since the end of the Cold War, a politically dysfunctional and economically bankrupt Pakistan's flirtation with Islamic extremism and terrorism, coupled with its nuclear and missile programs, had alienated Washington.

However, the 11 September 2001 attacks changed all that. Pakistan saw an opportunity to revive its past close relations with the United States, shed its near pariah status, and enhance its economic and strategic position vis-à-vis India by instantaneously becoming a "frontline state" in the international coalition fighting global terrorism. In return, Washington lifted sanctions and agreed to provide Pakistan with billions of dollars in aid and debt rescheduling. From Washington's perspective, courting Musharraf made geopolitical sense because the Pakistani military not only knew a great deal about the Taliban, Osama bin Laden, and al Qaeda, but also because any US military operation against Afghanistan could not be successful without the bases, logistics, personnel, and airspace in neighbouring Pakistan. In Beijing, as a result, there were great expectations of a sharp downturn in US-India relations, because in many ways what happens on the Indian subcontinent is unavoidably a zero-sum game and Pakistan's new relationship with the United States did affect India negatively.

However, tensions between South Asia's nuclear-armed rivals rose sharply after the terrorist attacks at the Kashmir Assembly in October 2001 and the Indian Parliament on 13 December 2001. The attack on the Indian Parliament triggered a major deployment of Indian troops along the border with Pakistan, with Islamabad responding in kind. New Delhi warned of retaliatory, punitive military strikes against terrorist camps inside Pakistani-controlled Kashmir. Although the Chinese Foreign Ministry spokesperson condemned these attacks, Chinese leaders and South Asia watchers were much more circumspect and ambivalent while lauding Pakistan's contribution to the war against terrorism. A South Asia specialist from China's National Defence University, Wang Baofu, noted with satisfaction that under the new circumstances, "The United States, considering its own security interests, readjusted its policies toward South Asian countries and started paying more attention to the important role of Pakistan in the anti-terrorism war, therefore arousing the vigilance and jealousy of India." Wang criticized India for "defin[ing] resistance activities in Kashmir as terrorism by taking advantage of the US anti-terrorism war in Afghanistan, thus putting more pressure on Pakistan through the United States," and praised General Musharraf for his "clear-cut attitude toward fighting against international terrorism)." Such a stance was not unexpected. For almost a decade, China had rejected India's proposal to issue a joint declaration against terrorism lest it be interpreted as a condemnation of Pakistan. Pakistan President General Musharraf made three trips to Beijing in less than a year (in December 2001, January 2002, and August 2002) for urgent security consultations with President Jiang Zemin and Premier Zhu Rongji and reportedly obtained "firm assurances of support in the event of a war" with India. At the time of heightened tensions in mid-January 2002, General Zhang Wannian, Vice-Chairman of China's Central Military Commission, met with

General Muhammad Aziz Khan, Chairman of Pakistan's Joint Chiefs of the Staff Committee, and was quoted as telling Khan: "For many years the militaries of our two nations have maintained exchanges and cooperation at the highest and all levels and in every field. This fully embodies the all-weather friendship our nations maintain." Zhang's reference to "cooperation... inevery field" (meaning the nuclear and missile fields) was a thinly veiled warning to India to back off. Later, Beijing matched words with deeds by rushing two dozen F-7 jet fighters, nuclear and missile components, and other weapon systems to shore up Pakistani defenses in the tense border face-off.Asecret "futuristic arms development cooperation" agreement was signed during General Musharraf's five-day visit to China in December 2001 to construct, among other weapons, an all-solid-fuel Shaheen III missile with a range of 3,500-4,000 kilometres to target all major Indian cities. The People's Liberation Army (PLA) troops from the Military Regions of Chengdu and Lanzhou and their respective subdivisions, the Xizang (Tibet) and Wulumuqi (Urumqi), along China's southern borders, were also put on alert in January to test their war preparedness should the conflict in the Indian subcontinent spill over onto Chinese soil.

The Chinese leaders had reportedly conveyed the following message to Musharraf: "China hopes Pakistan will not initiate any assault. Pakistan should not get involved in wars and instead focus on economic construction. However, if a war does break out between India and Pakistan, Beijing will firmly stand on the side of Islamabad." Soon thereafter, President Musharraf in a televised speech on 12 January 2002 announced a crackdown on extremist organizations waging jihad from Pakistani territory, and as a result, Indo Pakistani tensions somewhat subsided. The Chinese media claimed some credit for "mediating" between the two sub-continental rivals despite the Indian government's aversion to the dreaded "m" word: "Mediated by the United States, China, Britain, and Russia, leaders of India and Pakistan recently expressed their desire to try to control the tense situation." 12 Interestingly, this stance contradicted then Indian Foreign Minister Jaswant Singh's statement during Premier Zhu's visit to New Delhi in January 2002 that "China has neither any intention, nor shall it play any mediatory role between India and Pakistan." Not only that, the Chinese Foreign Minister also succeeded in persuading his Russian counterpart to issue a "Joint Declaration on the India-Pakistan Situation," signaling to New Delhi that, for the first time, Beijing and Moscow had a unified stand on the dispute. In concrete policy terms, it meant that New Delhi could no longer count on the Russian veto in the UN Security Council in the event of a war.

Then came the 14 May 2002 terrorist attack on a military base in Jammu that killed 34 people, mostly women and children, once again escalating tensions along the border where more than one million troops backed by heavy armor, warplanes, and missiles were deployed. There was renewed tough talk of war, including nuclear war, on both sides of the border. Beijing called for restraint from both India and Pakistan and emphasized the need for peaceful dialogue to settle outstanding disputes. Chinese Defence Minister Chi Haotian also urged both countries to desist from a military conflict and not to threaten each other with nuclear weapons. Describing the US diplomatic moves (i.e., the dispatch of Deputy Secretary of State Richard Armitage and Defence Secretary Donald Rumsfeld in early June 2002) to defuse the India-Pakistan military stand-off as "too little too late," the state-run media accused Washington of showing "no genuine desire to resolve the Kashmir issue." It noted that Washington had clearly not taken the tensions very seriously when it went on with a ten-day joint military manoeuvre with India on 16-26 May 2002, thereby implying that the Indo-US joint military exercise had emboldened India to up the ante against Pakistan. On 15 May, a Chinese official accompanying Foreign Minister Tang Jiaxuan during his visit to Islamabad told Pakistani journalists that China would back Pakistan in any conflict with India. Concerned over the "one-sided nature of public appeals" from Washington, Moscow, London, Paris, and Tokyo to General Musharraf to halt "cross-border terrorism" into Indian Kashmir, Chinese Foreign Minister Tang Jiaxuan told US Secretary of State Colin Powell on 27 May 2002 that "the international community should encourage direct dialogue between India and Pakistan in a more balanced and fair manner, which is the most effective way to lead South Asia towards peace and stability." Apparently, the growing threat of nuclear war and the prospect of Pakistani nuclear weapons falling into the hands of Islamic terrorists have made Washington lean heavily on Islamabad. In contrast, Beijing repeatedly asked New Delhi to do more to end the military stand-off while publicly calling for restraint by both sides and claiming to be even-handed. China continued to covertly side with its long-term ally, however, and is providing military wherewithal to Pakistan.

Meanwhile, in yet another television address on 27 May, Musharraf pledged that all militant infiltration across the Line of Control (LoC) would end, and he announced the banning of Lashkar-e-Toiba, the Jaish-e-Mohammad, and the Harkat-ul-Mujahideen—the three "*jihadi*" outfits at the forefront of terrorist activity in Indian Kashmir. From New Delhi's perspective, India's military deployment had succeeded in bringing the international focus on Pakistan as the home of pan-Islamic *jihadis* after the war in Afghanistan.

At the Conference on Interaction and Confidence Building Measures in Asia held in Kazakhstan in early June 2002, Chinese President Jiang Zemin pressed Indian Prime Minister Vajpayee to enter into direct talks with Pakistani President Musharraf to prevent the Kashmir conflict from exploding into a full-scale war. But the Indian government was so irked over Musharraf's playing of "the China card" that Vajpayee refused to budge. Later, in an interview with *The Washington Post*, the Indian Prime Minister complained that he saw "no basic change in China's policy. China continues to help Pakistan acquire weapons and equipment." In an article titled "Beijing as Guarantor of Pakistan's Security," a Russian weekly, *Nezavisimoye Voyennoye Obozreniye* (Independent Military Review), had reported that new security commitments have indeed been made to Pakistan by China since 9/11.18 New Delhi expressed its displeasure with Beijing by postponing scheduled visits by Indian Army Chief Padmanabhan and Prime Minister Vajpayee to China in October and November 2002.

The Nuclear Connection

There were other grounds for the cooling of relations between Beijing and New Delhi. In his testimony before the US Senate governmental affairs subcommittee in early June 2002, the Assistant Secretary of State for Nonproliferation, John S. Wolf, revealed that "China recently provided Islamabad with missile-related technologies, which include dual-use missile-related items, raw materials, and other accessories essential for missile manufacturing." In a sense, China's nuclear and missile assistance to a volatile Pakistan over the last two decades has now created the risk of a conventional conflict swiftly escalating into nuclear war. Beijing has not only provided Islamabad with nuclear bombs, uranium, and plants (all three Pakistani nuclear plants—Kahuta, Khushab, and Chasma— have been built with Chinese assistance) but also their delivery systems: readyto-launch M-9 (Ghaznavi/ Hatf), M-11 (Shaheen), and a number of Dong Feng 21 (Ghauri) ballistic missiles. This cooperation has continued despite Beijing's growing concerns over the "Talibanization" of the Pakistani state and society. When Islamabad carried out a series of missile tests amidst heightened tensions apparently to warn New Delhi to back off, the Indian government drew the international community's attention to the Pakistani missiles' China connection. "We are not impressed by these missile antics, particularly when all that is demonstrated is borrowed or imported ability.... The technology used in the missiles is not their own but clandestinely acquired from other countries," said a spokesperson of the Indian External Affairs Ministry.

Pakistan's test of its nuclear-capable, medium-range, Shaheen ballistic missile in early October 2002, just days before the parliamentary elections, once again provoked India to level accusations of missile technology proliferation by China. India's outspoken Defence Minister, George Fernandes, long a critic of China, said that Pakistan's military had always depended on support from China ever since it was carved out as a homeland for South Asia's Muslims in 1947 following decolonization of British India.

"Everyone knows what Pakistan will be without China. Its ego is boosted purely by the support it gets from China," Fernandes said at a party convention in Mumbai. Earlier, when India weaponized its nuclear capability through a series of tests in May

1998, Fernandes had described "China [as] the mother of Pakistan's nuclear bomb" and claimed that India's aim was to counter China's capability rather than Pakistan's, drawing protests from Beijing. When Pakistan came in the firing line following revelations in the US media about the missiles-for-nukes barter deal with North Korea, New Delhi argued that blame should also be put on China for making Pakistan a nuclear weapons state.

For New Delhi, Beijing's military alliance with Islamabad remains a sore point because the Sino-Pakistani nuclear nexus has introduced a new element of uncertainty and complexity in sub-continental strategic equations. While the attention of world leaders and the media has been focused on the nightmarish scenario of a nuclear Armageddon in South Asia and large-scale mutual assured destruction leading to the deaths of 12 to 30 million people, strategic circles in Islamabad and New Delhi have been discussing the pros and cons of a short, limited nuclear war in Kashmir. Media reports based on intelligence leaks have revealed the forward deployment by the Pakistani military of low-yield (five kilotons or less) tactical nuclear weapons (TNWs). Such small battlefield nuclear weapons have a one-mile destruction radius and could be used effectively against large troop concentrations and advancing tank formations along the LoC in Kashmir.

The Pakistanis seem to have taken a page out of China's book on tactical nuclear warfighting capability. Just as persistent Sino-Soviet disputes and the Soviet Union's conventional military superiority during the 1970s and 1980s gave China strong incentives to develop and deploy TNWs, the decade-long India-Pakistan border tensions and India's conventional superiority may have added momentum to Islamabad's efforts to deploy TNWs. Most of Pakistan's missiles acquired from China, such as the M-9, are short-range, solid-fueled, mobile, nuclear-capable missiles and can be used in a tactical mode. Asked to comment on reports that Pakistan has acquired TNWs, the Deputy Chief of the Indian Army, Lieutenant General Raj Kadyan, was quoted as saying that the "Indian Army has trained itself to cope with a tactical nuclear strike in the battlefield." Tactical nukes can be launched over an unpopulated area from field artillery guns or aircraft to halt an enemy advance or in an effort to intimidate a numerically stronger enemy. Since the damage is localized or confined to a certain area, the danger of affecting the civilian population is greatly reduced as compared to a strategic nuclear weapon of the Hiroshima kind and therefore need not evoke massive retaliation by enemy forces. The mountainous terrain in Kashmir provides the perfect setting for their use.

In addition to the United States and Russia, only China is believed to have a large stockpile of about 120 TNWs or "baby nukes." Some of these were apparently delivered to Pakistan following the visit of PLA Deputy Chief and military intelligence boss General Xiong Guangkai (arguably China's most important military figure and the man who calls Pakistan "China's Israel") to Islamabad in early March 2002.27 If the reports of China's transfer of TNWs to Pakistan are indeed true, the question then is: Would India, which does not possess TNWs but has strategic nuclear weapons in abundance, keep a nuclear conflict limited or escalate it to the strategic level and respond with massive retaliation? Though New Delhi has long maintained that even a tactical nuclear strike on its forces would be treated as a nuclear first strike, and would invite massive retaliation, some Pakistani generals believe that a tactical strike would circumvent retaliation from India, since such an attack on an advancing tank regiment or infantry battalion (in contrast to a strategic strike killing millions of civilians), would not be provocation enough for all-out retaliation. They contend that the many layers of bureaucracy surrounding India's nuclear capability, the strength of world public opinion, and the fact that strategic command remains in civilian hands places severe doubts on India's willingness and ability to retaliate with a massive nuclear strike against an opponent, particularly in the face of only a limited tactical strike from Pakistan.

Some analysts attribute the recent lessening of tensions to the belated recognition in India's strategic circles that New Delhi cannot afford to dismiss Pakistan's repeated threats of using nuclear weapons as "mere posturing" or "bluffing" on Islamabad's part. They point to the Pakistani military's strong aversion to fighting a 1965-or 1971-type conventional war with India and offer this as the rationale behind Islamabad's decision to pull back from the brink on several occasions in recent history (in 1987, 1990, 1999, and 2002). Others believe that the tendency of Indian strategic planners to discount the threat of nuclear escalation may well be based on some fundamentally erroneous assumptions:

- That the United States cannot allow Pakistan to be the first Islamic country to use nuclear weapons to settle a territorial dispute, as it would mean the end of the global nonproliferation regime and encourage other countries to go nuclear to settle their territorial disputes as well.
- That the presence of US forces in Pakistan will be a constraining factor.
- That the international community (the United States, United Kingdom, China, or the United Nations) will intervene in time to prevent such a catastrophe.
- And that India can count on American and Israeli military support to seize or take out Pakistan's nuclear and missile infrastructure. These assumptions do not seem to be based on cold, clear-headed calculations of the strategic interests and influence of major powers (especially the United States and China) and may well be a sign of wishful thinking on India's part. It is worth noting that new strategic and geopolitical realities emerging in Asia since 9/11 have put a question mark over Beijing's older certainties, assumptions, and beliefs.

China's Concerns

Much to Jiang and his Politburo's chagrin, the US-led war on terrorism has developed in ways that could not have been foreseen, with potentially disastrous consequences for China's core strategic interests. A major unintended (and unsettling, from Beijing's standpoint) consequence has been not only to checkmate and roll back China's recent strategic expansion moves in Central, South, and Southeast Asia, thereby severely constricting the strategic latitude that China has enjoyed since the Cold War, but also to tilt the regional balance of power decisively in Washington's favour within a short period. The supposedly brief Unipolar moment in history seems to have turned into a long-lasting Imperial moment—a Pax Americana *par excellence*. More important, recent developments show how tenuous Chinese power remains when compared to that of the United States.

The fast-changing strategic scene not only undercuts Chinese ambitions to expand Beijing's power and influence in Asia, but also hems in the one country in the world with the most demonstrable capacity to act independently of the United States. Not surprisingly, the beginning of 2002 saw Chinese leaders and generals shedding their earlier inhibitions about publicly expressing concern over the growing "southern discomfort"—that is, ever-expanding US military power and presence in southern Asia after 9/11. China's Chief of the General Staff Fu Quanyou warned the United States against using the war on terrorism to dominate global affairs by saying "counter-terrorism should not be used to practice hegemony." On an official visit in April 2002 in Iran, Jiang Zemin openly repudiated the US stance against the Iranian and Iraqi regimes, saying, "Our opinion [on terrorism] is not the same as the United States." In Germany, he told the *Welt am Sonntag*: "We all want to fight terrorism. But the states involved in the fight against terror each have their own specific viewpoint." China's initial optimism that new Sino-US-Pakistan triangular cooperation in the aftermath of 11 September 2001 would wean Washington away from New Delhi turned out to be wishful thinking as Bush Administration officials went out of their way to assure India that America's intensifying alliance with Pakistan would not come at India's expense. If anything, the current crisis has strengthened the American commitment to building stronger relations, including defence ties, with South Asia's preeminent power. However, China does not want to see India increasing its power, stature, and profile regionally or internationally. Beijing shares Islamabad's deep mistrust of India's strategic ambitions and seeks to prevent India's emergence as a peer competitor and a major strategic rival in Asia. That is why Chinese strategists have long argued that China's pursuit of great power status is a historical right and perfectly legitimate but India's pursuit of great power status is illegitimate, wrong, dangerous, and a sign of hegemonic, imperial behaviour. For its part, New Delhi has long accused Beijing of doing everything it can to undermine India's interests and using its ties with other states to contain India. Beijing is also alarmed over the growing talk in some con-servative policy circles in Washington and New Delhi of India emerging as a counterweight to China on the one hand and the fragile, radical Islamic states of West Asia on the other.

Earlier, when President Bush unveiled his missile defence plan, New Delhi responded far more positively than did most US allies. Some Indian strategic thinkers even see in the emerging US-India quasi-alliance an opportunity for "payback" to China. As G. Parthasarthy, former Indian Ambassador to Pakistan and Burma, put it: "Whether it was the Bangladesh conflict of 1971, or in the Clinton-Jiang Declaration in the aftermath of our nuclear tests, China has never hesitated to use its leverage with the Americans to undermine our security." Growing Chinese strategic pressure on the Malacca Straits has already led to maritime collaboration between India and the United States, with their navies jointly patrolling the straits. More significantly, US-India strategic engagement has scaled new heights with the announcement of a series of measures usually reserved for close US allies and friends: joint military exercises in Alaska that would boost India's high-altitude warfare capabilities in the Himalayan glaciers of northern Kashmir where it faces Pakistan and China; sale of military hardware including radars, aircraft engines, and surveillance equipment to India; joint naval exercises and the training of India's special forces; and intelligence sharing as well as the joint naval patrols in the Straits of Malacca. Washington also reportedly gave the green light for Israel to proceed with selling the Phalcon airborne early warning and control system (AWACS) to India—something that was earlier denied to China for fear of enhancing Beijing's air surveillance and early warning capabilities in the Taiwan Strait.

All of these measures send an implicit signal to China of India's growing military prowess. In a cover story in the authoritative *Beijing Review,* one of China's noted South Asia specialists expressed concern over the US sale of arms to India which "enables it to become the first country to have close military relations with the world's two big powers—the United States and Russia." To make matters worse, in early May 2002 Prime Minister Koizumi of Japan, Beijing's other Asian rival, which sees China representing a clear and future threat to its security, called for a broadening of Japan's security cooperation with India.

Many Chinese strategists believe India is using the war on terrorism as a pretext to militarily subdue Pakistan or to destabilize and dismember the country. Pakistan is the only country that stands up to India and thereby prevents Indian hegemony over the region, thus fulfilling a key objective of China's South Asia policy. 39 As South Asia watcher Ehsan Ahrari points out: "India may end up intensifying its own rivalry with China by remaining steadfast in its insistence that Musharraf kowtow to its demands, especially if China calculates that US-India ties are harming its own regional interests. China, though still concerned about the continued activism of Islamist groups in Pakistan and contiguous areas, is not at all willing to see the regional balance of power significantly tilt in favour of India." Though Beijing welcomes the new US commitment to prop up Beijing's "all-weather friend" after a decade of abandonment and estrangement, most Chinese strategists worry about the destabilizing consequences of a prolonged US military presence in Pakistan and increased influence on the future of Sino-Pakistan ties as well as on Pakistan's domestic stability. The Chinese are also believed to be "highly uncomfortable" with the four US military bases in Pakistan. Of special concern to Beijing is the US presence at Pasni in the Baluchistan region of Pakistan, where China is constructing a deep-water naval port at Gwadar, the inland Makran coastal highway linking it with Karachi, and several oil and gas pipeline projects.

Beijing has long been eyeing its construction of the naval base at Gwadar, at the mouth of the Strait of Hormuz in the Persian Gulf, as a bulwark against the US presence and India's growing naval power. Furthermore, the US military presence in Pakistan could sharpen the divide within the Pakistani military into pro-West and pro-Beijing factions, with China supporting the latter to regain ground lost since 9/11.44 The pro-Beijing lobby within the

Pakistani military is reportedly getting restive and waiting to strike if and when General Musharraf falters. The pro-China faction within the Pakistani military could also join hands with the pro-Islamic fundamentalist faction opposing the US military presence on Pakistan's soil. Alternatively, it could throw its support behind those nationalist elements that find Pakistan's loss of its "strategic depth" in Afghanistan for elusive diplomatic gains very hard to digest. The US arms sales to India and joint US-Indian military exercises may further sour China's and Pakistan's willingness to assist Washington in its war on terrorism.

War Scenarios

It is said that each conflict simply prepares the ground for the next one or every war contains the seeds of another. The AfghanWar of the 1980s against the Soviet occupation culminated in the war on terrorism in 2001. Whether the war on terrorism will lead to another war or a clash of civilizations or a nuclear jihad in South Asia, only time will tell. Pakistan is, in the words of former Italian Foreign Minister Gianni De Michelis, "the fuse of the world." The provinces close to the Afghan border and home to the US military bases are now controlled by Islamic parties that created the Taliban and are openly sympathetic to the aims and ideals of al Qaeda. The rising anti-American sentiment in Pakistan as demonstrated in the recent elections has made the country increasingly unstable. Violence levels in Indian Kashmir also continue to rise. Many observers believe that Washington may have to rethink its strategy vis-à-vis Islamabad if the war on terrorism is to be won decisively. The complete dismantling of the al Qaeda terrorist infrastructure in Pakistan seems unlikely because of the apprehension within the Pakistani military that doing so would devalue Pakistan's importance in the US security strategy and once again make the United States turn its back on the country and make the country vulnerable to Western pressure and sanctions. It would also deprive Pakistan of invaluable Western aid and leverage vis-à-vis Washington and New Delhi.

One Chinese national security analyst argues that "what worries China more is the possibility that it could be drawn into a conflict, not between Pakistan and India per se, but between

Pakistan and the United States, with the latter using India as a surrogate." With the top al Qaeda and Taliban leadership fleeing into Pakistan's Wild West and Pakistani-held Kashmir, Beijing knows full well that Pakistan is no longer the "frontline state" in the war on terrorism that it once was; it is, in fact, the battlefield in the war on terror. Should the India-Pakistani conflict escalate into a nuclear one, neither the geopolitical nor the radioactive fallout will remain limited to South Asia. Indeed, the most worrisome scenario would be one where Pakistan is losing a conventional conflict and uses tactical nuclear weapons in a desperate effort to win or to salvage a face-saving defeat that would allow the regime to survive. (The risk-taking nature of the Pakistani military leadership suggests that such a scenario cannot be completely ruled out.) Should India respond by launching strategic nuclear strikes resulting in the complete destruction of the Pakistani state, China would find it difficult to sit idly by. The next India-Pakistan war also could bring the United States and Pakistan on a collision course, with or without India acting as a US partner. Such a development would obviously present China with difficult choices. Open support for its closest ally would jeopardize China's relations with the United States and India. But nonintervention on Pakistan's behalf could encourage India to solve "the Pakistan problem" once and for all, with or without a nuclear exchange, and thereby tilt the regional balance of power decisively in its favour. As Zhang Xiaodong put it: "There is the real possibility that a new Indian-Pakistani war will take place in the future. This war would be disastrous, as it would change the whole political balance in Central and South Asia," which is currently tilted in China's favour. Unrestrained Indian power could eventually threaten China's security along its soft underbelly—Tibet and Xinjiang.

Should post-Musharraf Pakistan disintegrate or be taken over by Islamic extremists, a new level of instability would rock the region and increase tensions among Pakistan, India, and China. Another dreadful scenario is one in which Chinese-made Pakistani nuclear weapons fall into the hands of the United States, Israel, or even India in the event of a civil war should al Qaeda or the Taliban declare jihad against Pakistan—the weakest ally in the US-led anti-terrorism coalition. 51 India would be tempted to militarily intervene in Pakistan if Islamists gain control over the nuclear weapons of its neighbour, either through a coup or civil war. Such a scenario could reveal information regarding China's own nuclear program and the extent of help provided by Beijing to Islamabad. The scenario of Pakistan in splinters, with one piece becoming a radical Muslim state in possession of nuclear weapons, can no longer be simply rejected as an alarmist fantasy.

Difficult Choices

These scenarios put Beijing on the horns of a dilemma. Some Chinese strategists see in the current South Asian crisis an opportunity to recover lost ground and thwart India's ambitions to challenge China's future economic and military primacy in Asia. Should another war between India and Pakistan break out, New Delhi's high hopes of an India-US alliance to counter China may never materialize, a welcome development from China's perspective. Some hawks in the PLAsee China even benefiting from an India-Pakistani nuclear war. Hideaki Kase, a former special advisor to Japanese Premiers Takeo Fukuda and Yasuhiro Nakasone, believes that "China wants an Indo-Pakistan war, possibly a nuclear conflict, to weaken India." At the time of the 1999 Kargil War, one Chinese military official had reportedly told a Western diplomat that "should India and Pakistan destroy themselves in a nuclear war, there would be peace along China's southwestern frontiers for at least three decades, and Beijing needs 20 to 30 years to consolidate its hold over restive Tibet and Xinjiang provinces." However, this remains a minority viewpoint, as a nuclear war would have worldwide repercussions in terms of global economic depression, humanitarian crises, WMD proliferation, and China's developmental priorities.

Most Chinese analysts and policymakers believe that Beijing should have absolutely minimum involvement in a situation where there can be no clear winners. Some argue that Beijing should seize the opportunity to coordinate its South Asia policy with Washington as it is in the interests of both countries to avert the world's first nuclear exchange and to use India-Pakistan tensions to strengthen Sino-US ties.

While the Pakistanis are confident that if war comes with India, China will throw its weight behind Pakistan, diplomatically as well as militarily, the Indians remain adamant that the Chinese would not do so for fear of India playing "the Taiwan and Tibet cards." Interestingly, on 31 May 2002, the day Pakistan's new UN Ambassador, Munir Akram, issued an explicit nuclear warning to India, a Chinese Foreign Ministry spokesman denied a *Times of India* report that Chinese President Jiang Zemin had assured a US congressional delegation that China would not favour Pakistan in the existing tensions, and claimed that the report was "not based on facts." A Chinese South Asia analyst at Fudan University in Shanghai, Shen Dingli, told *The Wall Street Journal*: "China needs to send a message: For my own security I will intervene." Though Beijing may not overtly intervene in a limited war, China's geopolitical imperative requires it to come to Pakistan's defence if the latter's existence as a nation-state is threatened by India. Clearly, there is a great deal more to the Chinese role in South Asia than meets the eye. In the final analysis, Beijing's response to the next India-Pakistan war will be shaped by its desire to protect Chinese national interests, no matter what the cost.

7

China-India Border Conflict: Recent Perspective

INTRODUCTION

The China-Indian War, also known as the China-Indian Border Conflict, was a war between China and India that took place in 1962. A disputed Himalayan border was the main pretext for war, but other issues played a role. There had been a series of violent border incidents after the 1959 Tibetan uprising, when India had granted asylum to the Dalai Lama. In response to Chinese incursions, India initiated a Forward Policy in which it placed outposts along the border, including several north of the McMahon Line, the eastern portion of a Line of Actual Control proclaimed by Chinese Premier Zhou Enlai in 1959.

The Chinese launched simultaneous offensives in Laddakh and across the McMahon Line on 20 October 1962, coinciding with the Cuban Missile Crisis. Chinese troops advanced over Indian forces in both theatres, capturing Rezang la in Chushul in the western theatre, as well as Tawang in the eastern theatre. The war ended when the Chinese declared a ceasefire on 20 November 1962, and later withdrew from the disputed area. The Sino-Indian War is notable for the harsh conditions under which much of the fighting took place, entailing large-scale combat at altitudes of over 4,250 metres (14,000 feet). This presented enormous logistics problems for both sides. The Sino-Indian War was also noted for the non-deployment of navy or air force by either the Chinese and Indian sides.

Situation

China and India share a long border, sectioned into three stretches by Nepal and Bhutan, which follows the Himalayan mountains between Burma and what was then West Pakistan. A number of disputed regions lie along this border.

At its western end is the Aksai Chin region, an area the size of Switzerland, that sits between the Chinese autonomous region of Xinjiang, and Tibet (which China declared as autonomous regions in 1965). The eastern border, between Burma and Bhutan, comprises the present Indian state of Arunachal Pradesh (formerly the North East Frontier Agency). Both of these regions were overrun by China in the 1962 conflict. Most combat took place at high altitudes. The Aksai Chin region is a vast desert of salt flats around 5,000 metres above sea level, and Arunachal Pradesh is extremely mountainous with a number of peaks exceeding 7000 metres.

According to military doctrine, to be successful an attacker generally requires a 3:1 ratio of numerical superiority over the defender; in mountain warfare this ratio should be considerably higher as the terrain favours defence. China was able to take advantage of this: the Chinese Army had possession of the highest ridges in the regions. The high altitude and freezing conditions also cause logistical and welfare difficulties; in past similar conflicts (such as the Italian Campaign of World War I) more casualties have been caused by the harsh conditions than enemy action. The Sino-Indian War was no different, with many troops on both sides dying in the freezing cold.

Cause of War

The cause of the war was a dispute over the sovereignty of the widely-separated Aksai Chin and Arunachal Pradesh border regions. Aksai Chin, claimed by India to belong to Kashmir and by China to be part of Xinjiang, contains an important road link that connects the Chinese regions of Tibet and Xinjiang. China's construction of this road was one of the triggers of the conflict. Arunachal Pradesh (called South Tibet by China) is also claimed by both nations—although it is roughly the size of Austria, it is sparsely inhabited (by numerous local tribes) due to its mountainous terrain. The Indian state Arunachal Pradesh has a population of over one million as of today.

The Johnson Line

The western portion of the Sino-Indian boundary originates in 1834, with the Sikh Confederation's conquest of Laddakh. In 1842 the Sikh Confederacy, which at the time ruled over much of Northern India (including the frontier regions of Jammu and Kashmir), signed a treaty which guaranteed the integrity of its existing borders with its neighbours. The British defeat of the Sikhs in 1846 resulted in transfer of sovereignty over Laddakh, part of the Jammu and Kashmir region, to the British, and British commissioners contacted Chinese officials to negotiate the border. The boundaries at its two extremities, Pangong Lake and Karakoram Pass, were well-defined, but the Aksai Chin area in between lay undefined. In 1865, British surveyor W H Johnson came to an agreement with the Maharaja of Kashmir, in whose service he was employed, on a proposed "Johnson Line" which placed Aksai Chin in Kashmir. China rejected the arrangement, and the British government also harboured doubts, so decided to take up the issue in an attempt to reach a settlement.

However in 1892, before the issue had been resolved, China erected boundary markers at Karakoram Pass on the ancient caravan route between Xinjiang and Laddakh (which were disputed by the British Indian Government). Throughout most of the 19th century Great Britain and the expanding Russian Empire were jockeying for influence in Central Asia, and Britain decided to hand over Aksai Chin to Chinese administration as a buffer against Russian invasion.

The newly-created border was known as the MacCartney-MacDonald Line, and both British-controlled India and China now began to show Aksai Chin as Chinese. In 1911 the Xinhai Revolution resulted in power shifts in China, and by 1918 (in the wake of the Russian Bolshevik Revolution) the British no longer saw merit in China's continuing possession of the region. On British maps the border was redrawn as the original Johnson Line, but despite this reversion the new border was left unmanned and undemarcated. According to Neville Maxwell, the British had used as many as 11 different boundary lines in the region, as their claims shifted with the political situation.

By the time of Indian independence in 1947, the Johnson Line had become India's official western boundary. On 1 July 1954, Indian Prime Minister Jawaharlal Nehru definitively stated the Indian position. He claimed that Aksai Chin had been part of the Indian Laddakh region for centuries, and that the border (as defined by the Johnson Line) was non-negotiable. According to George N. Patterson, when the Indian government finally produced a report detailing the alleged proof of India's claims to the disputed area, "the quality of the Indian evidence was very poor, including some very dubious sources indeed". During the 1950s, China constructed a road through Aksai Chin, connecting Xinjiang and Tibet, which ran south of the Johnson Line in many places. Aksai Chin was easily accessible to the Chinese, but access from India, which meant negotiating the Karakoram mountains, was more problematic. Consequently India did not even learn of the existence of the road until 1957 — finally confirmed when the road was shown in Chinese maps published the following year.

The McMahon Line

In 1826 India and China gained a common border, including the area of what is now called Myanmar, following British annexations in the Anglo-Burmese Wars. In 1847, Major J. Jenkins, Agent for the North East Frontier, reported that the Tawang was part of Tibet. In 1872, four monastic officials from Tibet arrived in Tawang and supervised a boundary settlement with Major R. Graham, NEFA official, which included the Tawang Tract as part of Tibet. Thus, in the last half of the 19th century, it was clear that the British treated the Tawang Tract as part of Tibet. This boundary was confirmed in a June 1, 1912 note from the British General Staff in India, stating that the "present boundary (demarcated) is south of Tawang, running westwards along the foothills from near Ugalguri to the southern Bhutanese border." A 1908 map of The Province of Eastern Bengal and Assam (32 miles to the inch), prepared for the Foreign Department of the Government of India, showed the international boundary from Bhutan continuing to the Baroi River, following the Himalayas foothill alignment. In 1913, representatives of Great Britain, China and Tibet attended a conference in Simla regarding the borders between Tibet, China and British India. Whilst all three representatives initialed the agreement, Beijing later objected to the proposed boundary between the regions of *Outer Tibet* and *Inner Tibet* and did not ratify it. The details of the Indo-Tibetan boundary was not revealed to China at the time. The foreign secretary of the British Indian government, Henry McMahon, who drew up the proposal, decided to bypass the Chinese (although instructed not to by his superiors) and settle the border bilaterally by negotiating directly with Tibet. According to later Indian claims, this border was intended to run through the highest ridges of the Himalayas, as the areas south of the Himalayas were traditionally Indian. However, the McMahon Line lay south of the boundary India claims. India's government held the view that the Himalayas were the ancient boundaries of the Indian subcontinent, and thus should be the modern boundaries of India while it is the position of the Chinese government that the disputed area in the Himalayas have been geographically and culturally part of Tibet since ancient times. Months after the Simla agreement, China set up boundary markers south of the McMahon Line. T O'Callaghan, an official in the Eastern Sector of the North East Frontier, relocated all these markers to a location slightly south of the McMahon Line, and then visited Rima to confirm with Tibetan officials that there was no Chinese influence in the area. The British-run Government of India initially rejected the Simla Agreement as incompatible with the Anglo-Russian Convention of 1907, which stipulated that neither party was to negotiate with Tibet "except through the intermediary of the Chinese government".

The British and Russians cancelled the 1907 agreement by joint consent in 1921. It was not until the late 1930s that the British started to use the McMahon Line on official maps of the region. China took the position that the Tibetan government should not have been allowed to make a such a treaty, rejecting Tibet's claims of independent rule. For its part, Tibet did not object to any section of the McMahon Line excepting the demarcation of the trading town of Tawang, which the Line placed under British-Indian jurisdiction. However, up until World War II, Tibetan officials were allowed to administer Tawang with complete authority. Due to the increased threat of Japanese and Chinese expansion during this period, British Indian troops secured the town as part of the defence of India's eastern border. In the 1950s India began actively patrolling the region. It found that, at multiple locations, the highest ridges actually fell north of the McMahon Line.

Given India's historic position that the original intent of the Line was to separate the two nations by the highest mountains in the world, in these locations India extended its forward posts northward to the ridges, regarding this move as compliant with the original border proposal, although the Simla Convention did not explicitly state this intention. On Oct. 29, 2008, David Miliband, the British foreign secretary, announced that the previous British actions including the Simla Accord (1913) and thus the McMahon Line had been an anachronism and a colonial legacy. He apologized to China for not having renounced those actions earlier. He was supported by Chris Patten, the last British governor of Hong Kong, who called the British position embodied in the Simla Accord (1913) a "quaint eccentricity".

DALAI LAMA VISIT IGNITES SINO-INDIAN BORDER DISPUTE

In early November, the Dalai Lama is going to visit the majestic Tawang Monastery, perched atop a ridge in the Indian province of Arunachal Pradesh. Surrounded by thick clouds and perennial mist, the monastery sometimes seems almost to be suspended from heaven. It is also at the very centre of thousands of square kilometres of terrain claimed by both China and India, although India currently possesses it. It now risks becoming a proxy battleground on which both India and China seek to proclaim their sovereignty. The religious leader's visit can be seen as a card played by both India and the Tibetan exile community to keep pressure on China.

Home to one of the most sacred Buddhist monasteries, Tawang is the birthplace of the sixth Dalai Lama, Tsayang Gyatso, in the 17th century. The current Dalai Lama passed through this region when he fled into exile in 1959. Chhime Chhoekyapa, the exiled Tibetan spiritual leader's aide, told the media that the Dalai Lama is "going there for teaching. This has nothing to do with politics, there is nothing political about it." In Chinese eyes, however, and perhaps Indian eyes as well, everything the Dalai Lama does has something to do with politics. And this is a region that Beijing calls "Southern Tibet."

When asked about the Dalai Lama's upcoming visit, Beijing officials have fumed. "China expresses strong concern about this information," said Jiang Yu, the spokeswoman for China's Foreign Ministry. "The visit further reveals the Dalai clique's anti-China and separatist essence. China's stance on the so-called Arunachal Pradesh is consistent. We firmly oppose Dalai visiting the so-called Arunachal Pradesh." Tension has slowly been ratcheting up between the two Asian giants, with media commentators fanning the flames. "Is China itching to wage war on India?" asked Professor Brahma Chellaney in the September issue of the Far Eastern Economic Review. Reports have appeared in Chinese state media alleging that India was moving troops and fighter aircraft to the northeast, specifically into Sikkim and Arunachal Pradesh.

India, however, is acutely aware of its shortcomings in the territory it controls. The Chinese, with their extensive roads and railways, can actually come up to the Line of Actual Control, take a stroll and walk back. Two years ago, Chinese soldiers demolished a Buddhist statue that Indians had erected at Bumla, the main border pass above Tawang, according to a member of the Indian Parliament, Nabam Rebia. It takes several days for India's troops to get to the border. But slowly India is finding its voice as it struggles to speed up its own preparedness.

China claims around 90,000 square kilometres of territory, roughly the size of Arunachal Pradesh, regarding the area as "disputed." China lays claim to Tawang on behalf of the Tibetans. But in the exile community in Dharamsala, where the Dalai Lama and thousands of Tibetan refugees live, the community is not impressed. They do not claim Tawang as Tibetan, let alone Chinese territory. The Dalai Lama's travel plans were announced a week after his recent visit to Taiwan to visit victims of tropical storm Morakot. China denounced the Taiwan trip, although its complaints were remarkably muted. The visit to Arunachal Pradesh has now drawn further attention to China's treatment of Tibetan activists and the Dalai Lama's calls for cultural and religious freedom and autonomy.

Tawang became part of modern India when Tibetan leaders signed a treaty with British officials in 1914 that established the McMahon Line between Tibet and British-run India. Tawang fell south of the line. The treaty, the Simla Convention, is not recognized by China. "We recognize it because we agreed to it," said Samdhong Rinpoche, prime minister of the Tibetan government-in-exile. "If China agreed to it now, it would be a recognition of the power of the Tibetan government at that time."

Tawang's native population is almost entirely Buddhist. Its origin is obscure. It was a part of the kingdom of Tibet in medieval times although local tribal rulers have governed it from time to time. The British declared the area off-limits in 1873. India's independence from Britain severed it from Tibet. In 1962 Chinese troops conquered Tawang during the invasion of Tibet and for six months it was controlled by the Chinese. After their retreat, Tawang again came under Indian control.

India denied the Dalai Lama permission to visit Tawang the last time he requested to do so. This time it is playing the Dalai Lama card to the full. Officials in India's Ministry of External Affairs insist that "things are changing" and that India is getting more assertive. On Sept. 16, India's foreign minister, S.M. Krishna, rejected China's opposition to the visit.

In an interview on IBN7, the sister channel of India's CNN-IBN, Krishna said China's objections had no merit. While the government has not explicitly said the visit will be permitted, Krishna said: "Arunachal Pradesh is a part of India and the Dalai Lama is free to go anywhere in India. The only question is that he is not expected to comment on political developments." Analysts say the Tibetan leader's visit will reassert Arunachal's status as an Indian territory. "The timing of his trip [to Arunachal Pradesh] is significant. It comes while the debate over his visit to Taiwan is still hot," said Bhaskar Roy, a New Delhi-based China analyst. "Tibetans are as good at playing these games as the Chinese. They know such a visit will keep up the pressure on China."

In Dharamsala, Samdhong Rinpoche, Tibet's prime minister in exile, called Beijing's objections to the visit "absurd," adding that "Arunachal Pradesh and the Tawang region are an integral part of India. If the Dalai Lama, who has stayed in India for the last 50 years, is visiting any part of the country why does this bother China? If the Dalai Lama goes to Chinese territories it can raise objections but in this case has no business to interfere." The Arunachal Pradesh government is urging New Delhi to ignore the Chinese opposition. "Chinese claims over Arunachal Pradesh are simply baseless and not correct. Arunachal Pradesh is an integral part of India and would continue to be so," said Chief Minister Dorjee Khandu. "They [the Chinese] are opposed to everything that His Holiness does," said a spokesman for the Dalai Lama's private office in Dharamsala.

Tawang's strategic importance cannot be ruled out. The place provides the shortest route from Tibet into India. The Dalai Lama himself took this route to escape into India in 1959. Indian defence officials have already raised alarms declaring China and not Pakistan to be India's biggest threat. They believe that control over Sikkim and Arunachal Pradesh would enable Chinese forces to overrun the entire northeast border region. Chinese troops repeatedly have attempted to gain control of Sikkim's evocatively named Finger Area, a tiny but key strategic location where Beijing does not dispute the frontier.

In June this year, General J J Singh, governor of Arunachal Pradesh and former chief of army staff, announced the deployment of two army divisions of around 25,000 to 30,000 soldiers each along the Arunachal Pradesh border with China. The strength of India's Sukhoi fighter jet fleet in the Northeast is being increased. It remains to be seen if the Dalai Lama's visit will be the trigger that causes them to be used.

GLOBAL VARIABLES LEADING TO CONFLICT: INDIA

The three main variables motivating Indian behaviour towards conflict with China on the systemic level are: Indian national interests, the system's influence on Indian behaviour through structural constraints, and the relationship between Indian perception of the international structure and reality. To begin a systemic explanation of India's actions we must first identify its national interests, as it is what drives Indian action throughout the international structure. According to neorealist thought the primary end of all states is security. This being the case, not only is security the primary Indian national interest, but any issue relating to national security becomes a primary interest.

Official borders, and their enforcement is a primary interest of each state for obvious reasons. However, in the Indian case this issue takes on greater importance than it otherwise would for other nations. This can be attributed to two factors. The most prevalent factor was that India bordered a nation which not only questioned the legitimacy of the established border, but also violated it. The second factor is the modern international system is formed by the interaction of nation-states, which as defined by the Westphalian system are the only entities capable of legitimately exercising sovereignty.

A key component of nation-state status under the Westphalian system is the existence of demarcated and respected borders. These borders represent the extent of national sovereignty and define where each nation's authority begins and ends. The questioning of India's established border by China undermines both Indian sovereignty and security. Security is undermined first by the direct military and administrative challenge to Indian territory, and second by delegitimizing India's position as a nation-state. If India can neither defend nor define borders respected by other nations, other states may begin to question their position as a nation-state in the system and then their sovereignty. This was a chief concern for India as they regarded the Chinese threat to their border as one compromising their "independence, self-determination, and position as a great power in Asia".

Another issue of national security relating to Indian interests was defense of the McMahon Line. Two key issues aided the creation of security dilemma situation along the McMahon Line. The first was the discovery of the Chinese road connecting Xinjiang and Tibet through the Aksai-Chin area in 1957. The second was the imposition of martial law on Tibet in 1959 by the PLA. China argued that completion of the road southeast of the McMahon Line in Aksai-Chin was simply the reestablishment of a historical commerce route from Xinjiang to Tibet. This road not only represented a blatant Chinese violation of India's McMahon Line border, but it also caused armed tension in the region. Shortly after the roads discovery, PLA frontier guards began patrolling the Aksai-Chin region, but never more than 20km away from the road's location. The issue of the road in Aksai-Chin and the PLA's role in Tibet in 1959 became linked since the majority of Chinese troops entered Tibet via the road from Xinjiang. The surge of PLA soldiers into Tibet aroused suspicions of a forcible border assertion by the PRC. These tensions were heightened by the flight of the Dalai Lama from Lhasa, and the closure of Tibet to commercial and cultural access by India, guaranteed in the 1951 treaty. Defensive maneuvers or not, these activities created a security dilemma along the border as India felt that Tibet was "essential for mastery over South Asia, and the most economical method for guaranteeing India's security". Forced to account for increasing Chinese military power near or past the McMahon Line, India responded by deploying their military in forward positions along the border with China as early as 1960. Accounting for India's national interest with force posturing, they attempted to both affirm the legitimacy of the McMahon Line as a border and to account for the security dilemma created by the hardening of PLA positions in Tibet and Aksai-Chin.

The second way a systemic level analysis accounts for the 1962 war is the manner in which India's policy was defined by the structure of the international system. In looking at the geostrategic positioning of India within the system, it is immediately apparent that they attempted to remain neutral or unaligned in the bipolar structure. India remained a powerful enough state to deter the third world adventurism of either bloc within its territory, but weak enough to be challenged by hostile neighbours. An excellent example of this was the persistent threat of Pakistan on their Northwestern border. The poor relationship of Pakistan and India is rooted in domestic level variables, but a systemic level cause was a disputed claim over the sovereignty of Kashmir. Both sides claim the right to sovereignty over Kashmir, and this has resulted in a heavily armed border. Additionally, appearances of a Sino-Pakistani agreement to hem in India developed with Chinese diplomatic overtures to Pakistan for peaceful border settlement beginning in 1961. This forced India to take a hard-line stance in their border dispute with China out of fear that concessions would show weakness, and endanger their control of Kashmir in a Domino-Theory type logic train.

Another structural element of the international system was the existence of nuclear weapons. Nuclear weapons invalidated traditional calculations of deterrence, and thus the great powers were those whom possessed them. In India's regional calculations neither themselves, nor did any other surrounding nations possess nuclear weapons keeping intact the use of deterrence as a method of securing or defending interests. This being the case, the option of engaging in armed conflict with surrounding nations remained possible as long as in India's force calculations they were superior to their target. A prime example of India's employment of force to further interests was their invasion of Portuguese controlled Goa on December 17, 1961. This use of force to assert sovereignty over perceived territory is an excellent precedent for the October 9, 1962 offensive against the PLA in Ladakh. Force against PLA incursions remained off the table as long as the Indian military believed their strategic position and capabilities to be inferior to the Chinese. Returning from a 1960 diplomatic tour of the U.S., Nehru expressed the idea that due to Soviet and Western military aid, "the military balance had changed in favour of India". Thus in the absence of nuclear weapons, India disregarded the Chinese effort at deterrence and employed the use of force to settle their territorial claims.

Finally, it is necessary to point out how India's perception of the international system, which differed from reality, influenced their decision to employ force against the PRC. India perceived the international system as open to change from a bipolar to a multi-polar structure. This was based in their success of remaining unaligned to either bloc, while still receiving significant military and economic aid from both camps. Given India's strategic geographic position in the system, both superpowers sought to gain the allegiance of India to their side through the use of aid. Understanding this, India played both sides against each other, and assumed that either superpower would be willing to intervene on their behalf in the event of Sino-Indian hostilities for pragmatic and alliance building reasons. Thus, India viewed its use of force as a no lose situation. Either the force would succeed in attaining their national interests, or if Indian power proved to be inadequate, "the superpowers would intervene to prevent any large-scale war between India and China;" therefore, bailing out India from a potential catastrophe. This perception of Indian value to either superpower and the general misperception of the international system would cost them.

Ultimately the Indians failed to acknowledge that while the interests of the superpowers may partially depend on India's well being, the system is ultimately in anarchy and each nation is responsible for assuring their own security. Additionally, India had miscalculated both the willingness and ability of the superpowers to intervene on their behalf. In reality the Soviet Union could not exercise restraint on Chinese actions or compel them to drop the border issue. The Sino-Soviet split had not yet occurred, but its origin is in the late 1950's, and the attempt to restrain PRC actions towards India was a contributing factor in the decline of Soviet influence. Indian belief in U.S. intervention was based on a miscalculation of U.S. interests in Asia, as well as willingness to repel PRC advance based on the Domino Theory. While the U.S. intervened in Korea, Taiwan, and Indochina, India overlooked the essential element common to each. This element was the inability of each nation to resist communist advance on its own. In this case, the projected image of Indian power was a liability. The realities of the international system and its anarchic nature would ensure that their decision to use force would not be consequence free. Now the Chinese causes for war will be evaluated at the systemic level.

BORDER CONFLICT MORPHS INTO BROADER DIPLOMATIC JUJITSU

New Delhi has experienced diplomatic stare-downs over other issues such as Beijing's decision to issue stapled visas to Indians residing in certain parts of Jammu and Kashmir, Assam, and Arunachal Pradesh; states that border the contested Sino-Indian boundary. Stapled visas are not stamped on passport pages, but they are separately stapled on to the Indian passports. The message that the Chinese government is trying to deliver is that such visas are only issued to residents of Indian regions that are claimed by Beijing. In September 2010, General B.S. Jaswal of the Indian Army, who was based in the Indian-administered state of Jammu and Kashmir, was denied a Chinese visa. General Jaswal was to join an Indian army delegation visiting China as a part of bilateral dialogue. In response, India cancelled the military exchange with China that year.

Again in January 2012, India cancelled a 30-member military delegation's visit to China because a visa was denied to a delegation member belonging to the Indian Air Officer from Arunachal Pradesh, a state that borders Tibet. In November 2012, Indian along with several Asian countries reacted alarmingly to the new design of the Chinese passport watermarks that show nearly "90 percent of the South China Sea, Arunachal Pradesh and Aksai Chin, as well as famous tourist attractions in Taiwan" as part of People's Republic of China." India countered sharply by "stamping a round seal of the map of India" depicting the "correct external boundaries on visas stamped on such passports." Beijing's move was intended to be a clever ploy to force rest of the Asian states with which China has outstanding territorial disputes to acknowledge Beijing's territorial claim by stamping such passports with entry and exit stamps. In a testy exchange in New Delhi, the Former Chinese Ambassador to India, Zhang Yan, told an Indian journalist to "shut-up" at an official reception, when he was repeatedly questioned about Indian territory being depicted as belonging to China in a map enclosed in a folder that was included along with a bilateral business agreement.

India is not the only state that has felt the power of coercive and clever strategies employed by Beijing; several other Asian states, particularly Japan, Vietnam, and the Philippines, have been impacted by these aggressive strategies. Japan in its Annual Defense White Paper has pointed out that the People's Republic of China is using aggressive strategies to change the status-quo of the territorial disputes with Japan and other countries in the Asian sphere. Japan has identified specific activities such as intrusion into Japanese territorial waters, violation of its airspace, and instances when the Chinese Navy has locked its weapons radar on Japanese vessels in East China Sea. Even the United States has not been immune to Chinese military assertiveness. In April 2001, Chinese Air Force forced an American EP-3 spy plane to force land in the island of Hainan. The plane and the crew were only released after sustained negotiations between both countries. In 2009, Chinese warships forced an Indian submarine that was trailing them in the Gulf of Aden to surface. In August 2011 an Indian Warship *INS Airavat* that was completing a scheduled port call in Vietnam was challenged by the Chinese Navy and asked to identify itself when it was about 45 nautical miles from the Vietnamese coast.

New Delhi and Beijing's competition is not limited to the border issue; both have also become serious competitors in the economic and diplomatic arena. Beijing has engaged in diplomatic moves to keep India out of ASEAN, the UN Security Council, Shanghai Cooperation Group (SCO), Nuclear Suppliers Group (NSG), and sought to deny bank loans from Asian Development Bank (ADB) that was targeted for projects in Arunachal Pradesh that the Chinese claim as their own.

EVENTS LEADING UP TO WAR

Tibet and the Border Dispute

The 1940s saw huge change in South Asia with the Partition of India in 1947 (resulting in the establishment of the two new states of India and Pakistan), and the establishment of the People's Republic of China (PRC) in 1949. One of the most basic policies for the new Indian government was that of maintaining cordial relations with China, reviving its ancient friendly ties. India was among the first nations to grant diplomatic recognition to the newly created PRC.

At the time, Chinese officials issued no condemnation of Nehru's claims or made any opposition to Nehru's open declarations of control over Aksai Chin. In 1956, Chinese PremierZhou Enlai stated that he had no claims over Indian controlled territory. He later argued that Aksai Chin was already under Chinese jurisdiction and that the McCartney MacDonald Line was the line China could accept. Zhou later argued that as the boundary was undemarcated and had never been defined by treaty between any Chinese or Indian government, the Indian government could not unilaterally define Aksai Chin's borders.

In 1950, the Chinese People's Liberation Army annexed Tibet and later the Chinese extended their influence by building a road in 1956–67 and placing border posts in Aksai Chin. India found out after the road was completed, protested against these moves and decided to look for a diplomatic solution to ensure a stable Sino-Indian border. To resolve any doubts about the Indian position, Prime Minister Jawaharlal Nehru declared in parliament that India regarded the McMahon Line as its official border. The Chinese expressed no concern at this statement, and in 1951 and 1952, the government of China asserted that there were no frontier issues to be taken up with India.

In 1954, Prime Minister Nehru wrote a memo calling for India's borders to be clearly defined and demarcated; in line with previous Indian philosophy, Indian maps showed a border that, in some places, lay north of the McMahon Line. Chinese Premier Zhou Enlai, in November 1956, again repeated Chinese assurances that the People's Republic had no claims on Indian territory, although official Chinese maps showed 120,000 square kilometres (46,000 sq mi) of territory claimed by India as Chinese. CIA documents created at the time revealed that Nehru had ignored Burmese premier Ba Swe when he warned Nehru to be cautious when dealing with Zhou. They also allege that Zhou purposefully told Nehru that there were no border issues with India.

In 1954, China and India negotiated the Five Principles of Peaceful Coexistence, by which the two nations agreed to abide in settling their disputes. India presented a frontier map which was accepted by China, and the slogan *Hindi-Chini bhai-bhai* (Indians and Chinese are brothers) was popular then. However, Nehru in 1958, had privately told G. Parthasarathi, the Indian envoy to

China not to trust the Chinese at all and send all communications directly to him, bypassing the Defence Minister VK Krishna Menon since his communist background clouded his thinking about China. According to Georgia Tech political analyst John W Garver, Nehru's policy on Tibet was to create a strong Sino-Indian partnership which would be catalysed through agreement and compromise on Tibet. Garver believes that Nehru's previous actions had given him confidence that China would be ready to form an "Asian Axis" with India.

This apparent progress in relations suffered a major setback when, in 1959, Nehru accommodated the Tibetan religious leader at the time, the 14th Dalai Lama, who fled Lhasa after a failed Tibetan uprising against Chinese rule. The Chairman of the Chinese Communist Party,Mao Zedong, was enraged and asked the Xinhua News Agency to produce reports on Indian expansionists operating in Tibet.

Border incidents continued through this period. In August 1959, the People's Liberation Army took an Indian prisoner at Longju, which had an ambiguous position in the McMahon Line, and two months later in Aksai Chin, a clash led to the death of nine Indian frontier policemen.

On 2 October, Soviet Premier Nikita Khrushchev defended Nehru in a meeting with Mao. This action reinforced China's impression that the Soviet Union, the United States and India all had expansionist designs on China. The People's Liberation Army went so far as to prepare a self-defence counterattack plan. Negotiations were restarted between the nations, but no progress was made.

As a consequence of their non-recognition of the McMahon Line, China's maps showed both the North East Frontier Area (NEFA) and Aksai Chin to be Chinese territory. In 1960, Zhou Enlai unofficially suggested that India drop its claims to Aksai Chin in return for a Chinese withdrawal of claims over NEFA. Adhering to his stated position, Nehru believed that China did not have a legitimate claim over either of these territories, and thus was not ready to concede them. This adamant stance was perceived in China as Indian opposition to Chinese rule in Tibet. Nehru declined to conduct any negotiations on the boundary until Chinese troops withdrew from Aksai Chin, a position supported by the international community. India produced numerous reports on the negotiations, and translated Chinese reports into English to help inform the international debate. China believed that India was simply securing its claim lines in order to continue its "grand plans in Tibet". India's stance that China withdraw from Aksai Chin caused continual deterioration of the diplomatic situation to the point that internal forces were pressuring Nehru to take a military stance against China.

The Forward Policy

At the beginning of 1961, Nehru appointed General B. M. Kaul as army Chief of General Staff, but he refused to increase military spending and prepare for a possible war. According to James Barnard Calvin of the U.S. Navy, in 1959, India started sending Indian troops and border patrols into disputed areas. This program created both skirmishes and deteriorating relations between India and China. The aim of this policy was to create outposts behind advancing Chinese troops to interdict their supplies, forcing them north of the disputed line. There were eventually 60 such outposts, including 43 north of the McMahon Line, to which India claimed sovereignty. China viewed this as further confirmation of Indian expansionist plans directed towards Tibet. According to the Indian official history, implementation of the Forward Policy was intended to provide evidence of Indian occupation in the previously unoccupied region through which Chinese troops had been advancing. Kaul was confident, through contact with Indian Intelligence and CIA information, that China would not react with force. Indeed, at first the PLA simply withdrew, but eventually Chinese forces began to counter-encircle the Indian positions which clearly encroached into the north of McMahon Line. This led to a tit-for-tat Indian reaction, with each force attempting to outmanoeuver the other. However, despite the escalating nature of the dispute, the two forces withheld from engaging each other directly.

Chinese attention was diverted for a time by the military activity of the Nationalists on Taiwan, but on 23 June the U.S.

assured China that a Nationalist invasion would not be permitted. China's heavy artillery facing Taiwan could then be moved to Tibet. It took China six to eight months to gather the resources needed for the war, according to Anil Athale, author of the official Indian history. The Chinese sent a large quantity of non-military supplies to Tibet through the Indian port of Calcutta.

Early Incidents

Various border conflicts and "military incidents" between India and China flared up throughout the summer and autumn of 1962. In May, the Indian Air Force was told not to plan for close air support, although it was assessed as being a feasible way to counter the unfavourable ratio of Chinese to Indian troops. In June, a skirmish caused the deaths of dozens of Chinese troops. The Indian Intelligence Bureau received information about a Chinese buildup along the border which could be a precursor to war.

During June–July 1962, Indian military planners began advocating "probing actions" against the Chinese, and accordingly, moved mountain troops forward to cut off Chinese supply lines. According to Patterson, the Indian motives were threefold:

1. Test Chinese resolve and intentions regarding India.
2. Test whether India would enjoy Soviet backing in the event of a Sino-Indian war.
3. Create sympathy for India within the U.S., with whom relations had deteriorated after the Indian annexation of Goa.

On 10 July 1962, 350 Chinese troops surrounded an Indian occupied post in Chushul (north of the McMahon Line) but withdrew after a heated argument via loudspeaker. On 22 July, the Forward Policy was extended to allow Indian troops to push back Chinese troops already established in disputed territory. Whereas Indian troops were previously ordered to fire only in self-defence, all post commanders were now given discretion to open fire upon Chinese forces if threatened. In August, the Chinese military improved its combat readiness along the McMahon Line and began stockpiling ammunition, weapons and gasoline.

Given his foreknowledge of the coming Cuban Missile Crisis, Mao Zedong was able to persuade Nikita Khrushchev to reverse the Russian policy of backing India, at least temporarily. In mid-October, the Communist organ *Pravda* encouraged peace between India and China. When the Cuban Missile Crisis ended and Mao's rhetoric changed, however, Russia reversed course.

Confrontation at Thag La

In June 1962, Indian forces established an outpost at Dhola, on the southern slopes of the Thag La Ridge. Dhola lay north of the McMahon Line but south of the ridges along which India interpreted the McMahon Line to run. In August, China issued diplomatic protests and began occupying positions at the top of Thag La. On 8 September, a 60-strong PLA unit descended to the south side of the ridge and occupied positions that dominated one of the Indian posts at Dhola. Fire was not exchanged, but Nehru said to the media that the Indian Army had instructions to "free our territory" and the troops had been given discretion to use force. On 11 September, it was decided that "all forward posts and patrols were given permission to fire on any armed Chinese who entered Indian territory". However, the operation to occupy Thag La was flawed in that Nehru's directives were unclear and it got underway very slowly because of this. In addition to this, each man had to carry 35 kilograms (77 lb) over the long trek and this severely slowed down the reaction. By the time the Indian battalion reached the point of conflict, Chinese units controlled both banks of the Namka Chu River. On 20 September, Chinese troops threw grenades at Indian troops and a firefight developed, triggering a long series of skirmishes for the rest of September. Some Indian troops, including Brigadier Dalvi who commanded the forces at Thag La, were also concerned that the territory they were fighting for was not strictly territory that "we should have been convinced was ours". According to Neville Maxwell, even members of the Indian defence ministry were categorically concerned with the validity of the fighting in Thag La.

On 3 October, a week before the start of the war, Zhou Enlai visited Nehru in New Delhi promising there would be no war. On 4 October, Kaul assigned some troops to secure regions south of the Thag La Ridge. Kaul decided to first secure Yumtso La, a strategically important position, before re-entering the lost Dhola post. Kaul had then realised that the attack would be desperate and the Indian government tried to stop an escalation into all-out war. Indian troops marching to Thag La had suffered in the previously unexperienced conditions; two Gurkha soldiers died of pulmonary edema. On 10 October, an Indian Punjabi patrol of 50 troops to Yumtso La were met by an emplaced Chinese position of some 1,000 soldiers. Indian troops were in no position for battle, as Yumtso La was 16,000 feet (4,900 m) above sea level and Kaul did not plan on having artillery support for the troops. The Chinese troops opened fire on the Indians under their belief that they were north of the McMahon Line. The Indians were surrounded by Chinese positions which used mortar fire. However, they managed to hold off the first Chinese assault, inflicting heavy casualties.

At this point, the Indian troops were in a position to push the Chinese back with mortar and machine gun fire. However, Brigadier Dalvi opted not to fire, as it would mean decimating the Rajput who were still in the area of the Chinese regrouping. They helplessly watched the Chinese ready themselves for a second assault. In the second Chinese assault, the Indians began their retreat, realising the situation was hopeless. The Indian patrol suffered 25 casualties, and the Chinese 33. The Chinese troops held their fire as the Indians retreated, and then buried the Indian dead with military honours, as witnessed by the retreating soldiers. This was the first occurrence of heavy fighting in the war.

This attack had grave implications for India and Nehru tried to solve the issue, but by 18 October, it was clear that the Chinese were preparing for an attack on India, with massive troop buildups on the border. A long line of mules and porters had also been observed supporting the buildup and reinforcement of positions south of the Thag La Ridge.

SECTORS OF SINO-INDIAN BORDER: WESTERN SECTOR, MIDDLE SECTOR AND EASTERN SECTOR

The Sino-Indian border is generally divided into three sectors namely: (i) the Western sector, (ii) the Middle sector, and (iii) the Eastern sector.

The Western Sector

This 2,152 km long sector of the Sino-Indian border separates Jammu and Kashmir State of India from the Sinkiang province of China. The frontier between Sinkiang and Pakistan occupied Kashmir (PoK) is about 480 km long. The rest is boundary between Ladakh and Tibet.

The boundary in the western sector runs along the Muztagh Ata Range and the Aghil Mountain across the Karakoram Pass via Quara Tagh pass and along the main Kunlun Range to a point east of 80°E longitude and 40 km north of Hajit Langer. It forms a physical boundary between Gilgit area and Sinkiang following the main Karakoram watershed separating the streams flowing into the Indus basin from those flowing into the Tarin basin.

Farther south-east the boundary runs along the watershed across Lanak La, Kone La and Kepsang La, then follows the Chemesang River across Pergyon Lake and the Kailash Range. Here the boundary constitutes the watershed between the Indus system in India and the Khotan system in China. The western sector boundary is the outcome of the British policy towards the state of Jammu and Kashmir. These boundaries were defined by the treaties of 1665 and 1686 (known as Ladakh-Tibet agreements) and were confirmed by 1842 Dogra-Ladakh agreement among Kashmir, Tibet and China. However, this boundary was never delimited precisely on maps and has led to several boundary disputes between China and India. The Chinese claim rests mainly on ethnic grounds, and on the assertion that the wastelands of the Aksai Chin in disputed territory were always linked more with Tibet and Sinkiang. The Chinese claim that Aksai Chin is just an extension of Tibet with regard to language, religion and culture. But in Chinese documentation regarding the actual occupation of the area by Tibet in inconclusive.

The Indians, on the other hand, claim that the area has been historically administered by the state of Jammu and Kashmir since 1849, and that the Indo-Tibet Treaties of 1665, 1684 and 1842 confirmed the boundary between Tibet and Ladakh. China claims the Aksai Chin district, the Changmo valley, Pangong Tso and the Sponggar Tso area of north-east Ladakh as well as a strip of about

5,000 sq km down the entire length of eastern Ladakh. China also claims a part of Huza-Gilgit area in North Kashmir (ceded to it in 1963 by Pakistan), although the whole territory has been effectively under the British sovereignty since 1895.

Since 1954, the Chinese have repeatedly violated the international border between India and China and penetrated deep into the Indian Territory in the western sector. China renewed aggression in 1959 and the Line of Actual Control (LoAC) become of series of positions occupied by the Chinese forces rather than a well defined border between the two countries. In 1962, China waged a full scale war and its forces intruded far deeper into the Indian Territory. Currently the Chinese occupation line runs 16 to 240 km west of traditional line. China is in actual possession of about 54,000 sq km of the Indian Territory of which 37,555 sq km is in Ladakh area alone.

The Middle Sector

The middle sector boundary between China and India is 625 km long and runs along the watershed from Ladakh to Nepal. Two Indian states of Himachal Pradesh and Uttaranchal touch this border. The boundary of Himachal Pradesh follows the water parting between the Spiti and Para Chu rivers and continues along the watershed between the eastern and western tributaries of the Satluj. The Uttaranchal boundary is demarcated by the watershed between the Satluj on one hand and the Kali, the Alaknanda, and the Bhagirathi on the other. This boundary crosses the Satluj near the Shipki La on the Himachal-Tibet border. Thereafter, it runs along the watershed passes of Mana, Niti, Kungri-Bingri, Dharma and Lipu Ladakh. It finally joins trijunction of China, India and Nepal. This part of the border was approved by the Tibetan and the British governments under the 1890 and 1919 treaties. Although there are not much serious territorial problems between the two countries, the Chinese lay claim on nearly 2,000 sq km area in this sector.

The Eastern Sector

The 1,140 km long boundary between India and China runs from the eastern limit of Bhutan to a point near Talu-Pass at the trijunction of India, Tibet and Myanmar. This line is usually referred to as the Me Mahon Line after Henry Me Mahon, a British representative who signed the 1913-14 Shimla Convention. This line normally runs along the crest of the Himalayas between Bhutan and Myanmar. India has stressed that the Me Mahon Line is the international boundary between Tibet and India as was agreed to between the governments of India, China and Tibet. On the other hand China considers the Me Mahon line as illegal and unacceptable, claiming that Tibet had no right to sign the 1913-14 convention held in Shimla which delineated the Me Mahon Line on the map.

India challenges such a position, maintaining that Tibet was independent and in fact concluded several independent treaties which were considered valid by all parties, and were in operation for decades. China declined the validity of the Me Mahon Line as an international boundary and laid claims to areas south of this line up to the foot of the Himalayan range in the Brahmaputra valley. The whole of Arunachal Pradesh, measuring over 88 thousand sq km has been claimed by China as the Chinese territory. This area has been administered by India since 1947.

Chinese government never formally questioned the validity of 1913-14 Shimla convention until 1959. India has been striking at the two crucial points. First, Britain and India had been exercising jurisdiction over the area since 1914 and 1947 respectively and second China never disputed the Indian control over the area until 1959. Even in 1956 when the Chinese attention was drawn to certain maps drawn by China which showed these areas to be parts of China, the Chinese government promised to look into the 'cartographic errors' in their maps.

China's relations with India started taking a bad turn in 1950s when China started consolidating its position in Tibet and then in Ladakh. By 1956, China started intensifying its intrusions into the Indian Territory. India wishfully hoped that the insurmountable barrier of the Himalayas would prevent Chinese to attack Indian Territory. Indian apprehensions grew in 1956 when China built a road through Ladakh linking West Tibet with Sinkiang and quickly moved into Aksai Chin and eastern Ladakh. China also moved its forces into the North-East Frontier Agency (NEFA), the present Arunachal Pradesh. Reported small-scale armed clashes between 1959 and 1962 escalated into a full-scale war in October, 1962 when China launched a major offensive in Ladakh in the western sector and NEFA in the eastern sector. Indian armed forces were not well trained to fight a modern war in a rough and rugged mountainous terrain. They were outnumbered and outgunned by the Chinese forces.

Following lessons have been learnt from Chinese aggression over India:

(i) The myth that the Himalayas were an effective defense barrier was exploded.

(ii) India's naive confidence in China's friendliness had dulled its perception regarding effective security measures in the Indo-China borderlands.

(iii) The prompt and positive response of western countries in rushing military supplies to the war zone helped improve the image of the West in Indian eyes.

(iv) India realised that posture of "non-alignment" was no substitute for defense preparedness.

Surprisingly, Chinese forces pulled back without annexing the disputed territory in the eastern sector. In the western sector, however, they did not pull out of most of Aksai Chin. Perhaps they did so due to the fear that their advance troops would have been cut off from supply bases in Tibet in winter of 1962 when the high passes in the Himalayas would have been closed by snow. The Chinese justified their withdrawal by stating that they had no further territorial ambitions.

The primary aim of Chinese invasion was to deprive India of its moral leadership in the world especially among the Afro-Asian countries, and to put pressure on it to join the socialist camp. China's collusion with Pakistan is a clear indication of this political ambition. Perhaps China miscalculated its political power strategy. The support of the Western countries to India compelled China to rethink its strategy. India's unity in the face of Chinese aggression was another deterrent for China to achieve political mileage.

An uneasy truce had been prevailing for a long time since the October, 1962 war. Neither side made a serious effort to normalise the situation on the border. The Colombo powers, spearheaded by Ceylon (now Sri Lanka) and the erstwhile Soviet Union failed to bring about a respectable agreement between the two countries. Several countries condemned China as an aggressor. However, Cuba, Albania and Portugal supported the Chinese. Of late, leaders of both the countries have engaged themselves in improving the bilateral relations. Several meetings have been held to resolve the problem of border issues. A major development took place in October, 2003 when China made a significant change in its official website. It removed the mention of Sikkim from its list of nations.

In May, 2004, China recognised Sikkim as a part of India for the first time. The world map in World Affairs Year Book 2003/2004 does not show Sikkim as separate country in Asia. It also does not mention Sikkim in its index of countries.

The move was significant since it involves recognition of Sikkim-China border which is a part of the Me Mahon Line. If things go as planned, the two nations should be able to work out the guide lines for transforming the Line of Actual Control (LoAC) into a mutually acceptable and internationally recognised boundary. However, China still insists that Arunachal Pradesh is a disputed territory. China has also suggested a 'package deal'. It asked India to accept Chinese domination over Aksai Chin in return of China's acceptance of Me Mahon Line as the international boundary.

India, however, has advocated 'sector-by-sector' approach. Indian side is hopeful because China has settled border disputes with Russia and Vietnam.

8

India's China Policy: Importance of a Strategic Framework

For many political observers, the global political architecture is undergoing a transformation with power increasingly shifting from the West to the East. The two most populous nations on the earth China and India are on their way to becoming economic powerhouses and are shedding their reticence in asserting their global profiles.

Japan is gradually flexing its military muscle and the Southeast Asian tigers are roaring again after the 1997 "Asian Flu". Whether it is such hopeful prospects or the challenges ahead in the Korean peninsula, Taiwan, and Kashmir, it is clear that this new century will, in all likelihood, be an Asian century.

The future of this Asian century will to large extent depend upon the relationship between the two regional giants, China and India. According the United States National Intelligence Council Report on emerging global trends, by 2015, international community will have to confront the military, political and economic dimensions of the rise of China and India. The bilateral relationship between China and India will define the contours of the new international political architecture in Asia and the world at large. As of today, however, the trajectory of the Sino-Indian relationship remains as complex as ever to decipher despite some remarkable positive developments in the last few years.

This chapter attempts to explore this complex, multilayered relationship in all its dimensions, largely from the perspective of Indian foreign policy priorities. It mainly focuses on the recent developments in the Sino-Indian relationship. It reviews India's and China's view of each other and their policies. It examines the trends of convergence that have emerged in the past few years. Additionally, it looks at the points of divergence and possible areas of concern in the relationship between Asia's giants.

Sino-Indian Convergence: Bilateral and Global

Bilateral relations between India and the People's Republic of China (PRC) have indeed come a long way after they touched their nadir in the immediate aftermath of India 's nuclear tests in May 1998. China had been singled out as the "number one" security threat for India by India's Defence Minister just before the nuclear tests. After the tests, the Indian Prime Minister wrote to the US President justifying Indian nuclear tests as a response to the threat posed by China. Unsurprisingly, China reacted strongly and diplomatic relations between the two countries plummeted to an all time low.

However, some six years later, the relations between the two countries seem to be on an upswing. The visit of the Indian External Affairs Minister to China in 1999 marked the resumption of high-level dialogue and the two sides declared that they were not threats to each other. A bilateral security dialogue was also initiated that has helped the two countries in openly expressing and sharing their security concerns with each other. India and China also decided to expedite the process of demarcation of the Line of Actual Control (LAC) and the Joint Working Group (JWG) on the boundary question, set up in 1988, has been meeting regularly. As a first step in this direction, the two countries exchanged border maps on the least controversial middle sector of the LAC.

The Indian Prime Minster visited China in June 2003, the first such visit in a decade. The joint declaration signed during the visit stated that China was not a threat to India. The two states appointed special representatives in order to impart momentum to border negotiations that have lasted twenty two years, with the Prime Minister's principal secretary becoming India's political-level negotiator, replacing the India-China JWG. India and China also decided to hold their first joint naval exercise later in the year and discussions on joint air exercise continue. India also acknowledged China's sovereignty over Tibet and pledged not to allow "anti-China" political activities in India. On its part, China has acknowledged India's 1975 annexation of the former monarchy of Sikkim by agreeing to open a trading post along the border with the former kingdom and later rectified official maps to include Sikkim as part of India.

India and China have found substantial convergence of interests at the international level. Both share similar concerns about the growing international dominance of the US, the threat of terrorism disguised as religious and ethnic movements and the need to accord primacy to economic development. India and China have both expressed concern about the US ' use of military power around the world and publicly opposed the war in Iraq. This was merely a continuation of the desire of both states to oppose the US *hyperpuissance* ever since the end of the Cold War.

Like other major powers in the international system, India and China favour a multipolar world order where US unipolarity remains constrained by the other "poles" in the system. China and India zealously guard their national sovereignty and have been wary of US attempts to interfere in what they see as domestic affairs of other stares, be it Serbia, Kosovo or Iraq. Both took strong exception to the US air strikes on Iraq in 1998, the US-led air campaign against Yugoslavia in 1999, and more recently the US campaign against Saddam Hussein arguing that these violated the national sovereignty and undermined the authority of the United Nations system.

Both nations also favour more democratic international economic regimes. They have strongly resisted efforts by the US and other developed nations to link global trade to labour and environmental standards, realizing clearly that this would put them at a huge disadvantage vis-à-vis the developed world, thereby hampering their drive towards economic development, a top priority. Both have committed themselves to crafting joint Sino-Indian positions in the World Trade Organization (WTO) and global trade negotiations in the hope that this might provide them greater negotiating leverage over the developed states. They would like to see further liberalization of agricultural trade in the developed countries, tightening of the rules on anti-dumping measures and ensuring that non-trade related issues such as labour and environment are not allowed to come to the WTO.

In recent years, India and China have attempted to build their bilateral relationship on the basis of their larger worldview of international politics. As they have found a distinct convergence of their interests on world stage, they have used it to strengthen their bilateral relations. They have established and maintained regular reciprocal high-level visits between political leaders. There has been a sincere attempt to improve trade relations and to compartmentalize intractable issues that make it difficult for their bilateral relationship to move forward.

India and China have strengthened their bilateral relationship in areas as distinct as cultural and educational exchanges, military exchanges, and science and technology cooperation. Bilateral trade has recorded rapid growth from a trade volume of US $265 million in 1991 to US $3596 million in 2001. In 2001, bilateral trade saw an increase of 23.4 percent over 2000. It is expected to rise to $10 billion this year. The two nations are even evaluating the possibility of signing a comprehensive economic cooperation agreement and a free trade agreement by the end of this year, thereby building on strong complementarities between the two.

Both states are also taking steps to upgrade their military-related cooperation, leading to greater understanding on the bilateral military front, something that would have been unthinkable just a few years ago.As a first step in this direction, the Chinese and Indian navies carried out joint search and rescue operations off the Shanghai coast in November 2003. Both states are also seeking to cooperate on the nuclear front with China planning to import heavy water from India to be utilized in the pressurized heavy water reactors near Shanghai.

Many observers have also pointed out a subtle shift in Beijing's stance on Pakistan vis-à-vis India. China's "neutral" position during the Kargil conflict and the intense Indo-Pak crisis following the terrorist attack on the India's Parliament is seen by many as a reflection of China's sincerity in its attempts to improve ties. In keeping with China's attempts to project itself as a responsible regional player, China is seen by some as supporting peace and anti-terrorist efforts in South Asia by cooperating with the US and India. China is also seen as playing a central role in encouraging Pakistan to negotiate with India by using its leverage over Pakistan.

After assuming office Prime Minister Manmohan Singh's government made it clear that it favoured closer ties with China and would continue to work towards improving bilateral relations with China. In his first address to the nation, the Prime Minister, Manmohan Singh, also emphasized the carrying forward of the process of further development and diversification of Sino-Indian relations. The late J.N. Dixit, National Security Advisor in the current government, wrote that "the Congress will continue the process of normalizing, strengthening and expanding India's relations with China, which is the most important factor affecting Asian security and stability". One of the first foreign visits of the new Indian foreign minister, Natwar Singh, was to China to attend the Asia Cooperation Dialogue in Qingdao, in East China's Shandong province and apparently had "substantive discussions" with his Chinese counterpart.

All this reflects on India continuing to build its relations with China on the convergence of interests that the two nations have achieved in recent years. Aside from the positive developments, one should not ignore the enormous obstacles that confront this bilateral relationship. There has been a dominant tendency in the Indian foreign policy establishment to focus on the strengths of its bilateral relations with China while pretending that problems confronting the relationship would somehow take care of themselves. The challenges in the Sino-Indian relationship are by no means insignificant nor will China take care of Indian interests. It is for India to recognize them for what they are and evolve a coherent strategy to tackle them.

Divergences and Challenges

The number one priority for China's leadership today is economic growth and social stability. China soon underwent one of the most peaceful and orderly political transformations in its recent history, even though its exact ramifications remain far from clear. Hu Jintao became Communist Party chief in 2002 and President of China in 2003 replacing Jiang Zemin. He also finally ceded the effective control of the armed forces to Hu Jintao in September 2004. Hu Jintao is now formally in command of the vast party, government, and military bureaucracies that rule China. This shift, although important for the smooth working of the Chinese government, is unlikely to produce any radical change in China's foreign policy. China's focus is going to be on maintaining its high rate of economic growth in the coming years. It should be remembered that Hu Jintao is a product of the "evolutionary policies" of Deng Xiao Peng that emphasize economic growth and orderly governance. President Hu Jintao has made it amply clear that Western-style multiparty democracy is something that would not serve the Chinese people well, terming it a "blind alley" for China. Therefore, one can expect China to continue on its current economic trajectory and shaping its foreign policy accordingly.

China has enjoyed average annual rates of real income growth of around 10 percent in the last two decades of the twentieth century, something unprecedented historically. China accounts for about 5 percent of world trade and foreign direct investment (FDI) to China is predicted to reach an annual utilized rate of 100 billion in 2005. After its accession to the WTO, China 's already-high global economic profile is set to rise manifold. China will continue to focus on maintaining its high rates of economic growth in the coming years, even as some of the economic challenges China faces will become more acute. The burgeoning income disparities, restructuring of its states owned enterprises and the problem of non-performing loans in its banks are just a few of the economic problems China's economy is likely to face in the coming years. So far China has managed remarkably even though the future remains uncertain.

Broadly speaking, Indians either view China's economic growth as a façade or envy it. While India has achieved some remarkable growth rates in the last few years enjoying average annual rates of real income growth of six percent in the last two decades of the twentieth century, it still lags behind China. India accounts for less than one percent of world trade in goods and services. Currently, China outperforms India in terms of levels of growth, education, health, and living standards of its population, and global integration of its economy. China outpaces India, in sectors where the two compete for third country markets. Sino-Indian competition for these markets is bound to further intensify in the coming years.

Though some argue that the long term economic prospects of India are much better than China's, China remains the undisputed economic powerhouse of the moment driving the Asian and global economy with India somewhere far behind. The fact of the matter is so long as India does not place its own economic house in order; it will remain a second-rate power even in Asia. And China will remain the Asian power that the world will look up to when trying to manage problems in Asia.

What should be equally, if not more, significant for India is the fact that it is China's economic transformation that has given it the capability to become a military power with China spending as much as $65 billion a year on its military. China's military may or may not be able to challenge US supremacy in the next few years but it will surely become the most dominant force in Asia. According to authoritative sources, China is set to overtake Japan in the next decade to become Asia's major regional military power. The US involvement in the global war on terror has put the "containment" of China on the backburner and China has seized on this opportunity to strengthen its armed forces further.

China imbibed the lessons of US military undertakings such as the 1991 Gulf War, war in Afghanistan and the recent operation Iraqi Freedom. These have spurred China's pursuit of the latest Revolution in Military affairs (RMA) manifested in the buying, adopting of latest technologies and weapons systems (particularly from Russia) along with concomitant changes in doctrine and organizational structures. The People's Liberation Army (PLA) has been shedding its manpower since late 1990s to save funds so as to be able to focus on high tech. Despite a western embargo on China preventing transfer of military technologies, China has been able to deftly use US corporations to garner and apply dual-use technologies. China is simultaneously pursuing a qualitative and quantitative transformation of its nuclear infrastructure. China plans to deploy new road-mobile, solid-fuelled, long-range missiles over the next several years possibly to counter US ballistic missile defence.

Overtime, China 's enhanced military prowess will lead it to assert its interests more forcefully, thereby, adversely affecting Indian interests. As China becomes more reliant on imported oil for its rapidly growing industrial economy, China will develop and exercise military power projection capabilities to protect the shipping that transports oil from the Persian Gulf to China. The capability to project power would require access to advanced naval bases along the sea lines of communication and forces capable of gaining and sustaining naval and air superiority.

China 's assistance to Myanmar in constructing and improving port facilities on two islands in the Bay of Bengal and the Andaman Sea is the first step to securing military base privileges in the Indian Ocean. This can be used as a listening post to gather intelligence on Indian naval operations and a potential forward base for future Chinese naval operations in the Indian Ocean. India's traditional geographic advantages in the Indian Ocean are also increasingly at risk with deepening Chinese involvement in Myanmar. China's increasing naval presence in the Indian Ocean is of tremendous strategic consequence for India. There are also suggestions that the balance of air power in the China-India theatre has shifted in China 's favour with it acquiring an inventory of about 1500 modern combat aircraft for deployment in the theatre.

China remains the only major power in the world that refuses to discuss nuclear issues with India for fear that this might imply a de facto recognition of India 's status as a nuclear power. It continues to insist on the sanctity of the UN resolution 1172 which calls for India (and Pakistan) to give up its nuclear weapons program and join the Nuclear Non-Proliferation Treaty (NPT) as a non-nuclear weapon state. This was reflected in China's lack of response to the Indian Foreign Minister's proposal of a common nuclear doctrine for China, India, and Pakistan. China would not like to get into any sort of nuclear dialogue with India that might give the impression of China recognizing India as a nuclear power. Moreover, while both India and China have a "no first use" nuclear doctrine, China 's doctrine is not applicable to India as it is not a party to the NPT.

China has done its best to maintain a rough balance of power in Indian Subcontinent by preventing India from gaining an upper hand over Pakistan. It has consistently assisted Pakistan's nuclear weapons and ballistic missile programs to counterbalance India's development of new weapons systems. India's preoccupation with Pakistan reduces India to the level of a regional power while China can claim the status of an Asian and world power. China signed a charter to step up bilateral defence cooperation with Pakistan "to help maintain peace and stability in South Asia" even as it professes to improve its relations with India. Moreover, even as India and China share similar concerns regarding Islamic terrorism in Kashmir and Xinjiang respectively, China has been rather unwilling to make a common cause with India against Pakistan. China 's use of India's neighbours to curtail Indian influence has not been restricted to Pakistan. China has actively sought to contain India all around its periphery by engaging Nepal, Bangladesh and Myanmar.

Despite resolving most of its border disputes with other countries, China is reluctant to move ahead with India on border issues. India's discussion of border issues with China is seen as a concession. India remains satisfied with the "positive" and "satisfactory" Joint Working Group negotiations on the boundary issue. Despite the need for an expeditious demarcation of the Line of Actual Control, the talks seem to be continuing endlessly and the momentum of the talks itself seems to have flagged.

The momentum of the issue of Tibet seems to have been lost. Tibet has become a platform for the projection of Chinese military power. India's tacit support to Dalai Lama's government-in-exile has failed to have much of an impact either on China or on the international community. Today even Dalai Lama seems ready to talk to the Chinese as he realizes that in a few years Tibet might get overwhelmed with the Han population and Tibetans themselves might become a minority. The proposed opening up of the Nathula trade route that connects Tibet and Sikkim has been much trumpeted by the Indian government as a major achievement of Indian diplomacy.

However, this step is fraught with dangers as there is no certainty that internal security threat posed by Chinese infiltration would not get worse with the opening of Nathula. This has probably led to some rethinking in India on this issue.

There were disturbing reports during the Indian Prime Minister's visit to China, that Chinese troops had intruded into the Indian territory along a stretch of the unfenced border with Arunachal Pradesh. China refuses to recognize Arunachal Pradesh as part of the Indian territory, laying claim to 90, 000 sq. km. of its land. If recent reports are to be believed after a two-decade gap, China has resumed the supply of weapons to various insurgent groups fighting in northeastern India. China seems to be getting successful in hemming India in from both, the eastern and the western flanks.

China and India: Different Approaches, Different Outcomes

What the above discussion of the divergence and convergence between Sino-Indian interests reveals is the success of China in attaining its foreign policy objectives and the failure of India to preserve its vital interests vis-à-vis China. This cannot simply be attributed to China's economic and military strength. While China is definitely the bigger player in the region and the world at large but its success vis-à-vis India owes as much to its power as to the way that power has been cultivated and used. While realizing fully well that it would take China decades to seriously compete with the US, it has focused strategic energy on Asia. Its foreign policy is aimed at enhancing its economic and military prowess to achieve hegemony in Asia. China's recent emphasis on projecting itself as peaceful power is merely aimed at allaying the concerns of neighbours lest they try to counterbalance it. China's readiness to negotiate with other regional states and to be an economically "responsible" nation is also a signal to other states that there are greater benefits in bandwagoning to China's growing regional weight rather than opposing its rise in any manner.

However, while declaring that it will be focusing on internal socio-economic development for the next decade or so, China has actively pursued policies of preventing the rise of other regional powers. In case of India, this manifests itself in its cultivation of Pakistan as a close ally. From supplying it nuclear and missile technologies to building its military infrastructure, China has done all it can to build Pakistan as a counterweight to India. This policy has largely succeeded as India no longer enjoys its earlier conventional superiority vis-à-vis Pakistan possession of nuclear weapons by both nations ensures that any step that India takes to strengthen its nuclear weapons profile is viewed by the international community as highly destabilizing in the context of the "nuclear flashpoint" that South Asia has become for the world at large. China has thereby been successful in emerging as a "responsible" global player, despite its abysmal nuclear and missile proliferation record while the international community rails at India for making the world much more dangerous.

China's attempts to increase its influence in Nepal, Bangladesh, and Myanmar, its persistent refusal to recognize parts of India such as Arunachal Pradesh, its lack of support for India's membership to the United Nations Security Council and other regional and global organizations, all point towards China's attempts at preventing the rise of India as a regional and global player of major import. It is this strategy that China has consistently and successfully pursued without any apologies. In fact, this strategy has been so successful that today China no longer believes that India can be a serious rival for Asian hegemony and some have pointed out, India is off of China's diplomatic radar.

In contrast to China's well-laid out policy vis-à-vis India, India has from time to time oscillated from one extreme to another. George Tanham has famously pointed out that India has shown little ability to think strategically on national security. In the case of India's China policy, it needs to be realized that there is nothing really sinister about China's attempts to expand its own influence and curtail India's. China is a rising power in Asia and the world and as such will do its utmost to prevent the rise of other power centres around its periphery like India that might in the future prevent it from taking its rightful place as a global player. This is not much different than the stated US policy of preventing the rise of other powers that might threaten its position as a global hegemon. Just as the US is working towards achieving its strategic objective, China is pursuing its own strategic agenda.

There is also nothing extraordinarily benign in China's attempts to improve its bilateral relations with India in recent times. After working to curtail India's influence in various ways, China would not like to see India coming close to the US in order to contain China. In this geopolitical chessboard, both the US and China are using India towards their own strategic ends. India must resist the tendency of reacting to the actions of other. India 's attempt to come up a coherent strategy towards China based on identified strategic objectives is of paramount importance. Prime Minister Manmohan Singh declared that it wants to have friendly relations with China, a reasonable foreign policy objective. However, without a clear articulation of India 's national security objectives, pursuit of friendly relations with China should not become an end in itself. It should be a means towards achieving India 's larger strategic objective of emerging as a major regional and global player.

India 's China policy is also symptomatic of a larger misunderstanding in the Indian and political establishment with regard to a nation's foreign policy. For the left-liberal strand in the Indian polity, foreign policy is merely an extension of domestic policy. As such since India is a secular, democratic, and peace-loving nation, India 's pursuit of its relations with other states should merely be a reflection of these virtues. This has given rise to much of the moral rhetoric in foreign affairs. On the other hand, the Indian right, because of its preoccupation with establishing a "Hindu" nation and minority bashing, have extended its narrow sectarian view to foreign policy. The consequence has been its obsession with Pakistan as evil incarnate in its foreign policy agenda and its inclination to view the world in black and white, friends and enemies, evil and noble. Shaped by these forces, Indian foreign policy has merely been one of responding to events around it rather than anticipating them and evolving long-term strategies to deal with them. India's China policy is a casualty of this reactionary approach.

India needs to develop its economic and military might without being apologetic. It needs to clearly articulate its national interests and engage China on a host of issues, from the border problem to the alleged dumping of cheap Chinese goods in the Indian market. India needs to recognize that appeasing China is neither desirable nor necessary even as a direct confrontation with China is not something India can afford, at least in the near future. It must also be recognized that while for India, managing its relations with China is at the top of its foreign policy agenda, China does not view India as a significant global player and is largely indifferent to India's growing profile.

India is a rising power in Asia and there is nothing wrong in demanding its rightful place in the interstate hierarchy. Simply put India and China are two major powers in Asia with global aspirations and some significant conflicting interests. As a result, some amount of friction in their bilateral relationship is inevitable. The geopolitical reality of Asia makes sure that it will be extremely difficult, if not impossible, for *Hindi-Chini* to be *bhai-bhai* (brothers) in the foreseeable future. This reality should be accepted by the Indian policy makers, rather than wished away. India should make a serious attempt to manage this friction by expanding the zone of cooperation with China even as it tries to steadfastly pursue its national interests. India should display the confidence to craft a foreign policy that best serves its national security interests without always looking over the shoulders to make sure that China is not displeased. Again, India can learn a lot by examining how China has managed its relationship with the US in the last few years.

While India certainly needs to engage China in an effort at reconciling security and political perspectives, it is naïve to assert, as many do, that India should first be sensitive to China's concerns, real or imaginary, before defining its foreign policy goals and strategic agenda. Does China consult India in its pursuit of its own strategic objectives? It does not and neither should India expect it to. In a similar vein, India should define its foreign policy agenda in view of its own national security imperatives.

But for this to happen, the government of India will have to formulate a clear China policy and, more importantly, a broader national security strategy. Ad-hocism just won't do. This should be the top foreign policy priority of the Indian government if it wants India to emerge as a global power of any reckoning. India should heed to Sun Tzu's advice and recognize that a merely tactical foreign policy approach without the backing of a sound strategy will only lead to nowhere.

THE INFLUENCE OF INDIA'S SECURITY CONCEPT ON ITS CHINA POLICY

Earlier sections of this book explain changes in India's post-Cold War security concept and adjustments to its China policy. In the process of this discussion, we have distinguished two phases of adjustment to both the post-Cold War India security concept and China policy, and established that these changes were more or less simultaneous. We have also found that India's China policy reflects its security concept; in other words that adjustments to the content of India's China policy correspond to continuities and discontinuities in India's security concept. It may be said that this consistency demonstrates the important influence India's security concept has had on its China policy.

Policy-making, in any event, is the linking of concepts and policy; in other words, concepts, through government policy-making, crystallize into policy. Exploring the evolution of the Indian policy-making class and mechanisms, therefore, also benefits understanding of the manner in which security concepts of different eras and phases have influenced India's China policy.

India's foreign policy behaviour during the Cold War was largely determined by a few predominant personalities, both its foreign and security policies having long been dominated by Nehru and Indira Gandhi. The two leader's views on China had decisive influence on India's China policy. When considering India's defeat in the 1962 Sino–Indian Border Conflict and the open wound it represented to both the Nehru family and the INC, their adoption of an unyielding tack toward China was the sole political means of saving face. Sino–Indian relations consequently remained in stalemate for nearly 30 years. When Rajiv Gandhi replaced his mother in 1985, he seemed at first to follow her line on foreign policy. The rapidly changing international situation, however, forced him to veer from it, and specific improvements in Sino–Soviet relations compelled his adjustments to India's China policy. Soviet leader Mikhail Gorbachev urged Rajiv Gandhi during a visit to India in 1986 to improve relations with China, saying it would suit Soviet interests, and hinting at a press conference that the USSR would no longer be willing to provide support to India in the event of Sino–Indian conflict. In this situation, Rajiv Gandhi considered that India on its own would be powerless against a threat on two fronts. He was hence forced to change his preparations for a two-front war, as it was apparent that dispelling tensions along the eastern front through reconciliation with China would allow him to concentrate India's energies on the western front with Pakistan.

The Nehru family's stately bearing was absent after the Cold War, and the INC's power had declined. The insularity that had characterized India's foreign policy-making process since independence, however, did not change. The nation's foreign and security policy stayed in the hands of the prime minister and cabinet from 1991 to 1996, during which time the views of Prime Minister Rao and leaders of the INC government on security and foreign policy matters were decisive, and the influence of parliament, think tanks and academic institutions was negligible. It is notable, however, that Rao's background as home minister, defence minister and external affairs minister throughout the 1980s, as well as his status as the Congress Party's elder statesman, signified that he was a loyal adherent of Nehruvianism, and unrepresentative of any new type of thinking. The transformation of India's security concept during the Rao administration, therefore, can be understood as entirely the result of external forces.

The changes in the international and domestic situation compelled Rao to change his understanding of national strength.

He began emphasizing the strategic influence of economic strength and promoting restoration of the economy as a matter of urgency in withstanding security threats in the aftermath of the Cold War. This passive reaction to a complex situation gave the impression of India's overall foreign policy as passive and defensive. India adopted a focused approach to diplomacy during this period, directing its energies towards restoring the economy but maintaining a low profile in international affairs, as expressed in its China policy. Rao continued and furthered Rajiv Gandhi's adjustments by focusing on stabilization of Sino–Indian political relations and establishing tranquil borders as means to ensuring the recovery of India's domestic economy.

Two major changes occurred in India's foreign policy-making process during 1998. The first was the BJP's assumption of office that ended the long-standing INC power monopoly, and established foundations for a clean break with the traditional security concept. Although the BJP's domestic policies had a relatively ideological slant and promoted a Hinduist revival, the party was pragmatic as regards foreign policy. In contrast to the Congress Party, it dared to confront history, criticise India's previous foreign policy and introduce new thinking. Jaswant Singh, successively the Vajpayee government's External Affairs Minister and Finance Minister, published early in 1999 a book entitled *Defending India* in which he systematically describes his new security concept. Various views were thereafter expressed in government-issued articles. The BJP was obviously preparing to move on from the passive security concept of the Rao era. The second major change was India's refinement of its foreign policy-making mechanism. The November 1998 establishment of the National Security Council symbolized India's casting off of the influence and control of personality-based policy-making in favour of scientific research, inquiry and decision-making, and comprehensive long-term planning. The introduction by National Security Advisory Board subordinated to the National Security Council of scholarly authorities, reporters and former government and military officials demonstrated how much more open India's foreign policy-making process had become.

The BJP differed in its approach to China policy from both that of the Cold War era Nehru family, with its 1962 complex, and the early 1990s Rao government, which had been wearied and bound hand and foot by domestic and international pressure. The BJP's seizing of this historic opportunity confirmed India's rise as the nation's long-term strategic goal and placed its relationship with China on the strategic level. In other words, the BJP saw the Sino–Indian relationship as an important influence on India's rise. Although the two nations would be dealing with historically significant problems, they could be seen as a starting point.

The gradual opening of India's foreign policy-making process, moreover, made way for a vibrant exchange of ideas regarding China policy, which fell roughly into three groups: the first held that Sino–Indian cooperation suits both sides' interests and that post-Cold War China has no intention of making an enemy of India, desiring instead friendly relations and strategic partnership; the second that China is a long-term strategic threat to India because China's strategic objectives lie in establishing hegemony over Asia, which necessitates India's containment and, therefore, limitation of Indian influence. India, therefore, should adopt diametrically opposed policies; and the third group, situated between the two, held that the two nations could simultaneously rise to become main Asian powers and that competition and cooperation could coexist. Discussions on how to evaluate and understand China by Indian scholars and strategic circles are ongoing. After frequent debates among Indian National Security Council groups, the third, middle-ground viewpoint seems to be gaining acceptance.

When the INC regained power in 2004, a variety of factors led the new government to carry on with the previous administration's security concept. The new INC government's China policy was its predecessor's legacy, because the rise of India's international status during the BJP coalition government left the INC powerless to dispute the success of the previous government's foreign policy. The INC's democratized and more youthful leadership team was also willing to jettison historical baggage and look to the future. Although the Nehru family's leadership role within the Congress

Party remained uncontested, the influence of Prime Minister Manmohan Singh and Foreign Minister Mukherjee on foreign and security policy could not be disregarded. Moreover, the liberalization of India's foreign policy-making process was superimposed against a long-standing civil service system which ensured continuity of policy. In other words, many masterminds of BJP foreign policy still active in the external affairs ministry, defence ministry and other relevant functional departments under the INC, as well as in consultative committees, the media, think tanks and other non-functional departments, continued to exert influence.

Substantial changes occurred in India's China policy after the end of the Cold War whereby the nation's long-standing (1962–1988) antagonistic approach became one of reconciliation and engagement. These adjustments originated to a great extent in changes in the sub-continent's post-Cold War security concept, manifest in two major shifts which effected two major phases of adjustment in India's China policy. The new post-Cold War China policy nonetheless retained traces of the former, programme, imbuing it with a duality that reflected the overlap of India's old and new security concepts.

A change in India's security concept first became apparent during the period from the end of the Cold War to 1998. The first phase of adjustments this change triggered in India's China policy was evident in the sub-continent's extended concept of military might as national strength to one encompassing economic factors, and acknowledgement of the strategic value of economic strength in countering what it perceived as the looming threat of marginalization within the international community. Restoration of the domestic economy hence became a main measure through which to resist security threats in the post-Cold War era. Having made this shift in foreign policy objectives towards economic recovery, India set about creating a favourable environment within which to achieve this goal. Overall implementation of a China policy of preserving stable Sino–Indian relations by guaranteeing border tranquillity was vital to achieving this strategic objective. India consequently focused on the feasibility of reconciliation and, in view of China's reflective, inward-looking mood, no longer viewed China as an enemy. As regards India's specific policies, while focusing on the establishment of a progressive means to guaranteeing tranquil borders, thereby stabilizing Sino–Indian relations, India at the same time sought communication and cooperation in other areas. To avoid provoking China, the Indian government made tactical adjustments to its approach to Tibet from that of exploiting the issue and causing uproar to handling the matter in a low-key manner.

The new developments apparent in India's security concept in 1999 brought with it the second phase of adjustments to India's China policy. Indian leaders considered that the nation's security environment had improved to the extent that it constituted a strategic opportunity for India to rise to global-power status. This change in thinking and understanding caused the second shift of objective in India's foreign policy from that of improving the economy to the grand goal of global-power status. It corresponded to India's acknowledgement of the crucial nature of the Sino–Indian relationship and change of focus from border tranquillity and stable political relations to comprehensive considerations of how the two nations' relationship would strategically affect India's; rise. These insights compelled a shift of objective in India's China policy towards making China a positive factor in the sub-continent's rise; also recognition that this objective could be accomplished only by maintaining a stable basis for Sino–Indian relations. Official introduction during this phase of a comprehensive security concept signalled India's adoption of a more pragmatic, comprehensive handling of its relations with China. The specific steps it adopted were: increasing economic cooperation with China, thus benefiting India's economic development and stabilizing bilateral political relations; strengthening military communication and security dialogue, thus deepening understanding of China's strategic intentions towards India, increasing mutual trust, minimizing misunderstandings and avoiding conflict; and seeking Chinese support in its quest for a permanent seat on the UN Security Council, which would expand India's political power and international prestige.

In the course of research, however, it became apparent to the author that India's security concept did not undergo a thoroughgoing change after the Cold War ended, as elements of the Cold War approach remained in place.

Although India's security concept extended after 1988 to include both military and economic security, the ultimate purpose of national defence as regards a fundamental guarantee of security nonetheless remained that of increased military strength to safeguard national unity and territorial integrity. India abandoned its strategy of pursuing security through alliances, yet still viewed parity and the principle of checks and balances as hallmarks of its national defence.

Influenced as it was by traditional concepts, post-Cold War India's China policy was imbued with vigilance. Even though India did not perceive China as a threat in the short term, it was nevertheless concerned that the swing in balance of power between the two was not in its favour, and that China constituted a potential obstacle to India's rise. Indian leaders consequently embarked on a race against China to expand comprehensive national strength, particularly military force, including India's nuclear capability, as the means to a balance of power. India at the same time sought to offset Chinese influence both regionally and globally through development of strategic relationships with the United States, Japan and other nations. The sub-continent also remained vigilant in the long-standing issues of border disputes and Sino–Pakistani relations, and maintained pressure on China in this regard.

Changes in post-Cold War India's security concept were thus the result of both domestic and foreign factors. The first change during the early post-Cold War period was triggered by passive reactions to transformations in the nation's domestic and international situation that, in turn, prompted a passive transformation of thinking and understanding, manifest in passive defensiveness of India's foreign policy, specifically its China policy. The security concept that appeared during the late 1990s was comparatively proactive. The expanded strength of India's domestic economy and improvement of its external environment compelled a new understanding of security issues, as expressed in the proactive change in its security concept. This assertiveness was manifest in strategy and in an active, enterprising foreign policy. Seizing the historic opportunity to realize India's rise had become the common security objective of both major Indian political parties. Decentralization of political power and expanded openness of the foreign policy-making process, however, caused India's old and new security concepts to bind into one, and the resultant duality of India's hybrid security concept since the Cold War's end is reflected in its China policy. As India's dual security concept will continue into the foreseeable future, the duality of its China policy will be difficult to change.

9

Sino-indian Relations: A Chronology

On the eve of the 11th meeting of the Sino-Indian Joint Working Group (JWG) to discuss bilateral relations, with special reference to the pending border dispute, it would be useful to analyse the set-back to the bilateral relations since May, 1998, and the Chinese perception of its relations with India in the bilateral and global context after the Pokhran II nuclear tests.

An attempt has been made to cover all important Chinese statements since May 1998 in this chronology. From the chronology, one could notice three phases in the Chinese reactions. In the first phase (May to July, 1998), there was a strong barrage of criticism of the statements of George Fernandes, the Indian Defence Minister, and Prime Minister Atal Behari Vajpayee's letter to President Clinton portraying the threat from China as a motivating factor for the Pokhran II nuclear tests. The characterisation of the Chinese threat was condemned by China as hurting the Chinese people and projected as a mere pretext to cover India's hegemonistic ambitions. The tests were viewed as also indicative of India's desire to acquire a new political status through the possession of nuclear weapons. During this phase, the Chinese criticism of India related to the bilateral (damage to Sino-Indian relations) as well as global (damage to the global non-proliferation regime) aspects. There was rigidity in the Chinese attitude to both these aspects.

In the second phase (July-middle to December, 1998), there were signs of a mellowing down of the Chinese rigidity on the bilateral aspect. There was once again stress on the importance of Sino-Indian relations and repeated calls to India to make amends in a suitable manner so that the bilateral relations could be put back on track. After the initial hard-line comments on Kashmir suggesting a multilateral conference on the issue, Beijing reverted back to its 1996 and pre-1996 stance of neutrality as between India and Pakistan on this issue. In the third phase (since January, 1999), while welcoming the Indian initiatives for mending the damage to bilateral relations, Beijing continued to be rigid in its insistence that the international community should not accept India's concept of a minimum nuclear deterrence and that India and Pakistan should sign the NPT and the CTBT unconditionally and immediately. There was also a note of concern in Chinese pronouncements that other permanent members of the UN Security Council might ultimately accept India's need for a minimum nuclear deterrence.

During all these phases, Chinese inconsistencies in possessing a nuclear and missile capability for itself and opposing a similar capability for India were sought to be explained as follows:

- The Chinese capability was acquired in self-defence in the context of the cold war. China did not view the capability as conferring a political status on it. Moreover, China was already a permanent member of the Security Council.
- On the other hand, the Indian capability was acquired after the cold war was over when the contemporary trend was towards peace, harmony and non-proliferation. The Indian nuclear aspirations marked a revival of its hegemonistic designs and had the ulterior motive of seeking a new political status in the international community.

It is evident from the chronology that China's two-pronged policy is to continue to oppose India's nuclear aspirations and deny it any new political status at par with that of China through its emergence as a de facto nuclear weapon power, while at the same time not allowing this to affect the bilateral relations.

The Chronology

The setback process started with a statement by George Fernandes, the Indian Defence Minister, in the beginning of May

1998, in which he reportedly described China as a major military threat to India. However, he subsequently claimed that his observation made to a private TV channel was distorted.

On May 5,1998, Zhu Bangzao, a spokesman of the Chinese Foreign Office, described Mr.Fernandes' remarks as "absolutely ridiculous and unworthy of refutation" and added that China had noted with the "utmost regret and resentment" his statements on China since coming to office. He said:" The remarks by the Indian Defence Minister George Fernandes have seriously sabotaged the friendly atmosphere for improving bilateral relations between China and India…China does not pose any threat to neighbouring countries. His accusation concerning China's relations with relevant countries is utterly fictitious and has no basis in facts...His statement that China has built a sophisticated electronic surveillance base in Myanmar's Coco Islands and has installed missiles in Tibet targeting India is absolutely fictitious and entirely baseless…. It is extremely irresponsible."

On May 8,1998, an unidentified spokesman of the Chinese Foreign Office told pressmen that China had twice protested to India through the Indian Embassy in Beijing over the "ridiculous and fragile" statements of Fernandes.

On May 12,1998, Lin Shanglin, the Chinese CDA in New Delhi, issued a written statement at New Delhi stating as follows:" The so-called issue that China has been building a naval base in Myanmar is utterly fictitious, whose aim is to find grounds to the so-called China threat...Allegations of Chinese involvement in the development of Pakistan's Ghauri missile are a fabrication. It is irresponsible to assume that China is engaged in nuclear proliferation. The co-operation between China and Pakistan in the peaceful utilisation of nuclear energy is under the safeguards and supervision of the International Atomic Energy Agency (IAEA) and conforms to the international general practices."

After the suspected leakage to the "New York Times" by the US State Department of the letter written by Indian Prime Minister Atal Behari Vajpayee to President Clinton citing India's perception of a possible threat from China as one of the reasons for Pokhran II, Chinese Government spokesmen, govt-controlled media and strategic analysts started a barrage of vigorous criticism of India. The Xinhua news agency said on May 18,1998: "Political analysts are of the view that with the nuclear explosion, India seeks to develop nuclear weapons, barge into the world's club of nuclear powers and then seek regional hegemony."

Ye Zhengjia, a former Chinese diplomat posted at New Delhi and subsequently posted to the Chinese Foreign Ministry's Institute of International Studies, told Japan's Kyodo news service on May 18,1998: " By presenting a China threat scenario, India is trying to extract mileage out of ideological differences between China and the West while New Delhi is actually masking its own contradictions with the West to lessen the blow of sanctions." He denied that China's nuclear tests were carried out to raise the country's political status in the new world order. He added: " In any case, a country's international standing does not depend upon its capability to do a nuclear test. That time has passed."

The official "China Daily" wrote on May 20,1998: " India's improper move of attributing its nuclear tests at Pokhran to potential threat from China has made the international community realise that the new Indian Government is not only irresponsible, but also immoral. This is the first time in history that a nuclear country has denied its own responsibility for its nuclear tests and shifted the blame to others..To justify its series of nuclear tests, India uses the political tactic of making India-China ties tense....China had been taking a reserved attitude towards provocative statements from India in order to push forward Sino-Indian ties. However, India took China's forbearance as weakness."

Xinhua reported on June 2,1998, that at a meeting between the Chinese Vice-Premier Qian Qichen and the US National Security Adviser Sandy Berger both sides "believed that the international community must take effective and feasible measures to halt the nuclear arms race in the South Asian region and prevent nuclear proliferation in order to restore and safeguard peace and stability in the region." Sandy Berger had gone to Beijing to prepare the ground for Clinton's visit.

In an interview to the AFP news agency on June 3,1998, President Jiang Zemin denied that China had helped Pakistan make nuclear bombs and said: "The nuclear co-operation between the two countries is strictly peaceful in the area of technology of nuclear reactors and all the installations concerned are under the control of the IAEA."

He recalled his historic visit to India in 1996 "after a number of signals of friendship from New Delhi" and said he had received a warm welcome, " but the Prime Minister then was not the same person as the one today."

Jiang further said that Pokhran II which clearly showed that "India is targeting China and Pakistan" surprised him He added: "China hopes that Pakistan will not respond and will make a wise decision. But the Pakistani Government is faced with strong public pressure on the subject."

In an article on June 5,1998, the "Liberation Army Daily", the journal of the PLA, accused George Fernandes of recklessly using China's name as an excuse for India's nuclear ambitions and warned: " If this arrogant boast and military expansionism are not effectively checked, the consequences will be serious."

A signed editorial in the "China Daily" of June 6,1998, urged India to show wisdom by renouncing its nuclear weapons programme and said that a 14 per cent rise in India's defence budget was an unwise decision which would further escalate the arms race in South Asia.

It added: "Such a rise in defence spending reveals the South Asian country's ambition to be a military power and is adding fuel to the already heated arms race...It is unwise for the Indian Government to develop nuclear weapons and raise defence spending with no regard for its relations with the international community." It described Fernandes' statement in the Indian Parliament about the occupation of Indian territory by China as a "concocted excuse."

In an interview to the "Newsweek" on June 21,1998, Jiang Zemin said: "In November 1996, I paid a successful visit to India. I was accorded a very friendly reception by the Government and people of India. That visit has left me with very good memories. I was very surprised that they conducted the nuclear tests. I was even more surprised that they cited China as a reason for their nuclear testing. I really don't know what kind of threat China poses."

Jiang also said that if Clinton raised the question of alleged Chinese supply of missiles to Pakistan, "the answer very simply is that we don't plan to sell missiles."

A joint statement issued by Jiang Zemin and President Clinton on June 27,1998, after the latter's visit to Beijing in the last week of June, 1998, said: "Recent nuclear tests by India and Pakistan and the resulting increase in tension between them are a source of deep and lasting concern to both of us.

"Our shared interests in a peaceful and stable South Asia in a strong global non-proliferation regime have been put at risk by these tests, which we have joined in condemning.

"We have agreed to continue to work closely together, within the P-5, the Security Council and with others, to prevent an accelerating nuclear and missile arms race in South Asia, strengthen international non-proliferation efforts and promote reconciliation and the peaceful resolution of differences between India and Pakistan.

"The P-5 joint communiqué of June 4, which was endorsed by UN Security Council Resolution 1172, set out clear and comprehensive objectives and a plan for action to address the threat of a South Asian nuclear and missile arms race.

"We pledge our full support for the steps outlined in the joint communiqué and again call on India and Pakistan to stop all further nuclear tests and adhere immediately and unconditionally to the CTBT, to refrain from weaponisation or deployment of nuclear weapons and from testing or deployment of missiles capable of delivering nuclear weapons and to enter into firm commitment not to weaponise or deploy nuclear weapons or missiles capable of delivering them.

"The United States and China remain firmly committed to strong and effective international co-operation on nuclear non-proliferation, with the NPT as its cornerstone.

"We will continue to bolster nuclear non-proliferation efforts and reiterate that our goal is adherence of all countries, including

India and Pakistan, to the NPT as it stands, without any modification.

"States that do not adhere to the treaty cannot expect to be accorded the same benefits and international standing as are accorded to NPT parties. Notwithstanding their recent nuclear tests, India and Pakistan do not have the status of nuclear weapon states in accordance with the NPT."

Speaking at the Beijing University on June 29,1998, Clinton said: "We (the US and China) are now pursuing a common strategy to move India and Pakistan away from further testing and engage in a dialogue to resolve all outstanding issues."

Commenting the same day on the reference in the Clinton-Jiang statement to the nuclear issue in South Asia, the "China Daily" said that the US-China understanding on this subject "signified a healthy, stable China-US relationship." It added: " Such a relationship is not only in the interest of China and the US, but of the world peace and stability at large. "

Tang Guoqiang, a spokesman of the Chinese Foreign Office, rejected on June 30,1998, India's criticism of the Clinton-Jiang statement. He said that as major powers, the US and China had to act in the common interest of the international community to prevent a nuclear arms race in the region and promote reconciliation between New Delhi and Islamabad.

Accusing India of starting a nuclear arms race in South Asia, he said: "The joint statement expresses the strong determination of China and the US in further preventing nuclear proliferation and also promoting reconciliation and peaceful settlement of the differences between India and Pakistan.

"There is nothing reproachful about the joint statement on South Asia. While India opposed the joint statement, Pakistan has welcomed it. However, we have taken note of India's comments."

Writing in "The Hindu" of July 2,1998, F.J.Khergamvala, its Tokyo correspondent, quoted Robert Manning and James Przystup, former senior US State Department officials, who had visited China, as having stated in an article in the "Wall Street Journal" (date not mentioned) that during their visit a prominent Chinese analyst told them that "transferring material or technology to Iran is negotiable, but Pakistan is our Israel", implying thereby that Pakistan's security was as important to China as Israel's was to the US. However, in an interview to the State-run China Central Television before leaving China, Clinton said that the US and China had agreed to work together to prevent the spread of nuclear and missile technologies to countries like Pakistan that might misuse it.

He added: "China has agreed to work with the US to stop the transfer of technologies to countries that might misuse it, to not assist unsafeguarded nuclear facilities like Pakistan's and to consider joining the worldwide system that prevents the exportation of dangerous technologies."

At a meeting of the leaders of China, Russia, Kazakhstan, Kyrgyzstan and Tajikistan held at Almaty in Kazakhstan on July 3, 1998, Jiang Zemin failed to have a critical reference to the nuclear and missile arms race in South Asia included in the final communiqué. However, during a joint press conference by the leaders after the summit he condemned India for starting a nuclear race in South Asia.

While briefing pressmen on July 9,1998, Tang Guoqiang, the Chinese Foreign Ministry spokesman, avoided commenting on India's offer of a pledge of no-first-use of nuclear weapons. He merely said: "The most urgent task for India is to immediately abandon its nuclear programme and sign the NPT and the CTBT unconditionally as soon as possible."

However, in an interview to K.K.Katyal and C.Raja Mohan, the New Delhi correspondents of "The Hindu" the same day, Zhou Gang, the Chinese Ambassador to India, gave the first indication of the beginning of a mellowing down of the Chinese criticism of India. He made the following points:

- "It is up to the doer to undo the knot". Beijing would like India to provide responsible explanations for totally "unreasonable and groundless" accusations against China and, thus, create a favourable atmosphere for a new beginning in bilateral relations. The initiative for this must be taken not by China, but by India. It was China's set policy to develop a "constructive and co-operative partnership" with India towards the new millennium.

- It was impossible to call for a dialogue and establish best relations while keeping up attacks on China, which had been the victim of baseless accusations. China would like these charges to stop and "actual actions" initiated. China would not like the present situation to go on. "As two big powers, the high-level political contacts between India and China should be normal."
- He hoped that India and Pakistan would peacefully resolve their differences "including the Kashmir issue" through talks. "The position of the Chinese side is consistent". After the nuclear tests by India and Pakistan, the growing tension on Kashmir and the issue of peace and security in South Asia had caused widespread concern in the international community. "We will do whatever is beneficial for the improvement of India-Pakistan relations and peace and stability in South Asia, but never do otherwise."
- China's ties with Pakistan were State-to-State relations between two sovereign countries. China had not transferred to any country equipment or technology that could be used for making nuclear weapons. Some of India's concerns over Sino-Pakistan military co-operation were caused by misunderstandings and others arose out of unnecessary misgivings. China would like to exchange views on this subject with India through diplomatic channels, as used to be done in the past. He disapproved of the resort to media and exaggerations based on "rumours from the West."
- There was peace and tranquillity on the India-China border. "We hope the two sides would make joint efforts to maintain this situation." China had taken "a series of flexible measures" on Sikkim and he hoped that the Indian side " would also adopt a positive and flexible attitude so as to create a proper atmosphere and conditions for the disposal of this issue."

In a lead article on July 14,1998, the "China Daily" called for " a multilateral meeting attended by India, Pakistan, the US, China and Russia to help resolve the Kashmir dispute, over which India and Pakistan have fought two wars since 1947."

The article, quoting Ma Jiali of the China Institute of Contemporary International Relations, said: "Indian Government officials should stop spreading the China menace theory which will create suspicion and hostility between the two peoples. The Indian Government's unreasonable attacks on China deeply hurt the feelings of the Chinese people and undermined the mutual trust the two countries have been trying to build over generations." Quoting Ouyang Liping, another expert of the same Institute, the article said that China had consistently adhered to the policy of non-proliferation of nuclear weapons and denied that China was aiding Pakistan's clandestine nuclear programme.

Commenting on the annual report of the Defence Ministry of the Government of India for 1997-98, the article said: "In the report, the Indian Government did not examine its mistake in provoking a dangerous nuclear arms race. It vilified China as the main reason for the deterioration of South Asia's security environment instead."

The article described the BJP-led Government as head strong and alleged that the real purpose of Pokhran II was to gain regional hegemony.

It further quoted Ouyang Liping as saying: "India's recent nuclear explosions reflect a dangerous ultra-nationalism and its ambition to build a regional hegemony and become a major political power."

The article added: "Continuously denying its faults and spreading lies will not win sympathy or trust from others, but will make the international community more vigilant against its ambitions. India should first abandon its nuclear development plan unconditionally so as to convince Pakistan to follow in its foot steps."

The article again quoted Ouyang Liping as saying that the international community must press India and Pakistan to completely abandon their nuclear programmes and convert South Asia into a non-nuclear area. In this connection, he cited the examples of South Africa and Ukraine and said: "They (South

Africa and Ukraine) abandoned their nuclear capability in the 1990s under international pressure and for the good of their own peoples."

Despite this article, there was another indication of a possible mellowing down of the Chinese official criticism in an address by Zhou Gang, the Chinese Ambassador, in the India International Centre at New Delhi on July 25,1998. He made the following points:

- India's nuclear tests had led to "temporary difficulties" in Sino-Indian ties, but had not diluted Beijing's commitment to building a long-term friendly relationship with New Delhi." It is a firm policy of the Chinese Government to develop with India a long-term neighbourly and constructive partnership of co-operation for the 21st century.
- India and China could play an influential role in promoting Asian stability. "As the two most populous developing countries in the world, China and India can exert important influence in the affairs of South Asia and Asia as a whole."
- China did not seek hegemony in the region though it was naturally interested in the developments between India and Pakistan. China had normal relations with Pakistan, which were based on the five principles of peaceful co-existence. Pakistani nuclear weapons programme could not be linked to China's. Pakistan had, however, received conventional weapons from China, but the quantum of these exchanges was much smaller to the defence trade between India and a "powerful country" (an apparent reference to Russia).
- "Friendly relations between China and any country are not directed at any third country." China did not pose any security threat to India. "Fictitious charges against China have gravely hurt the feelings of the Chinese people and harmed Sino-Indian relations."
- China wished India "stability, progress and development" and sought "neighbourliness, friendship and progress" from New Delhi. The Chinese pronouncements were a

> refutation of some wanton attack and accusations by certain personages in India. They were meant to "safeguard the friendly relations between our two countries and bring them back on track."

Co-operation between India and China must diversify and should not be held hostage to the pending resolution of the border dispute. The boundary question could be resolved on the principle of mutual understanding and mutual accommodation. The Peace and Tranquillity accord of 1993 and the subsequent agreement of 1996 on confidence-building measures continued to be the cornerstone of the Sino-Indian security relationship.

In an interview to the "Al Ahram" of Cairo on July 26,1998, Prime Minister Zhu Rongji said: "I assure there is no Chinese threat to India. I confirm our keenness on good neighbourly relations and peaceful co-existence. Beijing had no time to threaten or scare other countries, as it is busy with its own economic development. Any view on China's fearful size came only from India. No other State took this view. India has utilised this theory as a pretext to conduct its nuclear tests. However, the real target behind the nuclear tests is practice of hegemony as well as settling the internal crisis facing the ruling party. Due to limited economic capabilities, China sets aside a limited percentage of its resources for defence purposes. It is less than that allocated by India and Japan. In fact, China needs some defence capabilities."

Jaswant Singh, who attended the ASEAN meeting at Manila as the Indian Prime Minister's special representative, met Tang Jiaxuan, the Chinese Foreign Minister, on July 27,1998. A Chinese spokesman later said that "both sides conducted frank discussions on the Indian nuclear explosions and Sino-Indian relations." He added that during the discussions, the Chinese Foreign Minister stressed that India, running counter to the world trend, conducted nuclear tests and that India, "in an attempt to find an excuse for the tests, groundlessly alleged that China poses a threat to India."

A joint statement issued by Tang Jiaxuan and his Filipino counterpart, Domingo Siazon after bilateral talks on August 2,1998, expressed the support of the two countries for the Security Council Resolution 1172 of June 6,1998. The two countries expressed "their grave concern over and strongly deplored the recent nuclear tests in South Asia. These had exacerbated tensions in the region and raised the spectre of a nuclear arms race."

In a statement in the Lok Sabha, the lower House of the Indian Parliament, on August 4,1998, Prime Minister Vajpayee said India was keen on improving its relations with China and asserted that his Government had never dubbed China as an enemy or a threat. He also said that India wanted to accelerate the efforts for a solution to the border problem.

Commenting on this statement on August 7,1998, Tang Guoqiang, spokesman of the Chinese Foreign Office, said: "We have taken note of the Prime Minister's statement in Parliament. We hope that the Indian side will take concrete actions so that the bilateral relations will return to normal."

Replying to a question on the Kashmir issue on August 11,1998, the same spokesman distanced himself from the views mentioned in the "China Daily" article and re-stated the traditional Chinese position. He said: " Kashmir is an outstanding issue between India and Pakistan. The Chinese position on that is consistent. The Chinese side hopes that India and Pakistan will solve their dispute through peaceful negotiations and maintain calm and restraint before the solution of the problem."

Addressing a meeting of industrialists organised at New Delhi on August 12,1998, by the Federation of Indian Chambers of Commerce and Industry, Zhou Gang, the Chinese Ambassador, made yet another reassuring statement. He said that despite the setback to the Sino-Indian bilateral relations, there was scope for increased bilateral trade and economic relations "because the reforms and the opening up of the economy in both the countries have provided great opportunities for expanding trade and economic relations."

He expressed his optimism that "on the eve of the next century trade and economic relations and cooperation between China and India would be pushed on to a new high." However, while talking to journalists after the meeting, he added that India's nuclear tests had severely damaged bilateral relations and "this will spill over to the economic relations also."

In reply to questions during the daily press briefing on August 13,1998, Tang Guoqiang, the Chinese Foreign Office spokesman, again evaded comments on China's reaction to India's no-first-use of nuclear weapons offer and repeated the Chinese demand that India should first give up its nuclear programme and sign unconditionally the NPT and the CTBT.

Addressing a meeting at the Bharat Chamber of Commerce at Calcutta on September 14,1998, Zhou Gang, the Chinese Ambassador, said differences between the two countries should not be seen as an obstacle to fostering trade. He added: "Expansion of economic relations, trade and technological co-operation between our two countries is beneficial for the overall development of bilateral relations and in conformity with the fundamental interests of the people of our two countries." He also claimed that China's nuclear tests were undertaken in the interest of self-defence.

China reacted sharply to a courtesy call by the Dalai Lama on Prime Minister Vajpayee in the third week of October 1998. On October 22,1998, a Chinese Foreign Office spokesman described it as a violation of India's commitment to keep itself away from the Dalai Lama's anti-Chinese activities. Rejecting the Chinese criticism, a spokesman of the Indian Foreign Office pointed out the next day that the Dalai Lama had been received in his capacity as a religious leader by successive Indian Prime Ministers and that leaders of other countries had similarly received him too. The 11th meeting of the JWG, which should have been held in the second half of 1998, could not be held due to the misunderstanding in the bilateral relations.

While talking to a group of visiting American journalists at New Delhi in the middle of November, 1998, a diplomat of the Chinese Embassy said that China had adopted an "active approach" to the subject and that the matter was under discussion through diplomatic channels.

In his briefing for the US journalists, the unnamed Chinese diplomat reportedly made the following points:

- China acquired a nuclear weapon capability in the context of the cold war. After the end of the cold war the trend was towards non-proliferation.

- The Indian tests were against the contemporary historical trend and seriously affected peace and stability in South Asia. The Indian tests had also dealt a heavy blow to international nuclear disarmament and the global non-proliferation regime.
- China did not agree that there was a nuclear apartheid. "The nuclear status of the five permanent members of the UN Security Council is a product of history. In our opinion, favouring the NPT doesn't mean that the nuclear weapon states will enjoy the permanent privilege of possessing nuclear weapons. China had all along urged countries with the largest nuclear arsenals to speed up the process of nuclear weapon reduction. As a nuclear state, China will never shirk its own responsibility for the complete prohibition and thorough destruction of nuclear weapons in the end."
- "China has always been committed, on the basis of the Five Principles of Peaceful Co-Existence, to the development of good neighbourly and friendly relations with its neighbouring countries, including India. China has made unremitting efforts to improve and develop Sino-Indian relations. This stand of China has not changed. Before and after India's nuclear tests, the Indian Defence Minister and other senior officials preached the China threat theory and made wanton accusations against China. All this cannot but affect the normal development of the bilateral relations. The responsibility for upsetting Sino-Indian relations at present is totally on the Indian side. As the ball is now in the Indian court, we hope that apart from expressing its willingness to improve the relations in words, what is more important for the Indian side is to take concrete actions to improve the relations."

A joint declaration signed by Russian President Boris Yeltsin and Jiang Zemin, at the end of the latter's visit to Russia on November 25,1998, cited South Asia along with Kosovo, Afghanistan and Korea as regions of "the most acute conflict situations, which, if they escalate, may pose real threats to the international community." It added: "On South Asia, Russia and

China confirm their position expressed in the UN and at other international fora and stress the paramount importance of the NPT and the CTBT for the global efforts to promote the non-spread of nuclear arms and nuclear disarmament. Russia and China call upon all countries which have not yet joined these treaties so far to do so without delay and without conditions."

Russian Foreign Office officials tried to play down the significance of the reference by saying that they had succeeded in toning down a harsh statement which Jiang wanted and in ruling out any reference to India by name. According to them, since Jiang insisted on some reference to it in the joint declaration they had to agree to a mild formulation which need not cause embarrassment to India.

In a letter to Jaswant Singh on December 15,1998, congratulating him on his taking over as the Minister for External Affairs, Tang Jiaxuan, the Chinese Foreign Minister, hoped that Sino-Indian relations could be consolidated and further developed during Singh's tenure. In his reply to the message, Jaswant Singh said:" India remains committed to the process of dialogue to address and resolve outstanding issues." He referred to his meeting with Tang at Manila and said that he looked forward to "continuing our interaction to further mutual understanding, co-operation and friendship, so essential for our two countries and peoples."

In his first press conference after taking office, Jaswant Singh stated that India was committed to improving its ties with China so that all outstanding issues were resolved in accordance with the five principles of peaceful co-existence.

In his daily press briefing on December 28,1998, Zhu Bangzao, the spokesman of the Chinese Foreign Office, said: " We welcome Minister for External affairs Jaswant Singh's remarks. China has always attached importance to the growth of its good neighbourly, friendly and co-operative ties with India on the basis of the five principles of peaceful co-existence. Normalisation of Sino-Indian relations complies with the fundamental interests of the people of both the countries."

The "Jane's Defence Weekly" reported in the last week of December, 1998, that the Chinese authorities had assessed that

India would take at least 10 years to establish an operational nuclear strike capability and, hence, India did not pose an immediate threat to China's security.

China strongly expressed its annoyance over the remarks of Ram Jethmalani, the Indian Urban Affairs Minister, that there was a strong case for India to recognise Taiwan as an independent country. He made these remarks in an interview to "The Week" of Kerala in the last week of December 1998.

The "People's Daily" wrote on December 31,1998: "We strongly urge certain Indian politicians to stop interfering in China's internal affairs and work towards improving rather than damaging the bilateral ties. Jethmalani's remarks have further hurt the feelings of the Chinese people. "

In a despatch on January 1,1999, Xinhua described Jethmalani's remarks as "evil-minded and dangerous." In an article on January 6,1999, the "China Daily" asked Indian leaders "not to test China's patience with irresponsible comments" and to adopt a coherent policy towards China. It added: "China's goodwill and repeated patience should not be returned with vile language." The criticism came down after the Government of India, through the Indian Embassy in Beijing as well as through its press spokesman in New Delhi, assured China that there was no change in India's policy on Taiwan.

There were clear indications in January 1999, that while showing readiness to restore the pre-Pokhran II normalcy to the bilateral relations, China remained determined in its opposition to India's acquiring any nuclear deterrence capability. Addressing a meeting of non-proliferation experts in Washington in the middle of January 1999, Sha Zukang, head of the Department of Arms Control and Disarmament in China's Foreign Office, reportedly stated as follows:

- "It is a direct violation of UN Security Council Resolution 1172 to negotiate, or to even discuss, with India on India's so-called minimum nuclear deterrence capability."
- "It is also unhelpful to publicly support India's permanent membership in the UN Security Council soon after its nuclear tests."

- The South Asian tests had become a litmus test for the effectiveness of the global non-proliferation regime. The international community should do its best to stop and reverse the nuclear weapons programmes of India and Pakistan.
- There were two essential requirements for the success of the international nuclear diplomacy in the sub-continent. First, " the international community should have sufficient patience and perseverance and should not lose hope because of the lack of progress in the short run." Second, "the major powers must have a consensus view and take concerted actions in this matter."
- "If any country seeks to exploit the South Asian situation to obtain unilateral, short-term political, economic or strategic benefits at the expense of the other countries and the international solidarity, it can only further undermine the already badly-damaged international non-proliferation regime, and, in the end, the long-term interests of that country will also be jeopardised."
- "We have noted with concern that after the Indian nuclear tests, some Nuclear Suppliers' Group members have taken a more pro-active stand on issues of nuclear co-operation with India. We hope that these countries could be more cautious in this area."

In an interview to the "Handelsblatt" of Germany on February 2,1999, Tang Jiaxuan, the Chinese Foreign Minister, rejected indirectly the idea of a Russia-India-China strategic triangle to which Prime Minister Yevgeny Primakov had referred during his visit to India in December, 1998. Tang spoke of China's "very good strategic partnership with Russia, which is full of vitality and regularly produces new elements" but clarified that Beijing's partnership with Moscow "includes neither alliances nor confrontation with third countries such as the US."

He described relations with India as far from ideal and blamed India for the deterioration in the relations. He urged India "to take practical steps towards the restoration of normal and healthy relations."

In an interview to the Press Trust of India on February 4,1999, Zhou Gang, the Chinese Ambassador to India, said: "India, instead of maintaining the so-called minimum nuclear deterrent, must accede to the CTBT and the NPT without delay and conditions."

Referring to speculation about the possible easing of sanctions against India by the US in the wake of the latest round of Jaswant Singh-Strobe Talbott discussions, he said:"Basically, China does not advocate sanctions."

On Primakov's strategic triangle idea, the Ambassador said:" China handles international affairs by proceeding from the fundamental interests of the people of China and the whole world and does not enter into alliances with any big power or group of countries. China's developing relations with any other country are not directed against another country."

In his daily press briefing on February 23, 1999, a spokesman of the Chinese Foreign Ministry welcomed the Vajpayee-Nawaz Sharif summit and the resulting Lahore Declaration. He added: "We hope the two sides will keep the momentum of dialogue and solve their differences through peaceful negotiations and consultations."

In his inaugural address to the budget session of the Indian Parliament on February 22,1999, President K.R.Narayanan said that India "seeks to strengthen and deepen its historic and friendly relations with China" and "is looking forward to continuing the dialogue with that country."

Addressing a seminar on Sino-Indian relations at New Delhi on February 25,1999, Zhou Gang, the Chinese Ambassador, said as follows:

- "We have consistently believed that the problems that cropped up in the Sino-Indian relations are temporary and can be surmounted. There exist extensive common interests between China and India and our commonalties far outweigh our differences."
- 'The outstanding issue between China and India is no more than the boundary dispute left behind by history." These differences could be resolved on the basis of the five principles of peaceful co-existence and in accordance with

the principle of mutual understanding and mutual accommodation.

- "We have noted that the Indian side has recently expressed its willingness to attach importance to its relations with China, not to view China as an enemy,and resume the dialogue, so as to find solutions to mutual concerns."
- China was not involved in the Pakistani nuclear and missile programmes."All co-operation between China and Pakistan in the field of peaceful uses of nuclear energy is under the safeguards of the IAEA. Non-existent is the issue of nuclear and missile proliferation to Pakistan. In fact, the Chinese side has already taken note of some concerns of the Indian side and, proceeding from the overall interests of friendly relations between China and India, it has taken a positive, flexible and pragmatic approach and made proper re-adjustment of certain policies concerned."
- The entire historical baggage of Sino-Indian differences could not be shed overnight, but only on the basis of reciprocity in a step by step manner. "All this needs a favourable atmosphere in our bilateral relations. Therefore, we hope that the Indian side will also adopt a flexible and pragmatic approach and solve the Chinese side's concerns earnestly."
- The attribution of a Chinese threat to justify India's nuclear tests by some personalities was mainly responsible for the recent deterioration in the Sino-Indian relations. "All this has deeply hurt the feelings of the Chinese people and seriously harmed the Sino-Indian relations. This is the main cause upsetting Sino-Indian relations."

The Ambassador's presentation coincided with the visit of a team of officials of India's Ministry of External Affairs to Beijing for three days from February 25,1999, to prepare the ground for holding the delayed JWG meeting.

In the daily press briefing on March 1,1999, Ms. Zhang Qiyue, a spokesperson of the Chinese Foreign Office, commented as follows on the talks with the Indian team: "Both sides discussed India's tests and their impact on Sino-Indian ties and expounded their respective positions on the issue. The two sides also focused on bilateral issues and re-affirmed their faith in the five principles of peaceful co-existence. The two sides agreed to work for the restoration and improvement of bilateral relations."

A spokesman of the Indian Embassy in Beijing said that India stoutly defended its position on the Pokhran tests and added: "We pointed out to them India's rejection of the UN Security Council resolution and our stand on the NPT and the CTBT." Addressing a press conference during the session of the National People's Congress, Tang Jiaxuan, the Chinese Foreign Minister, said on March 7.1999: "I expect, may be soon, the JWG on the boundary question between China and India will resume its activity." He again appealed to India and Pakistan to roll back their nuclear programme. Addressing a seminar on "India, China and Russia in the 21st century" organised by the Indian Council of World Affairs at New Delhi on March 9,1998, Zhou Gang, the Chinese Ambassador, said:

- The recent consultations in Beijing between officials of the two Foreign Offices marked a "new starting point" to improve bilateral relations.
- "We have noted that the Indian side has recently expressed its willingness to attach importance to and improve relations with China and not view China as its enemy. All this is welcome."
- China was pursuing an independent foreign policy vis-à-vis Russia, the US and India. "As powers of major influence and permanent members of the UN Security Council, China and the US share common interests on major issues related to peace and development in the Asia-Pacific region and the world as a whole. The two sides have decided to work together for the establishment of a constructive strategic partnership."
- The concept of a Sino-Russian strategic partnership did not have any military connotations. "Building a Sino-Russian strategic partnership is not aimed at forming an alliance and is not directed at any third party, but is aimed at abandoning confrontations between the two countries

so as to create conditions for the broadest equal exchanges and co-operation."

- "It is the firm policy of the Chinese Government to develop with India, a long-term neighbourly, constructive and co-operative partnership into the 21st century. The two countries had the foundation and potential for evolving mutually beneficial co-operation. India and China shared similar or common views on such issues as peace and development, human rights, environmental protection and population control."
- "Strict adherence to the five principles of peaceful, co-existence, mutual trust and shedding a threat image of each other were the key for laying a credible foundation for a healthy Sino-Indian relationship."
- China hoped that "South Asian countries will treat one another on an equal footing, live in harmony, develop friendly co-operation and settle their differences and disputes through peaceful means."
- When the bilateral relations were developing without a hitch, some personalities in India accused China of posing a threat to India's security so as to justify the nuclear tests. This was the main cause for upsetting the bilateral relations. Beijing's policy was defensive in nature and any fear of a China threat was entirely "unfounded and fabricated with ulterior motives."

In an interview to the PTI on March 21,1999, Sha Zukang, Director-General of the Department of Arms Control and Disarmament in the Chinese Foreign Office, said:

- "We have never posed a threat to India and history clearly shows that...We didn't have New Delhi in mind when we decided to go nuclear."
- Since China became a nuclear power, it had never threatened any country. "On the contrary, because of our own bitter experience of being blackmailed, we have declared to the world that we would never be the first to use nuclear weapons. To say China's nuclear weapons are threatening the security of India is hurting."

- China was willing to resume dialogue with India in the post-Pokhran phase, provided New Delhi took concrete actions to normalise strained bilateral relations. "We are prepared to enhance dialogue with India so as to clear misgivings, further mutual understanding and promote the goal of establishing a constructive and co-operative partnership between China and India. We hope that the Indian side will also take concrete actions in the same direction."
- "We continue to maintain that India and Pakistan should fully implement the UN Security Council Resolution 1172. To maintain peace and stability in South Asia and establish a nuclear-weapon-free world, both South Asian neighbours should abandon their nuclear weapons programmes and unconditionally accede to the NPT and the CTBT."

In an address to the United Services Institution (USI) of New Delhi on March 24,1999, Zhou Gang, the Chinese Ambassador, said as follows:

- "There exists profound traditional friendship between the people of the two countries. China and India sympathised and supported each other during their struggles of national independence and liberation against foreign aggression. The two countries share similar or identical views on many major issues such as economic development, human rights, environmental protection, combating drug trafficking and crime and population control."
- "There is nothing abnormal about some differences between the two countries. As long as both sides proceed from the overall interests of bilateral friendly relations and handle these concerns on the basis of mutual trust, with a positive, flexible and pragmatic approach and in a truth-seeking and forward-looking spirit, the differences will be narrowed gradually and problems resolved instead of coming in the way of the normal development of the bilateral relations."
- "Good neighbourly relations between India and China will not only conform to the fundamental interests of the two countries, but will encourage peace, stability and development in Asia and the world at large."

- "The outstanding issue between China and India is no more than the boundary dispute left behind by history. The Chinese Government has maintained that while positively seeking a solution to the boundary issue, the two sides should work hard to develop bilateral relations in various fields so as to create a favourable atmosphere for the final solution of the boundary issue. China stood for a peaceful, fair and equitable solution to the boundary issue on the basis of the five principles of peaceful co-existence, in accordance with the principle of mutual understanding and mutual accommodation through friendly talks, while taking into account the historical background and the present reality and the national feelings of the people of the two countries."
- "China welcomed the resumption of talks between the two Foreign Office officials in February. This useful meeting provides a new starting point for the improvement of Sino-Indian ties." He hoped that the two sides trust each other and treat each other with sincerity and strictly adhere to the five principles of peaceful co-existence.

Talking to pressmen on April 2,1999, Brajesh Mishra, Principal Secretary to the Indian Prime Minister, said that an official dialogue with Beijing had already commenced and that the forthcoming JWC meeting might result in a visit to China by the Indian Minister for External Affairs.

During a meeting with a visiting delegation of the Congress (I) led by K.Natwar Singh, at Beijing on April 8,1999,Hu Jintao, the Chinese Vice-President, asked India to pursue a long-term policy on Sino-Indian relations in view of the "complex and dynamic international situations unfolding at the turn of the century." He said that under the changing international situation today, India and China should "look closely at and handle the relations between the two countries from the historical perspective and a long-term viewpoint."

He noted that the bilateral relations had progressed on the normal track over the past decade "thanks to the joint efforts of the leaders of the two countries ", and regretted the chill in the bilateral relations after Pokhran II. The process of progress had consequently suffered "undesirable disturbances", he said.

Reports of Chinese reaction to the Agni II missile test available so far indicate that the spokesman of the Chinese Foreign Office expressed regret and concern at the test which, he pointed out, was a violation of the Security Resolution 1172 and added:" We have taken note of the remark by the Indian Prime Minister that this test is not directed against any country."

The annual report of the Indian Defence Ministry for 1998-99 released on April 16,1999, said as follows on Sino-Indian relations:

- Sino-Indian relations have improved in recent years and New Delhi regards China as "a great neighbour."
- India does not regard China "as an adversary and would like to develop mutually friendly relations with it."
- India has expressed its interest time and again in resolving its boundary dispute with China peacefully and through bilateral negotiations as quickly as possible.
- The September 1993 agreement on peace and tranquillity and the subsequent accord on confidence-building measures provided a reliable framework for the maintenance of peace and tranquillity in the border areas.
- Contacts between the two sides such as the meeting between Jaswant Singh and Tang Jiaxuan at Manila and the earlier visit to India by the Chinese Chief of General Staff serve the objective of furthering mutual understanding between the two countries and reassuring each other about their peaceful intentions.

SINO-INDIAN RELATIONS: A GROWING UNEASE

The dramatic rise of two Asian giants set against the backdrop of a troubled diplomatic history has propelled India and China into a trajectory that will likely prove difficult to navigate in the coming years. With the world riveted by Chinese aggression against Japan and Southeast Asian states in recent months, one country was not surprised: India. After all, New Delhi has been grappling with the challenge of China's rapid rise for some time. Bilateral ties between China and India nosedived so dramatically last year that Indian strategists were even predicting'the year of the Chinese attack on India'; it was suggested that China would attack India by 2012 primarily to divert attention from its growing domestic troubles. This suggestion received widespread coverage in the Indian media, which was more interested in sensationalizing the issue than interrogating the claims.

Meanwhile, the official Chinese media picked up the story and gave it another spin. It argued that while a Chinese attack on India is highly unlikely, a conflict between the two neighbours could occur in one scenario: an aggressive Indian policy toward China about their border dispute, forcing China to take military action. The Chinese media went on to speculate that the'China will attack India' line might just be a pretext for India to deploy more troops to the border areas.

A Growing Unease

This curious exchange reflects an uneasiness that exists between the two Asian giants as they continue their ascent in the global inter-state hierarchy. Even as they sign loftily worded documents year after year, the distrust between the two is actually growing at an alarming rate. True, economic cooperation and bilateral political, as well as socio-cultural exchanges are at an all time high; China is India's largest trading partner. Yet this cooperation has done little to assuage each country's concerns about the other's intentions. The two sides are locked in a classic security dilemma, where any action taken by one is immediately interpreted by the other as a threat to its interests. At the global level, the rhetoric is all about cooperation, and indeed the two sides have worked together on climate change, global trade negotiations and demanding a restructuring of global financial institutions in view of the global economy's shifting centre of gravity. At the bilateral level, however, mounting tensions reached an impasse last year, when China took its territorial dispute with India all the way to the Asian Development Bank. There China blocked India's application for a loan that included money for development projects in the Indian state of Arunachal Pradesh, which China continues to claim as part of its own territory. Also, the suggestion by the Chinese to the US Pacific fleet commander last year that the Indian

Ocean should be recognized as a Chinese sphere of influence has raised hackles in New Delhi. China's lack of support for the US-India civilian nuclear energy cooperation pact, which it tried to block at the Nuclear Suppliers Group (NSG), and its pro-Pakistan position on anti-India terrorist groups operating on Pakistani soil, including the orchestrators of the November 2008 Mumbai attacks, have further strained ties.

Sino-Indian frictions are growing, and the potential for conflict remains high. Alarm is rising in India because of frequent and strident Chinese claims about the Line of Actual Control in Arunachal Pradesh and Sikkim, where Indians have complained of a dramatic rise in Chinese intrusions into Indian territory over the last few years, most along the border in Arunachal Pradesh, which China refers to as "Southern Tibet". China has recently upped the ante on the border issue. It has been regularly protesting against the Indian prime minister's visit to Arunachal Pradesh, asserting its claims over the territory. What has caught most observers of Sino-Indian ties by surprise, however, is the vehemence with which Beijing has contested recent Indian administrative and political actions in the state, even denying visas to Indian citizens of Arunachal Pradesh.

The recent rounds of boundary negotiations have been a disappointing failure, with a growing perception in India that China is less willing to adhere to earlier political understandings about how to address the boundary dispute. Even the rhetoric has degenerated to such an extent that a Chinese analyst connected to China's Ministry of National Defence claimed in an article last year that China could "dismember the so-called 'Indian Union' with one little move" into as many as 30 states. Pakistan, of course, has always been a crucial foreign policy asset for China, but with India's rise and US-India rapprochement, its role in China's grand strategy is bound to grow even further. Not surprisingly, recent revelations about China's shift away from a three-decades' old cautious approach on Jammu and Kashmir, its increasing military presence in Pakistan, planned infrastructure linking Xinjiang and Gwadar, issuing stapled visas to residents of Jammu and Kashmir and supplying nuclear reactors to Pakistan, all confirm a new intensity behind China's old strategy of using Pakistan to secure its interests in the region.

India's Formidable Challenge

While it has not yet achieved the economic and political profile that China enjoys regionally and globally, India is increasingly bracketed with China as a rising or emerging power-or even a global superpower. Indian elites who have been obsessed with Pakistan for more than 60 years suddenly have found a new object of fascination. India's main security concern now is not the increasingly decrepit state of Pakistan but an ever more assertive China, a shift that is widely viewed inside India as one that can facilitate better strategic planning.

India's defeat at Chinese hands in 1962 shaped the Indian elite's perceptions of China, and they are unlikely to alter them anytime soon.

China is thus viewed by India as a growing, aggressive nationalistic power whose ambitions are likely to reshape the contours of the regional and global balance of power with deleterious consequences for Indian interests. Indian policymakers, however, continue to believe that Beijing is not a short-term threat to India but needs to be watched over the long-term. However, Indian defence officials are increasingly warning in rather blunt terms about the disparity between the two Asian powers. The Indian naval chief has warned that India neither has "the capability nor the intention to match China force for force" in military terms, while the former Indian air chief has suggested that China posed more of a threat to India than Pakistan.

China's recent hardening toward India could well be a function of its own internal vulnerabilities, but that is hardly a consolation to Indian policymakers who have to respond to an Indian public that increasingly wants the country to assert itself in the region and beyond. India is rather belatedly gearing up to respond with its own diplomatic and military overtures, setting the stage for a Sino-Indian strategic rivalry. Both India and China have a vested interest in stabilizing their relationship by seeking out issues on which their interests converge, but pursuing mutually desirable interests does not inevitably produce satisfactory solutions to strategic problems. A troubled history coupled with the structural uncertainties engendered by their simultaneous rise is propelling the two Asian giants into a trajectory that they might find rather difficult to navigate in the coming years. Sino-Indian ties have entered turbulent times, and they are likely to remain there for the foreseeable future.

The Indian and Chinese Experience

One of the cruel ironies of today's world is that India which is applauded as the world's largest democracy has the largest number of poor and destitute in any country, and China which has achieved, a steady rise in people's living standards and has also acquired the status of a world power has failed to develop democratic institutions and practices. It is also interesting to note that despite the absence of liberal democratic freedoms the West has a deep fascination with China which is reflected not only in the tourist inflow to China but also in the flow of foreign investment and government good will. Operation of democratic institutions such as free and fair elections, existence of competitive politics and dissent do not particularly attract either Western tourists or Western capital to India. On the contrary the geopolitics of South Asia has been governed by the US and other Western countries as compared by India's pre-eminent position and therefore they have followed by an large a policy of containment of India vis-a-vis its neighbours. The functioning democratic system of India has had little effect on their policy. The experience of India and China have put the theory of democracy to a severe test. Two old questions need to be asked again about democracy. In addition, two new questions have to be raised. Do formal political institutions and practices constitute democracy or does it involve appropriate socio-economic conditions which enable citizens to exercise their political rights. On this issue India scores poorly with nearly forty per cent of its people below what is statistically called a "poverty line". China has asserted that it is engaged in creating better living conditions for its people after overthrowing semicolonial and semifeudal domination. Today, however, this dichotomy between economic and political conditions of democracy is seriously questioned. Their mutual dependence is emphasised. Therefore both India and China have to achieve yet more conditions of democracy.

The other familiar question relates to equality and freedom. Western liberal democratic theory asserts the priority of freedom over equality even though the radical stream in liberalism stresses that gross inequalities are detrimental to the exercise of freedom. On this criterion pre-Reform China scored higher marks than India. Social inequalities were reduced in China to a very large extent with the abolition of landlordism and formation of cooperatives and Communes and also takeover of the bourgeoisie owned industries by the state. The wage system was directed towards promoting equality and limiting income differences within the six point grade system. In India too there were a number of measures taken in the early decades following independence to curb monopoly in industry, abolish zamindari system and carry out land reforms.

In both the countries the stress on equality declined in the 1980s and almost disappeared in the 1990s. In the past decade or so equality has been a low priority in both China and India. The "equalitarianism", "theory of eating from the iron rice bowl" and such ideas of the Cultural Revolution were severely criticised by the Chinese reformers as being obstacles to the development of the productive forces. The perspective of the present day leadership in China is to "allow some people to get rich first" so that the general level of growth is raised steadily. In India the introduction of the Structural Adjustment Programme promoted the ideology of profit and the egalitarian programmes of social transformation took the back seat.

The two new issues arise from the great democratic upsurges of the past few decades, namely the social movements such as the women's movements, the environmental movement, the autonomy movement and the human rights movements. One question posed by them is to concretise freedom as freedom from multiple forms of domination so that freedom to realise the potentialities of the human being is advanced. Patriarchal domination continues substantially in all the countries of the world as evident from the deliberations at the Fourth World Congress of Women in Beijing and as documents in the 1995 *Human Development Report.* China and India have only marginal difference among them. As to ethnic self-determination there has not yet been a scientific measurement. But both the countries have fairly centralised regimes and both have regions manifesting popular discontent. The caste hierarchy and disabilities in India are targets of public attention and social action. There is no comparable social problem in China though new forms of social stratification have emerged in the recent years.

The other issue is response of the modern state to these expanding democratic demands. All ruling elites would like to have an appearance of being popular and responsive to the demands of the various unprivileged groups. And they engage in innumerable measures of legitimation to create a climate of acceptability among the people. Thus the modern state is coercive, responsive and legitimative at the same time. For this purpose it has developed sophisticated systems of management of society, complex methods of propaganda and innovative techniques of manipulation.

Bibliography

Amitabh Sikdar: *India and China : Strategic Energy Management and Security*, Manas, Delhi, 2009.

Anderson, J.: *Transnational Democracy: Political Spaces and Border Crossings*, Routledge: London and New York, 2002.

Anil, K.C.: *Military and Democracy in South Asia : Challenges, Politics and Power*, Sumit Enterprises, Delhi, 2009.

Cheek, Timothy: *Mao Zedong and China's Revolutions: A Brief History with Documents.* Boston: Bedford/St. Martin's, 2002.

Coakley, J.: *The Territorial Management of Ethnic Conflict*, London: Frank Cass, 2003.

Deepak, B R : *India and China : 1904-2004 : A Century of Peace and Conflict*, Manak, Delhi, 2005.

Digumarti Bhaskara Rao: *Military Conversion : Impact on Science and Technology*, Discovery, Delhi, 2003.

Donnan, H. and Wilson, T. M.: *Borders: Frontiers of Identity, Nation and State*, Oxford: Berg, 1999.

Evelyn Goh, *Meeting the China Challenge: The U.S. in Southeast Asian Regional Security Strategies*, DC: East-West Center, 2005.

Gaur, Mahendra : *Indian Policy of Neighbour*, Delhi, Kalpaz Pub., 2006.

Gupta, S.: *Disrupted Borders: An Intervention in Definitions of Boundaries*, London: River Oram Press, 1993.

Hans J. Morgenthau: *Politics Among Nations: The Struggle for Power and Peace*, New York, Knopf, 1960.

Huntington, S.P.: *The China Modernisation Military and the State*, N.Y., Vintage Books, 1964.

Jagannath P. Panda: *China's Path to Power : Party, Military and the Politics of State Transition*, Pentagon, Delhi, 2010.

Kapur, C.K. : *Chinese Military Modernisation*, Manas, Delhi, 2003.

Mary, W.: *Military Space Force: the Cultural Dimensions of Authority*, Cambridge, Belknap Press, 1985.

Nayyar, K K : *National Security : Military Aspects*, Rupa, Delhi, 2003.

Prabir De: *India and China in an Era of Globalisation : Essays on Economic Cooperation*, Bookwell, Delhi, 2005.

Radhakrishna: *Military Ethics: Guidelines for Peace and War*, Sumit Enterprises, Delhi, 2009.

Stuart R. Schram: *The Political Thought of Mao Tse-Tung*. New York: Praeger, 1969.

Wilson, T. M.: *New Borders for a Changing: Cross-border Cooperation and Governance*, London: Frank Cass, 2003.

Index

❑❑❑